EUROPE
IN THE MAKING

JOHAN GALTUNG

CRANE RUSSAK
A Member of the Taylor & Francis Group
New York · Philadelphia · Washington, DC · London

USA	Publishing Office:	Taylor & Francis New York Inc.
		79 Madison Ave., New York, NY 10016-7892
	Sales Office:	Taylor & Francis Inc.
		1900 Frost Road, Bristol, PA 19007
UK		Taylor & Francis Ltd.
		4 John St., London WC1N 2ET

Europe in the Making

Copyright © 1989 Taylor & Francis New York Inc.

First published 1989
Printed in the United States of America

Library of Congress Cataloging in Publication Data

Galtung, Johan
  Europe in the making / Johan Galtung.
    p. cm.
  Bibliography: p.
  Includes Index.
  ISBN 0-8448-1619-1.—ISBN 0-8448-1622-1 (pbk.)
    1. Europe—Politics and government—1945– 2. Europe—Defenses.
3. Europe. I. Title.
D1058.G28   1989
320.94—dc20   89-34082
                                                      CIP

Contents

Contents

Preface

This book is about Europe. It is about that wonderful, incredibly diverse, and rich, but not always symbiotic continent stretching from Nordkapp at the top of Norway way down to the south of Spain, Malta, Crete, and Cyprus; from Ireland, Portugal, and Brest-Bretagne way out in the Atlantic to—yes, to where? To Brest-Litovsk? No, not to a random border town at a random border that happens to make for puns like Europe from Brest-to-Brest. To the Urals, then? Not much of a mountain range and not even an internal border in one, by far the largest, of the 15 Soviet republics.

To Vladivostok? Perhaps. But what then about the Asian part of the Soviet Union, including Siberia? Would "Europe" include the five Central Asian Republics? Would it include Gruziya, Armeniya, and Azerbaydzhan? Why should Ukraina, Belo-Russiya, and the Russian Republic be "European" and they not? Maybe the others are European. And then maybe not. Maybe somebody should ask them how they want to be classified; I mean not asking Moscow but asking them. Or maybe the world should simply accept that the Soviet Union is all of this and much more, a great experiment like the United States, in the coexistence of very different ethnic and racial groups. European or Asian? Both and neither.

So is the author writing a book about something he cannot define clearly? Yes, and it does not bother me in the slightest. Maybe that is the first European contradiction: nobody knows exactly what Europe is. Include the Soviet Union, or at least much of it, and there are 30 countries in Europe. Exclude it, and there are the 29 countries of *Europa Major*, not counting the mini-states (Faroe, Aland, Liechtenstein, San Marino, Monaco, Andorra, Gibraltar, Vatican City) and the rather maxi Greenland—at any rate more than the 12 countries of *Europa Minor* that today are members of the European Community, the minority group sometimes arrogating to itself the very name "Europe." This book is about all five Europes as spelled out in the Introduction: Europe with the present superpowers, *Europa Major*, *Europa Minor*, the Europe of local government, and the Europe of the Peoples.

The 10 chapters in this book about all of Europe are loosely divided into five parts, with two chapters in each, all seeing Europe in different light.

The first part deals with *Europa Major* and *Europa Minor*. Chapter 1 is
an effort to answer the old question "What is Europe?" by using two simple
intellectual tools: macro-geography and macro-history. "Which are the major subdivisions of Europe and how do they relate to each other?" is a question of European anatomy and physiology. "How did the Europe we know
today evolve historically?" is a question of genealogy. Both questions can
be answered in many ways. The two chapters together give one approach
with contradiction as the main theme. The analytical task is to identify the
contradictions, not only to talk vaguely about them, and this is attempted
here in geo-historical terms. The focus of Chapter 1 is on *Europa Major*,
the Europe of 29 countries divided into five regions or sub-Europes; and the
focus of Chapter 2 is on *Europa Minor*, the European Community, tracing
its growth from communities to community with scenarios into the future
to union and superpower. Readers may not agree with the thesis that the
European Community is a superpower in the making but might agree that
the thesis is worth discussing. Moreover, if one superpower is waxing, could
it be that the other two are waning?

In Chapters 3 and 4, concerning the two superpowers, the major actors
in the Europe of the Cold War and of the Conference on Security and Cooperation in Europe are identified, with an effort to explore their myths. The
first myth is the superpower system, meaning neither United States nor the
Soviet Union in particular, but the shared myth of having a mission in the
world so important that everybody else should stand at attention. Some of
the myths are deadly in their consequences. Much of the mythical material
is shared between the superpowers, but then each of them has a specialty
or two of its own. The second myth is the nuclear deterrence system, meaning neither NATO nor the WTO in particular, but the total system built
around the ideology of nuclear exterminism, not significantly reduced by
removing 4 percent (the INF agreement), possibly "compensating" with much
more.

In the third and fourth parts, dynamism is introduced. Four sources are
identified as representing something qualitatively new. Two major expressions of Europe of the peoples and two major expressions of Europe of the
politicians are discussed in the chronological order of their appearance on
the European scene. The historical role of the peace movement is explored
and discussed using the geographical map of Europe as developed in Chapter
1 including some reflections on the role of the peace movement in other
parts of the world. The Green Movement is placed on the European historical agenda as a new phenomenon, but completely within the historical logic
of the European project. What happens in the Soviet Union, in the West

conveniently and wrongly wrapped up under the one name heading "Gorbachev," is also seen as dynamic, with the potential for a second socialist revolution. And I do see all these three—the peace movement, the Green Movement, and the Gorbachev movement—as the most significant factors behind the INF agreement of December 1987. On the other hand, the Europe of Chapters 3 and 4 is still there, even very much so, following its own logic, so Chapter 8 ends with a list of warnings about what to watch out for.

Finally, in the last part alternatives are discussed, focusing on "alternative security policies," and on "active peaceful coexistence," with some remarks on Europe of local government in other words on the peaceful use of military and economic power. And in the conclusion, the general political dimensions of a new European peace order are summarized, using material from all 10 chapters.

Most of the chapters in this book have been "tried out" as they were presented at various conferences during the last years. I am indebted to organizers and discussants in these places, and particularly to *Die Grünen* and the German and European peace movements in general (Chapters 1, 5, 6, and the Conclusion); to students at the College of Europe in Brugge for inviting a lecture critical of the European Community (Chapter 2); to the Right Livelihood Award Foundation (Chapter 8 is my acceptance speech for the 1987 award); to the Defense Commission of the German Parliament and the Political Commission of the European Parliament for inviting me to testify at their hearings in 1984 and 1987 (Chapter 9); and to many municipalities in Europe for invited talks on the foreign policies of local government (Chapter 10).

The major source of inspiration, however, remains the two superpowers, mainly negative because of their myths (Chapters 3 and 4), mixed because of the INF agreement (Chapter 8), but also positive. Gorbachev has launched a major Soviet effort to accommodate the power structure to the needs of their citizens and the interests of the world, and not vice versa (Chapter 7). The best hope for peace now would be a much needed U.S. *glasnost'* and *perestroika,* but that will have to be the subject of two other books.

Priscilla B. Olsen did an excellent job with the manuscript when I was Visiting Professor of World Politics of Peace and War at Princeton University, as did Carolyn DiPalma, Claus Otto Scharmer, and Professors George Kent and Manfred Henningsen during my present stay as Professor of Peace Studies at the University of Hawaii.

Honolulu, Hawaii,   Johan Galtung
May 1989

Introduction: The Five Europes

There are at least five Europes (EI–EV); four of them governmental or territorial and one of them nonterritorial, the Europe of the peoples. Together they make up the Europe we know.

EI: The Conference for Security and Cooperation in Europe

This is Europe with the superpowers and Canada. There are potentially 32 governments participating in EI if we do not count the mini-states and the maxi-state of Greenland (see Europe IV), and include the absent Albania. EI is an outcome of World War II and the Cold War, and will probably disappear when the last residues of these calamities have withered away. But we are not yet through with that unfortunate phase in history. EI is indispensable as it permits the superpowers to participate in Europe in a reasonably open, symmetric, and accountable manner. Of course, they are both parts of Europe in their own ways, irrespective of the history of the last 50 years. The United States of America received most of its population from the "Old World" and still retains some unmistakably European characteristics. The Soviet Union, particularly the Baltic States, Moldavia, and Ukraina-White Russia-Russia are geographically, historically, and culturally contiguous to Europe. Both superpowers are present today in unacceptable, hegemonial roles, and EI is a setting offering them some legitimacy.

Quite conceivably, EI will soon be at the peak of its life cycle. The other Europes are already gaining in self-confidence. In the future the United States and the Soviet Union may become observers rather than participants in EI. Their governments may relate to the other Europes as governments do, bilaterally and in multilateral intergovernmental organizations. But EI will not become a dominant construction, for at least two good reasons.

First, both superpowers have major extra-European projects of high, even top priority. Apart from the obvious economic problems of running mega-

1

formations that have been suffering for a long time, not only under the arms race but also under orthodox capitalism and orthodox socialism, they are engaged in major geopolitical pursuits. I am not thinking of their old projects with a global reach fueling the Cold War confrontation since they were obviously incompatible. They have by and large been given up.[1] Both superpowers are now focusing more on their regional arenas.

The United States is engaged in a *pax americana* project in the Western Hemisphere, with a free trade area from Yukon-Hudson Bay to Tierra del Fuego as a major construction pillar,[2] in addition to the old political (OEA/ OAS) and military systems (TIAP/Rio de Janeiro Treaty). Down the road the United States may have visions of an American Community like the European Community. The Soviet Union is engaged in a *pax sovietica* project, in the Soviet Union itself, building the Soviet Community if not from scratch at least endowing the construction with a new structure (*perestroika*) under conditions of a relatively open dialogue (*glasnost'*). They are deeply concerned and involved elsewhere; but these two projects will keep them more than busy for years to come. Two exhausted, stalemated superpowers securing their multinational core areas for survival.

The second reason lies in the European ambivalence between wishing and fearing independence. Out of 29 European countries, an incredibly high number, 13 NATO members (not counting France) and 6 WTO countries, a total of 19, or two-thirds of the countries, are the client states of the superpowers. At least officially they exchange superpower protection for "subpower" submissiveness, including general agreement with the superpower in the assessment of the geopolitical situation.[3] Quite some humiliation for a continent with far from humble perceptions of its own geopolitical role! But it serves the useful function of having somebody to blame. Thus the Italian and Polish political systems have an important characteristic in common: they both try to keep their opposition out of governmental roles on the ground that "their" superpower might intervene.[4] If the superpowers no longer cared, both regimes would have to face their *compromesso storico*[5] and both systems could mature and benefit. That time is now.

EII: Europa Major, The Europe of 29 Countries

Generally speaking, this Europe, the real Europe, is unknown. Most Europeans do not even know the number of countries on their own continent.[6] Of course, we may discuss to what extent we should also include the eight mini-states and the maxi-state of Greenland—all of them interesting constructions at different levels of independence—and to what extent the Soviet

Union belongs. I have chosen to place the Soviet Union in EI, partly because of their alternative, clearly extra-European project, partly because of the difficulty with any construction admitting only one of the superpowers to the "Common European House." And I have chosen to place the mini/maxi-states in EIV. However, the argument that double membership is a part of the generally contradictory nature of Europe holds in both cases. No dogmatism works in these matters.

But there is also firm reality to EII, the Europe from Brest (Bretagne) to Brest (Litovsk) concept. Both historically and geographically, EII is agonizingly complex and contradictory—to be spelled out in Chapter 1 below. This is where the real Europe is located, nowhere else. The other four are important, but mainly because *Europa Major* is weak, badly treated by itself and by history. As a matter of fact, EII is so invisible that any change will be upward, meaning competing with the others.

EIII: Europa Minor, The Europe of 12 Countries

This is, of course, the European Community, explored in some detail in Chapter 2. A minority in number of countries but a clear majority in population,[7] *Europa Minor* becomes increasingly significant because of its possible future superpower status. Given enormous resources and ambitions a minority of countries dwarfs the totality, creating new tensions in the European space.

EIV: The Europe of Local Governments

This is the first Europe below the governmental surface: the Europe of regions, of provinces/departements/republics down to the Europe of the counties/municipalities. The number of actors immediately gets much higher. The local identification may vary from zero or negative (people may want to get away, as they may also want to get away from their countries) to an identity so high that it overshadows all others. Particularly interesting in this connection are two projects that come from different sources politically but in no way are incompatible: the impressive twinning of local governments in the European space, and the movement for nuclear-free municipalities. Both movements engender an outreach from the inward-looking municipality, beyond the country in which they are "local" to even very distant countries, penetrating the governmental crust, attaching itself directly to an "opposite number," to other municipalities on the other side. If this is done within sub-Europes—and the European Community is one of those only so important that it is counted here as a Europe in its own right—then this serves to cement the relationship. If the outreach goes beyond, then an infrastructure for more encompassing Europes is taking shape.

The mini-states may show the way into the future, precisely because they are residues of the Europe of a distant, medieval past, spared by the project of nation-building.[8] They are dependent on one country (Andorra on two), but also enjoy levels of independence above local governments. There is something anarchic about them that must be deeply disturbing to people wanting all points of world geography unambiguously allocated to countries enjoying equal sovereignty. Instead of regarding them as retarded nation-states, they can be seen as advanced local governments, in many fields exercising relatively independent foreign policy. One of them, Aland, is even a very interesting model of demilitarization.[9]

EV: The Europe of The Peoples

This is the second Europe below the governmental crust, and by far the most important of them all. We are speaking of 540 million human beings,[10] more than one-tenth of humankind. This Europe is also organized, but in nonterritorial people's organizations (I refuse to use that word coming out of governmental arrogance, "nongovernmental"). The organizations vary from the most informal movements to highly formalized, even very old organizations; and from organizations for the promotion of interests to value-oriented organizations. Some of them are local, some national, some regional, some all-European, and many go beyond that and reach for the world level. Very important are movements organized around nationalism, one of the strongest sources of human identity. Particularly strong are national movements in search of a land of their own, through secession, occupation, or both. But also very strong are the two most important recent movements, the peace movement and the green movement. Paraphrasing Marx, we may even talk about "a specter—haunting Europe—the green specter."[11]

EV is the real Europe on which the other four depend, if we are to believe European theories of the primacy of the individual even if sometimes it looks as if the state comes first. If states depend on the consent of the governed, then those who rule without that consent will suffer the consequences sooner or later. And the map of Europe will change as it has before, not only the geographical map reflecting the borders between the countries, but also the invisible, nonterritorial maps reflecting the countless ties spun between individuals and organizations all over Europe.[12]

For easy reference and recall, we might better refer to these five Europes as CSCE, E29, EC12, ELocal, and EPeople. They are not the only European constructions or projects. More particularly, we probably have to take into account at least four other projects, again in the French sense of *projet,* as possible building blocs competing with others now that the House of Europe is under reconstruction (to use again the expression made famous by Gorbachev even if the Soviet Union is only at the doorsteps of that house). More particularly, we have:

1. The *NN Project of neutral and nonaligned countries,* involving the inner six (Finland, Sweden, Austria, Switzerland, Yugoslavia, and Albania, even if the latter does not participate in CSCE), possibly also the outer three (Eire, Malta, and Cyprus).
2. The *Nordic Project,* involving five countries, two mini-states (Faroe and Aland), one maxi-state (Greenland), and one nation without fixed land, the *sami* nation up in the north.
3. The *Central Europe Project,* involving essentially countries of the old Austro-Hungarian (Habsburg) Empire or Dual Monarchy. As a construction it lasted only from the "constitutional compromise" of 1867 until the end of World War I, 1918, with one part consisting roughly of Austria, Czechoslovakia, Slovenia, and parts of Poland; and the other part consisting of Hungary, parts of Romania and Croatia. By far too important to be disregarded[13] and highly successful as a cultural project; being strongly felt even today.
4. The *Eastern European Project,* involving the six WTO countries in Eastern Europe, with the difficulty of being very closely tied through WTO and CMEA to a superpower with strong extra-European commitments and projects.

At present it is unclear how strong these projects are as alternatives to the most dynamic project in Europe right now, EC12, the European Community, a topic discussed later. The NN project is actually mainly interesting in a CSCE context, as bridge-builders between the two blocs, and has already played a certain role in that connection.[14] They suffer from the basic deficit of lack of contiguity, being scattered all over Europe, like EFTA with which they have a certain overlap.[15]

The Nordic and Central European projects, however, are based on geographical contiguity and a considerable tradition in European history even if the former never became a unified political actor and the latter only for half a century. They are political realities as opposed to the geographical abstractions explored in Chapter 1, dividing Europe into four geographical parts that obey a certain historical logic.

And Eastern Europe is too recent and at present so torn by conflict within and without, not necessarily related to socialism and the Soviet Union,[16] that anything may happen. The construction may fall apart together with the Socialist mystique. But it may also be given new life to stand up against the pressures from the West and the reforms in the East. Unlike Western Europe they depend very much economically on their superpower, which is in a process of basic and agonizing change.

More important, however, is the preliminary conclusion: we have a multiplicity of Europes and sub-Europes. Instead of deploring this we should celebrate. We may need all of them for a solid House of Europe and not lament that "in my father's house there are many rooms." As developed below, there may also be a blessing hidden in all this contradictory diversity. Precisely because it is so contradictory it is hard to believe that Europe as a whole, E29, can ever come together and become a major threat to any part of the rest of the world. With contradictions engineered away a part of Europe, EC12, may certainly be threatening; with contradictions left in Europe, E29, is not.

Nobody has expressed this better than Laotse:[17]

A man is born gentle and weak.
At his death he is hard and stiff.
Green plants are tender and filled with sap.
At their death they are withered and dry.
Therefore the stiff and unbending is the disciple of death.
The gentle and yielding is the disciple of life.
The hard and strong will fall.
The soft and weak will overcome.

For *Europa Major* there is no such danger, at least not for the foreseeable future. Too contradictory to become hard, strong, and dead, it cannot administer death to others. But *Europa Minor,* given the recent historical record of many members of belligerence and colonialism, may be a very different story.

1

Europe the Contradictory: A Macro-Geographical and Macro-Historical Overview

Europe the contradictory, the double-faced; Europe the Janus. Europe from the Atlantic to the Urals and beyond; of course, Russia is a part of Europe, and, of course, Russia today stretches to the Pacific and is a part of Asia. As noted, that is already one of the contradictions.

As a point of departure, it is intellectually difficult to talk about Europe as a whole, and this is perhaps a major reason why so few people do. The difficulty derives from one single circumstance: *Europe is so contradictory*. That is the major theme of this chapter, which explores that theme geographically, historically, and culturally.

GEOGRAPHY, HISTORY, CULTURE

Take geography as a point of departure. There is Europe *east* and *west,* as we know only too well (see Fig. 1). There is the abominable division of Europe by the blocs, euphemistically referred to as "the alliances," although they are mainly autistic expressions of superpower hegemony,[1] exercised in different ways. They are certainly pitted against each other militarily; they are divided politically; and from a social, economic, and cultural point of view one champion's capitalism with a liberal/conservative underpinning and one champion's socialism with a marxist underpinning. This is certainly one more contradiction. But even more contradictory are the socialist elements in capitalism found very clearly in the West in the welfare states of Western Europe, more or less successfully achieved. And the capitalist ele-

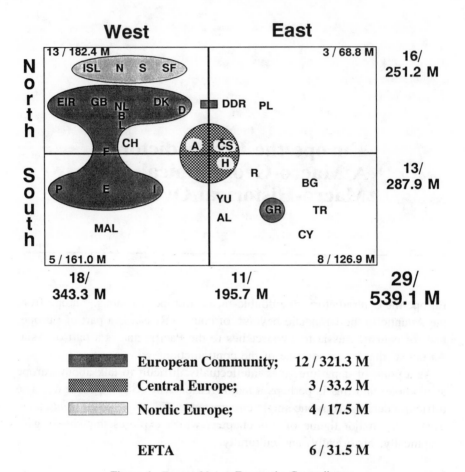

Figure 1. *Europa Major:* Europe the Contradictory

ments in socialism found increasingly clearly in the East as market principles operating on the side of society, increasingly move toward the center of the social formation under Gorbachev.

Then there is Europe *north* and *south* (Fig. 1), roughly speaking, divided by levels of technical-economic development, with more developed Europe in the north and less developed Europe in the south. But there are pockets of low development among the high, and high development among the low.[2] Not to mention the obvious circumstance that human development may be high when economic development is low, and *vice versa*. Hence, there are plenty of contradictions also along this geographical dimension, which cuts across the East-West divide in Europe, making the total set of contradictions extremely rich indeed.

In fact, it might be fruitful to combine the two divides and think in terms of four Europes. There is the more developed, capitalist *northwest* with the five Nordic countries (including Finland), England with Scotland and then Ireland (although it possibly belongs more to the Catholic southwest), Be-Ne-Lux, the Federal Republic of Germany, Switzerland, and Austria. Then there is the *southwest* consisting of the mainly Catholic, mainly Latin countries of France, Italy, Spain, Portugal, and Malta; possibly adding Ireland and subtracting half of France. There is a European *northeast* consisting of Poland, the German Democratic Republic, and Czechoslovakia. And finally a European *southeast,* often referred to as the Balkans, consisting of Hungary, Rumania, and Bulgaria; Yugoslavia and Albania; Greece, Turkey (at least the European part), and Cyprus. Thirteen countries in the northwest, five in the southwest, three in the northeast and eight in the southwest: 29 European countries all together when we do not include the Soviet Union.[3]

Added to this division of Europe of 29 countries into four parts comes the very important concept of Central Europe, *Mittel-Europa.* It has a reality. I sense it even though I do not know its geographical borders. Its nucleus is the *Doppelmonarchie,* the Habsburgian, Austro-Hungarian construction in other words, with Wien with all its nostalgia in the middle and for that reason also in the very center of Europe. Central Europe at its very minimum would include Austria from the northwestern corner, Czechoslovakia from northeast, and Hungary from southeast. But then Poland (particularly southwest) and Yugoslavia (particularly northwest) also somehow belong.[4] With this very concept east moves west, west moves east, north moves south, and south moves north.[5] They meet in the middle, but bring with them the imprint of the corners from where they come.

Why all these differences in such a small area of world geography? Of course, because their histories were different even if there is a common European agenda, political tasks that are done, that have to be done, and may have to be carried out in something of the same order.[6] There are both liberal/conservative and marxist theories in this field, all of them rightly famous, none of them capturing the richness of Europe as a whole. Add to those efforts the very simple approach used above, dividing power into four: the distribution of *cultural, economic, political,* and *military* power. The point of departure would then be the general image of the European prince in the late period of feudalism, still retaining in his hands considerable control over all four types of power. If not himself exercising cultural power— that was the prerogative of the church—he at least had to come to terms with the church. He was not ruling quite alone, but together with his court he was very close to having a monopoly on economic, political, and military power.

Enter the new age, the challenge to absolutism. In the field of cultural power human rights, freedom of expression, and so on. In the field of economic power the rise of the independent entrepreneur, of private capital, of market forces. In the field of political power, in other words basic decision making, the rise of democratic institutions. And in the field of military power: no change. There was conscription of the general male population, in France from 1793, imitated by other countries. Absolutism remained at the top, if not exercised by the prince then by the successor to the prince, the state. Feudalism continued in the military field with monopoly, secrecy, and— significantly—the exclusion of women from the corridors of power.[7]

It stands to reason that the parts of Europe have not come equally far in these four processes. They are not synchronized, except that none of them has shown much inclination to go very far when it comes to the final battle on this list: demonopolization in the field of military power. As a general rule we might perhaps say that the northwestern corner has made most progress along the other three roads. Eastern Europe in general has made a transition from the feudal prince to a modern state, but then has vested in that modern state the monopolistic prerogatives of the feudal prince with total control over cultural and economic and political and military power, all four at the same time. For some interesting ideological reasons, this particular type of latter-day feudalism has been given a special name. It is referred to as "socialism," even as "the really existing socialism." Southern Europe is in general more concerned with economic aspects and so is western Europe although in a slightly different way; more concerned with standing up against the pressure from outside Europe, the United States and Japan, than with any real need to grow further, for reasons entirely their own.

As mentioned, there is no reason why the four parts of Europe should be proceeding synchronically along these four roads. That would presuppose a homogeneity across European geography and a parallelism in the history of the parts that would be totally unreasonable, or at least extremely improbable given the absence of an all-European government. Moreover, such differences would tend to accumulate in significance. Leads and lags tend to become more prominent over time.[8] And the result is a Europe that becomes increasingly contradictory, particularly when compared to the (perhaps overly romantic) image we have of a relatively homogeneous Europe sometime back in the Middle Ages, united in the Christian and Latin/Greek traditions, to a large extent carried through the ages by Arab scholars.

So, what is Europe, then, if we cannot catch it in an unambiguous way, neither geographically nor historically? The answer that it is unity in diversity only begs the question; where is that unity in a continent that never was united?

I might say that this is exactly the point. The only noncontradictory way of describing Europe is to say that Europe is not only diverse, except for being mainly Christian and Indo-European in languages, but also basically contradictory. And there is a particular reason for this having to do with what seems to be the most fruitful way of conceiving of Europe geographically and historically: as a *cultural project*. The Indian philosopher who was also India's first president, Radhakrishnan, said in one of his books (he was at that time professor of religion at Oxford University): characteristic of the West is its roots, and they are Jewish, Greek, and Roman. From Judaism the West learned to see itself as a Chosen People; Christianity, a derivative of Judaism, is also an expression of that. From the Greeks the West learned some particular rules of thinking, such as the (Western) "laws of thought" with heavy emphasis on the inadmissibility of contradictions; this made theory-formation, deductive thinking in general, and theology in particular, possible. And from the Romans the Europeans learned how to build empires and statecraft in general, a habit they have practiced ever since.[9] In short, the Europeans see themselves as a Chosen People with a very disciplined, special way of thinking, and also highly expansionist. And they end up with so many contradictions precisely because they are engaged in so many efforts to become noncontradictory.

I think what Radhakrishnan says is true. But it is not the whole truth. It leaves out what we might call "the other Europe," much more inclined toward itself, contracting rather than expanding, less rigid in its way of thinking, more willing to see itself as one region among several, not particularly chosen for any particular missionary activity. *There is Europe hard, and there is Europe soft*. Moreover, it is almost impossible to think of one without also mentioning the other. In fact, it looks as if anything European comes in two versions: hard and soft Christianity, hard and soft liberalism, hard and soft Marxism. And no doubt this might also one day be the case for the Green party, which today appears mainly in a soft form but with a solid, hard, fundamentalist core (the German *Fundamentalos, Fundis* as opposed to the softer *Realos*) when they go networking with other green parties. The result might one day become a very hard organization in order to fight the other hard Europes coinhabiting the softer Europe with which most Greens identify. One may, of course, argue that this division can also be found in other parts of the world, which undoubtedly is true for the Islamic world and for the parts dominated yesterday or today by (neo)colonialist Europe. But it is less true for countries in the Hindu-Buddhist sphere, or at least not to the extent that it can be formulated as a principle, like "double-faced" Europe.

The Europe of high culture, of the sublime, of the highest in culture and science (much of it Arabic and Jewish) as well as the Europe of imperialism, of domination and aggressiveness, even genocide (much of it against Arabs and Jews). Which Europe is the real one? Of course, it is easy to focus on the hard and denounce, and equally easy to choose the soft and praise. But in either case we shall do violence to truth. The truth about Europe is not some position inbetween, that is a very misleading metaphor. The truth comprises both. Europe *is* contradictory. Are you, or am I, "for" or "against" Europe? Both, of course. To be only for or only against says more about the person (simple-mindedness, for instance) than about Europe.

But if the truth of Europe is so contradictory, what then about the "laws of thought," themselves a part of the European cultural tradition and a very important part, ruling out contradictory thoughts? In this there is also a contradiction.[10] And that contradiction makes victims out of all of us in a very particular way. We become less able than we should have been to think about, leaving alone to talk about, Europe as a whole. Precisely because we have a tendency to shrink away from stating the contradictory, we would also tend to divide Europe so that we can think noncontradictory thoughts about either one. And the most tempting division is always the most concrete one: geographical subdivision. Of course we have a tendency to end up with two Europes regardless of how we subdivide, east and west, socialist and capitalist, north and south, Protestant and Catholic, or what not. That makes it easy to be for one and against the other.

EUROPE HARD AND SOFT

But the division of Europe into hard and soft is not a division of that kind. It is not the division of Europe into geographical parts. It is rather an effort to point to inclinations in all Europes, at all points in European space and time: now with the hard as dominant and the soft as recessive, now the other way around, with the soft on the upper side and the hard lurking underneath.[11] In other words, there will also always be hard elements in the soft and soft elements in the hard, making the conceptualization of Europe even more problematic.

What would be the concrete consequences that can be drawn from this abstract, daoist type of image? I see three consequences, all of them easily said, not so easily translated into practice.

First, to accept intellectually that this is Europe, and give up any effort to produce images of Europe as *either* hard *or* soft when in fact it is *both-and,* and even *both-and* at the same time and at the same point in space.

European colonialism was outrageous in its exploitation, its killing, and maiming—but at the same time it also brought values of solidarity and compassion, of tolerance. One might even say that every European message comes with a countermessage, and the total message can be understood only if one is willing to accept both sides of the coin. Europe brings in its wake terrible damage, but also efforts to repair and undo that damage. A creative continent, indeed; and intellectually demanding to comprehend.

And that leads to the *second* point: trying to learn to think, talk, and write about Europe as a whole. When we project into the future for "Europe," then this very word should stand for *Europa Major* and not for Western Europe or the even smaller *Europa Minor,* the European Community. The latter is still often referred to as the European "common market," revealing in its very name its merchant imprint.[12] We have to think in terms of the entire variety of European culture, Christian, Jewish, and Muslim; Protestant, Catholic, and Orthodox; Germanic, Latin, and Slavonic, and all the others—an incredible diversity, much too much for any one human being to contemplate, let alone to comprehend fully during a lifetime. And we would do well to learn to enjoy this diversity rather than trying to diminish it through giant schemes of mega-markets or mega-plans, cultural homogenization, giant political communities with military superpower connotations.

Third, and most important: a project of systematic efforts to strengthen the soft Europe and to weaken the hard Europe. The problem is, of course, that in fighting something hard one might oneself become hardened, and thus continue the vicious circle. One way out would be the way of nonviolence, of cultivating new patterns of political struggle, and more particularly new forms of social contracts between leader and led. Another perspective would be solidarity with the weak, with the victims of the hard Europe everywhere—certainly including such major victims as women and nature itself. And all of this in a pattern of fundamental democratic mobilization, not reducing this word to parliamentarism alone, but meaning by democracy exactly that, the rule of the people, not of parliamentarians, not of technocrats.

In emphasizing these four themes—nonviolence, solidarity, ecology, and basic democracy—four basic principles of the Green parties have also been mentioned. In short, Green Politics. But with the important reminder that we are all carriers of that European cultural gene, the tendency for the soft to become hard and for Europe to continue its cyclical move through history, oscillating between the sublime and compassionate on the one hand, and the base and suppressive on the other. And just as much as the greens may not always remain soft, the others may not be that homogeneously hard either.

A GLIMPSE OF HISTORY

To explore macro-European dynamics today a glimpse of history is indispensable. For this purpose let us return to the division of Europe into five
parts by drawing lines, adding a circle in the center. One of the lines co-
incides with the Alps and their continuation in the Carpathians. That line
might be continued toward the West, cutting through France, perhaps ending
with the Pyrenées. It may be argued that *Occitanie* is to the south of the
line. The other line runs from north to south, following the linguistic border
between the Slavonic and Germanic speaking people, down to the Adriatic,
placing in the eastern part of Europe the Hungarians and the Rumanians,
the Albanians, and the Greeks and the Turks. The "pure" East would be
orthodox and would use Cyrillic letters. It is not, however, so important to
define the lines in very precise terms since the conceptual tools used here
are only rough ideas about a distinction between northern and southern Europe on the one hand, corresponding to the old distinction between *cis-al-
pina* and *trans-alpina,* and anybody's intuitive notion of a distinction between western and eastern Europe. The division is almost the same as in
the preceding chapter, but more historical and less contemporary political,
dividing France instead of Germany.

What is important, however, is that this conception of southern Europe
could be extended to include North African (Maghreb) and West Asian
(Mashreq) coastal states, together composing the *Mediterranean region.* This
would add to the concept of Europe the Arab states bordering on the Mediterranean, and Israel/Palestine. Maybe this leads to almost 25 countries.
In extension this notion of southern Europe would not be too different from
the Roman Empire at its heyday except for its northern and eastern outposts;
enclosing the *mare nostrum,* the Mediterranean sea itself. In what follows,
however, we shall mainly stick to a more conventional conception of Europe.

The problem to be discussed can now be framed using the concept of
power gradient: given the two axes, where are the highs and lows of power
in Europe, in various phases of history? We shall then use the same four
types of power: *military* power ultimately defined as *"who occupies/invades
whom"*; *economic* power ultimately defined as *"who exploits whom"* (whether
through simple robbery, taxation, or the more intricate practices of investment in capital goods and transfer of surplus characterizing industrial capitalism, or corresponding practices in mercantile capitalism); and *cultural*
power roughly defined as *"who forms (shapes) whom."* Needless to say,
these forms of power are related and have all kinds of spillover effects from

one to the other. They are, in fact, the three classical types of power: the stick, the carrot, and the idea; coercive, remunerative, and normative power.[13] On top of this there is also *political* power, the power to decide over others, including over which type or which mix of power types, to use.

There is no doubt that the *Roman Empire* put the center of power in the *south*. They invaded the north, they exploited the north, and they shaped the north. The latter was so successful that even in this century the concept of being a person with culture, with *Bildung,* is related to internalization of southern European culture, for instance, knowledge of Latin and Greek, in other words southern languages that today are not even spoken in the region. Nobody in the south derives cultural prestige from speaking Norwegian; in fact, not even from speaking more important languages like English and German that are seen as carriers of politics and commerce rather than culture. The power center was in the actual southwest rather than in the southeast by virtue of the fact that Rome was located in that part. But the Western Roman Empire collapsed in the fifth century, and after that there was a transfer of power from southwest to southeast until the Muslims equalized the south ultimately, after 1453, conquering the southeast, balancing the Iberian empires.

The *Middle Ages* can perhaps be seen as a period in which the power distribution among the four parts of Europe we are discussing became more symmetric, with the exception of the cultural power emanating from Rome, now in the form of the Catholic Church. It was only with the advent of Protestantism that a certain symmetry in cultural power was obtained, with strong islands of Protestantism established in the Catholic sea in an almost unchanging pattern for the last 300 years or so. The economic counterpart included the Hanseatic League, started much earlier (thirteenth century), and the industrious economic activity of the Low Countries. Gradually the northwest was to emerge as the European power center. It still is.

It may perhaps be said that Protestantism gave a more clear expression to some basic items of Western social cosmology carried over from Greek/Roman antiquity: a strong accent on individualism and competition, expansion in space, and a highly dramatic (but not cyclical) conception of time. Life was perhaps safer, more protected, more collective under Catholicism than it became under Protestantism after the Reformation, although the difference should not be exaggerated. At the same time mercantile capitalism was so successful in the north that large-scale capital accumulation started taking place.

All of this contributed to the industrial revolution in the northwestern corner of the European region. It was probably based on a combination of cap-

ital accumulation (that actually partly derived from Spanish *conquista* capital) used for *investment* in capital goods, not only for *buying* merchandise
like the Spaniards did[14] *and* the clear expression of individualizing Western
cosmology found in various types of Protestant thinking, also expressed in
the Magna Carta/Glorious Revolution syndrome in England and the French
Revolution in France.[15] Alone none of these factors would have made it.
Together they probably account to a large extent for the rise of modern
capitalism in the northwestern corner of Europe. And with that the relative
symmetry of the Middle Ages came to an end. The rest of Europe, south
and east, kept the more hierarchical, but also more collectivist, Catholic and
Orthodox traditions, less individualizing and "entrepreneurial," not only
economically, but also religiously.

In short: the power center shifted toward the north and toward the west—
later on to proceed to the far west, the United States. Europe became once
again a highly lopsided region with political/military, economic, and cultural gradients running from west to east, and from north to south. The
Swedes, the French, and the Germans invaded the Slavs, not the other way
around. It was they who had command over the trade between west and
east, not the other way around. And it was they who, particularly since the
times of Peter the Great, started shaping the east, not the other way round.

And similarly for the north/south gradient: the trade pattern quickly became industrial goods from the north against foodstuffs and such from the
south, after the British, the Low Countries, and the Hanseatic League had
balanced the traditional trading superiority of the Italian city-states much
like Protestantism balanced Catholicism. The north also invaded the south,
an early example being northern France relative to southern France.[16] Later
came the establishment of the colonies, mainly by the French and the British
on the southern and eastern Mediterranean seaboard.

All this makes an image of concentric circles more adequate than the four
boxes for this "modern" period. There is a first circle with center in the
northwest, including United States/Canada; a second circle consisting of the
southwest, the southeast, and the northeast of Europe; and then a third circle
of the southern and eastern Mediterranean seaboard and Russia ultimately
extended through colonialism all over the world. The U.S. historian W. H.
McNeill calls this "The Dominance of the West," but seems to think it changed
into "Global Cosmopolitanism since 1850."[17] It did not. There were reactions to Western dominance, producing a more balanced picture. But the
general pattern was Western penetration, and that is not the same as global
cosmopolitanism.

The Muslim Ottoman Empire enters this picture as a barrier and a menace that lasted almost 500 years but was restricted to the southeastern corner. After its breakdown its function became more clear: as a bulwark against northwestern penetration that immediately took place—politically/militarily, economically, culturally—when the Ottoman Empire collapsed after World War I and the northwest invaded the Mashreq as they (France) had done with the Maghreb before. The same holds for the Soviet Union and its hegemonic position relative to most of eastern Europe: northwestern economic and cultural penetration would probably have been even more pronounced had it not been for the balance created after World War II. That the balance had to be maintained with coercive means only proves the point. Under Gorbachev that coercion is breaking down, but as a consequence northwestern penetration will probably take place.

In fact, I would see the whole gamut of northeastern, southeastern, and southwestern revolutionary populism, left or right, between the world wars, from Lenin/Stalin via east-southeast European dictators (Pilsudski, Horthy, Antonescu) and Kemal Atatürk to Mussolini, Franco, and Salazar as *the second circle trying to stand up against the first*. (Pétain could also be seen in this light; after all, Vichy is located far south of Paris.) Mussolini made a gigantic effort to reestablish the equilibrium of antiquity, using not only the renaissance but also antiquity as model.[18] Direct violence against structural violence to put it in those terms.

In this chapter we are concerned both with the east-west and the north-south axes. They are both important in any understanding of Europe. The east-west axis prevails today since the East has military power, the South does not. But it is important to think not only in terms of contradictions and conflicts along the west-east gradient, but also along the north-south gradient, pitting Northern Europe not only against Southern Europe, but against more of the south, the whole Mediterranean region as such, including— indeed—Palestine. Thinking should not lag too much behind reality. And reality today is that the northwestern corner once more is penetrating into the south, using the European Community as its instrument, probably with a second uprising in the coming, sooner or later.

The contemporary power gradient has forms well known to any observer of current world affairs. The military political headquarters of the world are in the north: Washington and Moscow to mention the superpowers, NATO (in Brussels) and the Warsaw Treaty Organization (WTO) to mention the alliances. It is they who use the Mediterranean for the deployment of their ships, not the south that uses the northern waters for the deployment of theirs. The bloc system meets at times in a network of conferences, usually in the north. The leaders of the superpowers of the alliances meet each other in summit meetings; also usually in the north (Geneva, Reykjavik, Washington, Moscow). There is little contact of a politically/militarily meaningful kind between the more peripheral members, and particularly not in the south. Economically the headquarters are all in the north: New York for the American economy, Brussels for the European Community, Moscow for the CMEA system. This is where decisions are taken regarding the south, not *vice versa*. The economies of the south are shaped by the demands from the north, not *vice versa*. With the integration of Portugal and Spain from the southwest and Greece from the southeast into the European Community, break-away tendencies of a fascist type will have been reversed—at least for a while. But that does not mean that tensions disappear.

The inter-European currency is the dollar, the inter-European lingua franca is English, and the *International Herald Tribune* the closest there is to a European newspaper. None of this is south, much of it is not even European. Ultimately it will probably become European, but then hardly south.

Then, the *third circle*. Again, we could do the same exercise and divide the world into four parts, with a First world of rich capitalist countries ($10–12,000 per capita annual income), a Second world of not-so-rich ($4–6,000) Socialist countries, a Third world of very poor ($300), mainly capitalist countries and then a Fourth world, the world southeast of East and Southeast Asian countries, headed by Japan (with the richest individuals having more than $1 billion in annual income).[19] But we do not need that much specificity. Suffice it to say that the first country to get into the world capitalist market from the third circle, Japan, already is second to none in most economic fields and that there are other countries in the same region following suit. Japan was the first country to practice the basic idea of the New International Economic Order, that the economic object should become an economic subject, one century before it was conceived. How many will or can follow in Japan's wake outside East Asia remains to be seen.[20]

The point made here is very simple. The third circle is not a passive or dependent variable any longer; it is on the move. There are efforts to co-opt, to tame (Trilateral Commission, OECD, European Community); even to coerce (U.S. interventions). The first world is certainly not a part of the third circle and feels immensely threatened by non-first circle religions and ideologies. The spiritual/cultural challenge hit the youth of the late 1960s traveling east along the "hippie trail" (Turkey-Iran-Afghanistan-Pakistan-India-Nepal) to sources of wisdom. The economic challenge, above all from Japan but also from OPEC and NIEO, hit everybody in the 1970s. The military challenge is not there except in the form of terrorism. Of course, it will come some day if the first world continues trying to dominate, in atomic and/or chemical forms. The export of drugs and relocation of people ("refugees," "foreign workers") should also be seen in this context.

The pressure on the rest of Europe from the northwestern corner was and is tremendous. The northwest had the basic instruments, science and technology, industry and commerce, efficient politics and military. A feeling of despair must have engulfed the rest of Europe. As mentioned, fascism and communism can both be seen in this perspective, as second circle efforts to catch up quickly, with obvious parallels in today's Third World. They both aimed at building strong states. They were both economically defensive relative to the outside, wanting to become self-reliant. And they could both point to the obvious: the northwest became strong first and democratic later, even much later. So why should they not try the same, starting with an "early modern" autocratic period?

One interesting question is why the (Orthodox) east of Europe became communist, the (Catholic) south fascist, and the (Orthodox and Catholic) southeast of Europe both fascist and communist, in that order. Difficult to say. From the point of view chosen here some could be attributed to "chance." There was a basis in the highly vertical, hierarchical structures created by the Orthodox and Catholic churches compatible with the single party, authoritarian state constructions. Maybe the two churches predispose for the two ideologies, with the Orthodox Church being more all-embracing, *God loves all of us,* more optimistic, and the Catholic Church more vertical and selective, although not so pessimistic as the Protestant churches. However that may be, popular mobilization and a strong state as bulwarks against the northwest in the attempt to become as rich, valid, and strong as they. England was the centerpiece of the northwest and the country to the southeast, Germany humiliated by a Versailles Treaty imposed by its northwest (including the United States), became the centerpiece of the reaction, with both fascist, anti-Semite, socialist, and violently anti-British features.[21]

But how could it be otherwise? How could the first circle believe that the second circle would accept northwestern dominance and not revolt sooner or later? How naive is it possible to be, even for hardline Europeans? World War II came as a clash between northwestern Europe (minus Germany) and fascism, and between fascism and the far northeast, the Soviet Union. It was actually the fight of the south against the north in Mussolini's terms (the second coming of the Roman Empire), of the Center (in the sense of Germany-Austria) against the rest from Hitler's point of view (*Neuordnung*). The north won, of course, being stronger with the Soviet Union and the United States added.

But the two parts of the north fell out against each other, belonging to different circles. The northwest learned again that resistance against north-western dominance could take communist, not only fascist form. New types of penetration were tried: Marshall aid, and ultimately incorporation into the European Community. And this is more or less where we stand today with the European Community making great inroads into the south, even into the southeast, possibly also the east. The first circle again tries to incorporate the second, this time finding formulas for joint exploitation of, and defense against, the third, using such weapons as terrorism and immigration.

It is important to try to understand the giant forces at work here. The northwest had an edge over the other parts that they did not want to give up. The rest of Europe admires and imitates, yet wants to preserve its identity, autonomy, perhaps also trying to obtain parity relative to the northwest. One does not exclude the other. And thus it is that in second circle Europe we have both those who try to become self-reliant and those who prefer the status as periphery. A struggle that will continue still for a long time, with an equilibrium more like what we had during the Middle Ages as the only stable, but not easily obtainable, outcome.

My basic thesis is that no effort to dominate Europe from any self-appointed center will succeed in the longer run, be that from the northwest or the northeast; or from the center, from the north or the south. There is so much strength in Europe, so much tradition to preserve that there will always be independence movements whether against London and its successor Washington/New York; against Berlin and Rome; against Moscow; *and* against Paris and Brussels when they try to step into any "vacuum" created when the superpowers loosen their grips. If anything is the lesson from European history, this is it. Fiercely expansionist and fiercely independent tribes—with some capacity for cooperation when exploiting and defending themselves against others. But also with some capacity for equilibrium as seen today among the European Community, the Nordic countries, perhaps also among some CMEA countries. You name it, the Europeans have it.

Looking at the total European scene against the backdrop of this macro-historical overview, I would identify the following contemporary projects, in the French sense of *projet*; dialectically related to each other:

1. First circle expansion into the second circle using the European Community and the Western European as the vehicle.
2. First circle effort to reconquer lost territory in the third circle, using development assistance in general and the European Community/Yaoundé-Lomé system in particular.

3. Resistance against expansion in Europe in the shape of four alternative projects:
   a. the neutral-nonaligned countries
   b. the Nordic project in the northwest
   c. the Central European project in the center
   d. a possible Eastern European Community in Eastern Europe.
4. Resistance against expansion into the third circle in the shape of four alternative projects.
   a. the United States project to keep the Western Hemisphere
   b. the Soviet Union project to keep the Soviet Union together
   c. the Japanese project to reestablish the Greater East-Asian Co-prosperity Sphere
   d. many, usually weak, Third World projects, marked and marred by terrorism and fundamentalism.

General rule: The stronger the penetration; after some time, the stronger the resistance. Contradictions lead to dialectics. History moves in waves and counterwaves. And so does European history. Charlemagne, Charles Quint, Napoléon, and Hitler—and the NATO-WTO system—tried to freeze European history into some design. They failed. So will their successors.

2

Europe the Contradiction-Free: From Community to Superpower

Macro-historically, the European Community can be seen as an effort by the northwestern corner of Europe, since the Industrial Revolution onward by far the strongest part, to heal war wounds and to regain the power lost in the rest of Europe and in the Third World. The EC countries, particularly the eight former colonial powers among the 12—France, Germany, Belgium, Netherlands, and Italy from the first six members, and England, Spain, and Portugal from the next six—had seen their power curtailed in two significant ways after World War II. Eastern Europe had become Communist under heavy Soviet influence; and the colonies were all heading for independence. In addition something had happened before the war, indeed leading up to it: Germany with Austria and much of Southern Europe had become *fascist* with terrible bellicose, even genocidal consequences. The European Community was created to solve problems two and three; and ultimately, possibly, number one.[1]

Being by far the most dynamic of the five Europes mentioned in the introduction—not strange given its tremendous cultural, economic, military, and political resources—the process EC is undergoing is changing the topology of the European space; both in *domain* (the number of countries that are members and associate members), *scope* (the range of agenda items), and *level of integration* (of members as well as of agenda items).[2] Those who object that the changes affect only the EC members might contemplate that even big neighbors next to a union or superstate with 320 million inhabitants suddenly start looking like San Marino or Andorra.

Since the thesis here is that superpower status for the European Community is in the cards and has been for a long time,[3] it is worth reviewing the development of the European Community until now, adding some educated guesses as to what comes next.

READING THE CLOCK

Let us take what has become the EC flag as a point of departure: 12 golden stars arranged in a circle, suggesting both wealth and closure, on a blue base, suggesting conservatism as basic orientation. The flag is today found at border crossings to EC member states, with the name of the country well protected inside the circle, and no national flag visible any longer. The EC passport conveys the same message, with the translation of the European Community appearing above the name of the country. National symbolism comes second to EC symbols.

But the flag can also be read as a clock, from 12 midnight to 12 noon, with 11 intermediate stages. Certainly, 12 midnight, 1945–50, was dark, indeed. There were the three problems noted above. But the third problem was not only a cataclysmic war between the Allies (mainly from the northwestern corner of Europe) and the Axis (Germany/Austria and Italy together with some countries in southeastern Europe). The continent had experienced a Self-Other gradient[4] based on an inflated self-image and a dehumanized image of others, derived from religion and ideology, nationalism and racism sprouting on European soil. Any such barbarism in the European mind or body had to be exorcised given the smallness of the continent and the destructive impact of modern weapons. The image of Europe as the root of modern civilization was at stake.

The solution is well known to peace theory: conflict avoidance through associative (bringing them together cooperatively) rather than dissociative (keeping them apart through balance of power/terror, deterrence) structures.[5] The *European Coal and Steel Community* was proposed by Robert Schuman on behalf of the French government 9 May 1950 (the EC birthday) and started working in 1952 (generally the year when treaties etc. came into force, not when they were proposed, signed, or ratified are referred to). An act of genius, bringing together France and Germany that had fought three devastating wars during only 75 years, in a context of Belgium-Netherlands-Luxembourg and Italy. A very concrete beginning. *One o'clock.*

But then the cart was put before the horse because the theory was wrong (or there was no theory at all). Winston Churchill had already called for a United States of Europe in his Zurich speech of 1946.[6] What came about, the Council of Europe, quickly stagnated at a relatively low level of scope

and integration. But appetites were whetted. Two major European politicians, René Pleven (1950) and Paul-Henri Spaak (1952) proposed a European Defence Community (EDC) and a European Political Community (EPC),
respectively, only to see the EDC defeated August 1954 by the French parliament, and the EPC filed away. But the work on a European treaty was
carried on in Fouchet Plans I and II of 1961–62, and surfaced in the European Parliament "Draft Treaty establishing the European Union" of 1984.[7]
The military project became a weapons/energy project.[8] "Economics first,"
both liberals/conservatives and marxists would have warned politicians believing in the primacy of politics and military power under state monopoly
command.[9]

But military and political integration had to yield to the primacy of economics. The domain was reminiscent of Charlemagne, a name very frequently invoked by the EC, but not the scope. In 1958 the Treaties of Rome
expanded the scope with two more communities: the *European Atomic Energy Community* (also known as Euratom), and the *European Economic
Community*. The former was later to play a major integrative role centered
around nuclear reactors.[10] The latter was the clearest possible expression of
the primacy of economic interest. *Two o'clock.*

With the Treaties of Rome concluded, problem three was by and large
solved. Time had come for problem two. Decolonization took place all over
the globe as the colonial system fell apart after the liberation of India. From
1964 the series of conventions known as Yaoundé I and II and Lomé I, II,
and III, with accessions by the ACP states (Africa with Madagascar, the
Caribbean, and the Pacific)—expanding from 18 to 66 as expansion of the
EC core brought new sets of former colonies into the ACP system—came
into force. As for the empire of Charles Quint, the sun could no longer set
on the total construction, the outer market. *Three o'clock.*

From 1967 on the three communities were merged, sharing the four key
institutions: council, commission, parliament, and the court (the first two
being executive, the third legislative, and the fourth judiciary; in line with
European theory for state-building). In 1968 the customs union was achieved,
and from 1970 direct funding of the European Community.[11] *Four o'clock.*

The European parliament was still underdeveloped as there had been no
direct elections. The first direct elections for 410 (later 518) Members of
the European Parliament (MEP) came in 1979 with 61 percent overall turnout, ranging from 91.4 percent and 85 percent for Belgium and Luxembourg
where voting is obligatory to 47 percent for Denmark and 32.6 percent for
the United Kingdom.[12] In 1979 the currency "snake" became the *European*

Monetary System (EMS) based on the European currency unit (ECU) and exchange/information/credit/transfer arrangements. *Five o'clock.*

With elections every five years, it can be argued that much of this touched the individual citizens of the member states only indirectly, rarely, or not at all. With the introduction of an EC passport in 1984, frequently used for identification, a very concrete step was taken to promote an EC identity. Add to this the flag and the hymn (Beethoven/Schiller "Ode to Joy"), and the difference between domain and scope in cooperative arrangements and level of integration as transcendence is clear. The European Parliament then passed the resolution on the "Draft Treaty establishing the European Union" in 1984. Halfway. *Six o'clock.*

From 1986 on the expansion of the European Community from 6 member states to 12 was completed, via 9 members from 1973 (United Kingdom, Denmark, and Ireland), 10 from 1981 (Greece) to 12 in 1986 (Spain and Portugal). Two countries had rejected membership: Norway in the 1972 referendum with 53.5 percent voting "no," and Greenland in the 1982 referendum with 52 percent "seeking new type of relationship," reducing the EC territory by about one-half. With 322.6 million inhabitants, the European Community as an integrated polity now becomes number 3 in the world after the two Asian giants of China and India; well ahead of the two superpowers, the USSR with 278.6 million and the United States with 239.3 million, and much ahead of Japan, with "only" 120.8 million. In territory, however, the Soviet Union is far ahead with 22.4 million square kilometers as against only 2.3 million for the European Community. And the United States is also much larger with 9.4 million, but not Japan with 0.38 million. *Seven o'clock.*

In 1987 came a decisive step on the road to integration: the *Single European Act* (SEA), amending the original treaties. By now the European Community starts looking more like one country, opening for decisions by a qualified majority rather than by unanimity (meaning veto power for the member state least disposed toward integration) and for a far greater input from the European parliament into the entire process. In retrospect the Single European Act will probably stand out as the major step toward the European Union envisaged by those leading this process, many of them French, from the first stages of EC history. The SEA also put the *European Political Cooperation* (EPC, "C" only standing for "cooperation," not for the more ambitious "community" of the earliest years) on a treaty basis for the first time, with all this implies for consultation, cooperation, and common action in foreign affairs. *Eight o'clock.*

And then we enter the future, this book being written between eight and nine o'clock. To make educated guesses is risky. The guesses may be wrong. But not to have an image of the future is worse than risky. It is stupid.

One point is easy: 1993, the *Internal European Market*. Time has come to eliminate all nontariff barriers that impede the "four freedoms," the free flow of goods and services, of persons and capital. What this will mean economically remains to be seen. The EC predicts potential gains to the tune of 210 billion *ecu* from removal of barriers, economies of scale, and intensified competition, and in the medium term two to five million new jobs and 5–7 percent extra noninflationary growth. Maybe. But there may also be tension if lagging countries slow down the leading one, the Federal Republic of Germany.[13] *Nine o'clock*.

But the "educated guess" would then make a triple leap. There are still serious gaps in the economic and political configuration. The internal market will never be complete without a single European currency, concrete bills and coins to hold in the hand (and with a more evocative name than "*ecu*"— how about a napoléon?). And no serious financial planning can be done without the instrument of a central European bank. Sooner or later they will both have to come, like flag, hymn, and passport. But there is still no EC president, only a president of the European Parliament and of the Commission. The Draft Treaty establishing the European Union introduces a new European Council as the fifth institution of the Union (Art. 8), consisting of the Heads of State or Government of the Member States (Art. 31). But who shall "stand up to/against" the presidents of the United States and the USSR? Who shall speak with that famous one voice? Who shall inspect the troops, salute the flag, and stand at attention when the supranational anthem is played? A European President. *Ten o'clock*.

With these problems solved, economic, political, and cultural integration are in place. The cultural common ground has actually been the point of departure. The European patrimony includes cruelty to nature; repression of women including witch-burning; racism, and slavery to the point of colonialism; class exploitation to the point of working people to early death; nationalism and imperialism to the point of devastating warfare and exterminism; intolerance and persecution of those who think differently to the point of inquisition and *gulag*. And it includes environmental protection, human rights extended to women, nonwhites, and those who think differently; trade unions and socialism; international universalism and in general the highest in philosophy and the arts, rule of law and democracy, human rights and individual dignity; technical and social innovations, market and plans, corporations and bureaucracies. Collectively suppressed and collectively celebrated memories combine into a negative and positive, but solid basis for common action.[14]

Still missing is the European Defence Community for real military integration. As joint arms production and as nuclear energy cooperation, it has taken place all the time. But real military cooperation has been either bilateral, e.g., France-Germany and Germany-Netherlands, or multilateral in such contexts as the Western European Union and/or Euro-NATO.[15] There are the four problems of three European NATO-countries not members of the EC (Norway, Iceland, and Turkey) and one EC country not member of NATO (Ireland); easily solved by expanding EC membership and/or making Ireland a *de facto* NATO member, in return for certain concessions in Northern Ireland.[16] In short, time will soon be ripe for the European Defence Community, with a high level of integration not only of arms and arms production, but also of armed forces with all this implies in terms of C^3I (command, control, communication, and intelligence). *Eleven o'clock.*

At that point very little is needed to complete the construction. ECSC belongs to history with the waning of coal and steel. The EEC has indeed been realized with the internal market. EMS will become an EMC, with a central bank and common currency, a European Monetary Community. In the EPC the "C" will stand for community. The EDC completes the configuration. The institutions are all there. And there is a rich infrastructure for most areas covered by ministries in the member countries, such as the common agricultural policy (CAP), the European Social Fund (ESF), the European Regional Development Fund (ERDF). All that is needed is to make use of the basic working equation that *the Community of all European Communities = the European Union,* using the blueprint of the Draft Treaty, say, by the year 2000. Given its size and resources,[17] level of integration, and the possession of nuclear arms, *European Union = European Superpower* (see Fig. 2). And we are back at the point of departure; big power politics, albeit "at a higher level," global rather than regional, with tremendous economic and awesome military power. *Twelve o'clock.*

From this point on the discussion usually proceeds in two directions: "this is not going to happen," or "it is going to happen but is all to the good;" as opposed to "it is going to happen and is bad."

Those who argue against the scenario will often bring up the position of the United Kingdom in general and the present prime minister, Margaret Thatcher, in particular, for instance, her stand against a central European bank. No doubt she is right in asserting that a European Monetary Union (as opposed to only cooperation) would mean a significant sovereignty re-

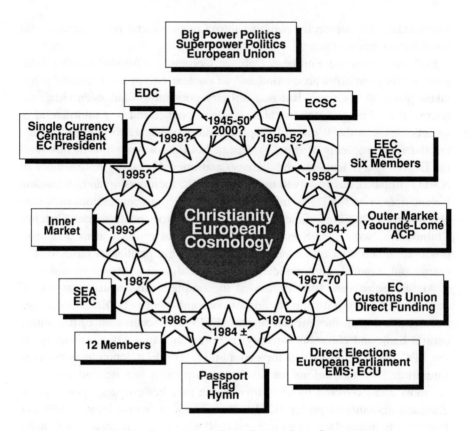

Figure 2. Europa Minor: From Community to Superpower

duction for EC members. But there have been strong stands before in the short history of the EC. And one of the strengths of the EC is the tremendous range of issues on the quickly rolling EC agenda, making absolute stands yield to some bargain, like a central European bank for a Briton as the first EC president, clearly placing Margaret Thatcher above her rival, Queen Elizabeth? And if that does not work, there is always "two-speed Europe."

Another argument sometimes heard is that the nine official languages of the European Community preclude any real integration, leaving alone union-superstate-superpower as no single leading EC nation will be permitted to impose their language as union language (like English for the United States and Russian for the Soviet Union). The latter is true, but not the former. To the contrary, language diversity, regardless of the costs in money and paper for translations, is a source of strength. Moreover, the EC may end up with three working languages (English, French, and German, the latter in deference to the economic strength and locomotive function of the Federal Republic), and make active knowledge of at least one and passive knowledge of the other two a condition for any role of importance in the organs of the EC. Switzerland is run on that basis, and successfully moved from nominal confederation (Confederatio Helvetica) to federation a long time ago.

In short, it is hard to believe that the process will not unfold more or less as presented here, give or take a couple of years, some procrastination, and some change of order. Significant opposition from the electorates is hardly to be expected when not even the Greens or the Rainbow coalitions seem to be able to come up with a united stand against the last stages of this process. Visions of the type presented here might be important for people in nonmember states to vote against joining. But they are outside. And even inside the type of scenario presented here is not in the discourse developed for discussing the future of European integration. That discourse covers economic growth and distribution, and the ability of the EC to handle the many problems of the environment; political and military union being on the sidelines. But even if that discourse is included, it is hard to believe that there would be a majority against a union.

TOWARD UNION

There are five reasons why I believe in this scenario.

First and very simply: the EC leaders themselves want it this way. The range of statements over time, across countries, and across leaders is one indicator.[18] More important is the solid preparation of the blueprints linked to meetings at the highest level, combined with a keen awareness of the role of timing in an integration process. They behave like a textbook in integration theory when it comes to priorities: knowing that the cultural base is in order, meticulously shaping economic cooperation and common action with a relatively weak institutional superstructure, proceeding all the time with *de facto* military integration, only making it look like economic cooperation, deepening considerably the level of political integration, adding on the way important integrative symbolism until all the components are in place, waiting for the final assembly of the European Union. Symbolic date: the year 2000.

Second, the configuration is shouting, even crying: *complete me!* The superstate has the same *Gestalt* as the states they know so well. Why should one or two elements be missing from the configuration? What, if anything,

would stabilize an equilibrium one or two steps short of completing the configuration? For instance, what if anything would make the European Union
decide not to have weapons of mass destruction, including nuclear arms and
laser/particle arms? What would make them say that this is for the United
States, the Soviet Union and China, and maybe Japan has or will get something of the kind; it is also for two of our members. But for us? Never!
Somehow that does not sound right. The process leading to an integrated
superweapon command may be long and cumbersome and may not involve
all countries until a (much) later stage. But given how far this process is
already known to have come, it would be naive to rule it out of court as
impossible.

Third, this is what they know how to do. The EC leaders are not busi-
nessmen. They are politicians, even statesmen. Some of them are leaders
of states that only one generation ago were "great powers," the superpowers
of those days; two of them Allies, two of them Axis. Had they been busi-
nessmen the item on top of their agenda would probably have been how to
make the biggest corporations the world has so far seen. But statesmen would
put on top what they can do well: building states, *in casu* a superstate, using
the raw material that they are presently sculpting into shape. As mentioned
above the task is done in a highly professional way, learning from the mistakes of the *Sturm und Drang* period. *To assume that they do not do what
they know is as erroneous as to assume that they do not know what they
do.* Like termites they are enacting their 16th/17th Century code.

Fourth, the skills and knowledge at the conscious level are supplemented
by the underlying code, the social cosmology embedded in their collective
subconscious. There is nothing mysterious in this even when referred to as
a *European mystique*. We can safely assume that most of them, when pressed,
would agree that they share Euro-centric assumptions such as these: that the
center of the world was and should be again in Europe; that the periphery
of the world is exactly that, a periphery waiting for the Word and the Deed
(except for a recalcitrant circle of Evil nations and countries rejecting both);
that progress for Europe is also progress for the world and that both of them
are somehow inevitable; that Western science and technology are superior
to other "knowledges" in other civilizations; that Man is destined to rule
over Nature; that the society based on competition between individuals in
all fields is the society that will produce the best results; that Christian religion and liberal ideology are superior to others.[19] They may feel this European mystique so strongly that it needs no articulation, except on some
festive occasions. Arrogantly they distance themselves from other civilizations. European propaganda, by the trained and the bribed will hide reality

until it explodes in their faces; like the Iranian revolution in the face of unprepared U.S. leaders.

Fifth, the skillful administration of challenges along the road; to the point of needing, even creating enemies for internal cohesion. There is a long tradition in Europe of seeing itself as pitted against the dark forces of "Oriental Despotism,"[20] ranging in a semicircle from the Maghreb via the Mashreq countries to Russia. The "Yellow Peril" concept can easily be fitted into this image. The tradition of a Europe united against such perils, in defense of Christianity, European civilization (meaning civilization in general), or "peace," is an old tradition in European history, at least from the beginning of the fourteenth century.[21] There is much to build on. More particularly, the image of "Muslim fanatics" is fed into the concreteness of terrorism, with the obvious function of integrating EC security forces, including intelligence services. Then there is the "Soviet threat" with its long-standing function as major integrative stimulus at the military level. With Soviet withdrawal already in process, in all likelihood to be followed by U.S. withdrawal, the integrative pressure can be more concentrated on Europe alone and not deflected into Atlanticism. The function of Japan (what could be more "oriental"?) as economic challenge is equally obvious.[22] That police, military, and economic integration demand a high level of political integration in order to engage in cooperation and common action is obvious. One integration feeds and is fed by the other.

But there are two important gaps in the picture. If the Soviet Union is vacating the position as external military threat, then where is the military threat? And where is the cultural challenge? One possible reaction would be to deny that anything fundamental has happened in the Soviet Union, claiming that *glasnost'/perestroika* is only a cloak for sinister designs. The lack of response to what to the rest of the world looks like a genuine peace offensive would be in the subjective interest of such forces in order to preserve the integrative function of the Soviet threat. Nonaccommodating, nonrewarding responses to Soviet ouvertures may disrupt the virtuous circles of disarmament and peace and bring us back to point zero again, or subjectively worse because of the expectations engendered. A more moderate course of action would be to do nothing, neither for nor against the Soviet initiatives, merely pretend they do not exist and continue as usual, possibly fearing the competition of a growing, democratizing Soviet Union.[23] Moreover, no substitute for the Soviet Union as challenge/enemy is easily available. Enemies that big, that close, with a recent history of despotism in addition to being a member of long standing of "oriental despotism" do not grow on trees. Fortunately, one might add. So there is a gap here.

The problem of cultural challenge has to be solved in a different manner. Since by definition no culture is superior to European culture, there cannot be any challenge from the outside, beyond some "exotic" features as condiments for specialists and museums. Thus anybody interested in, say, Buddhism, is a mystic with a romantic weakness for "Asia"; leaving alone that Buddhism is almost brutally rational relative to the amount of irrational faith of the *credo quia absurdum est* variety needed to embrace the mysteries of Christianity.

The challenge can come only from the inside, as weakening of Western culture, not so much because of defection to other cultures as because of internal erosion. But if the European self is essentially healthy, only disunited, and there is no challenge worth mentioning from the non-Western Other, then the only source of cultural danger would be from that Other-in-Self known as the United States. Just as acceptance of U.S. political-military leadership in the Cold War formation has been accomplished by (overacceptance of) U.S. populist culture, the rejection of this U.S. role may well be accompanied by purification of Europe of U.S. influence, and not only of U.S. language. No more *chien chaud* and *perros calientes* for "hot dogs."

It is difficult for many people to draw the thin line between being anti-U.S. foreign policy—whether this is rooted in being against superpower policy in general, or because U.S. policy is seen as standing in the way of European superpower roles,[24] and being anti-American in the sense of being against anything American, including Americans (in the same way as many Europeans were anti-German for a long period after World War II). More likely, and regrettable, would be a generalized anti-Americanism, hitting a U.S. culture at present in a less creative phase with an unimpressive production of movies, theater—except musicals—novels, art (rock/pop music being a possible exception). A general movement to protect Europe against presumably debasing U.S. cultural influence after 45 years of exposure to exactly that might catch on easily. Included would be general critique of U.S. lifestyle and U.S. food habits and exports.

With the archetype of Oriental Despotism including the Yellow Peril component, and the United States added to compensate from the humiliation of having been U.S. client states, a rich reservoir of challenges/enemies can be administered. This would apply to all EC members states with the exception of Ireland where indirect clientelism in foreign affairs, via Britain, would be a better description, and with the important exception of France which can claim leadership precisely because the country was the first to challenge the United States to the point of withdrawing from NATO as a military alliance. Thus it may well be that France already had its bout of anti-Americanism and that we are talking about time-delayed explosions elsewhere in a richly mined political landscape, for instance in Germany.

The scenario using challenges for the progressive integration of the European Community to a European Union gives a creative minority the opportunity to come up with a number of responses, to be imitated by the internal proletariat (people in the member states) and the external proletariat (other countries, including the ACP countries)—to use Toynbee's powerful metaphor. The response then creates new challenges and whether they will, or can, be solved equally creatively remains to be seen.

One such challenge is located in the domain rather than the scope of the EC; in other words the problems accompanying future expansion. The European Union is open to "any democratic European state" (art. 2), according to the Draft Charter. Imagine that the remaining 17 European countries pass the democracy test. How many of them can be expected to apply and to become members? A long list of applicants is a measure of success; hence a factor reinforcing the process. At the same time there are limits to the expansion that may be attained before the integrative level corresponding to union has been reached, and this may cool the enthusiasm. Too much diversity; too many voices. But regardless of how that may work out, let us look at the possibilities and make some guesses.

The countries that *a priori* fit best are the 13 countries of northwestern Europe, seven of them already EC members. In this part of Europe, however, there are four competitive projects: *neutralism* for Austria, Switzerland, Sweden, and Finland; the *Nordic Project* that in addition to Sweden and Finland would apply to Norway and Iceland and to the defector from that project, Denmark; the *EFTA Project* and the *Central Europe* project clustering around Austria. It is highly unlikely that Switzerland, Sweden, and Finland will give up the neutralism project; and two of them can bolster that with efforts to launch an economically/politically more solid Nordic project.[25] Norway and Iceland might become EC members, however, particularly if the EC learns from the two referenda lost and produces an acceptable fisheries formula.

In southwestern Europe four of the five countries are already members. The fifth country, Malta, might prefer the neutralism project. And in northeastern Europe the three countries are all nonmembers; except for the *de facto* economic membership of the DDR via the Federal Republic, since the latter does not recognize the border between the two. For Poland and Czechoslovakia the question is how quickly the alternative projects of a *Cen-*

tral Europe and an *Eastern Europe* could emerge, and with the present discreditation of socialism the latter may need more time than is available to be a credible competitor.[26]

The southwestern corner with eight countries and only one EC member (Greece) offers more possibilities. In spite of NATO, Turkish membership seems unlikely. The Christianity project underlying the European Community is incompatible with the Muslim character of Turkey, regardless of how secular the republic, and how democratic it may one day become. In the same vein Albanian membership is unlikely not only because of its strict adherence to the neutralism project, but also because underneath the country is Muslim. If we then rule out Cyprus (here treated as one country) as hopelessly divided still for some time to come, we are left with Hungary and Yugoslavia, and with Romania and Bulgaria. Again the problem is not whether they would like to join something—they probably would—but whether the two alternative projects of Central and Eastern Europe arrive in time. If not it should not be ruled out that all four, and also Czechoslovakia, DDR, and Poland, would apply for EC membership when they become "pluralistic democracies." In that case the first problem mentioned in the beginning of this chapter, the "loss of Eastern Europe," would be solved.

Evidently, the Soviet Union can hardly be expected to relinquish its grip on these countries (six, if we do not count Yugoslavia), only to see them disappear into a European Community with military, even superpower connotations, next to the Soviet Union. To prevent this potentially highly controversial issue from escalating, all parties might find it in their interest that the two alternative projects are promoted, possibly with double membership for Poland, Czechoslovakia, Hungary, and Yugoslavia, and with the Baltic states as the Hong Kongs of the Soviet Union. This would not only be the process least disruptive of the present reality in Eastern Europe, but also permit a recent sediment in European archaeology, the Habsburg construction to surface. On the other hand, too much diversity to digest.

Conclusion: Norway and perhaps Iceland may become members, having insufficient faith in any alternative project, at the same time as a stronger Nordic project takes shape and at the same time as neutralism, Central Europe and Eastern Europe also become more meaningful. Countries may try to join more than one project. But even with the addition of Norway alone (perhaps even without Norway) the European Union is already of very respectable superpower size. Moreover, whatever the outcome of the peaceful struggle for membership among these alternative projects, there is always the possibility of national or regional agreements with the European Community afterward, like an expanded free trade area with EFTA, combining the neutral and Nordic projects. And EC and CMEA are now relating to each other directly.[27]

Let us proceed to the second question, is this good or bad? There is the argument that it makes a Europe independent of the United States more able to make deals with the Soviet Union, and the counter-argument that a Western power center, Paris-Brussels, comes closer to the Eastern power center, Moscow, than Washington ever was. Both arguments have a certain validity, but will probably be believed by different people, given how unable people are to accommodate dissonant arguments.

For this debate the frame of reference is the Atlantic theater of the Cold War familiar to Europeans West and East, to Americans far away from their Western coast and Russians far away from their Eastern coast. But there are other contexts. A European superpower would be much more capable of a *de facto* reconquest of Africa, most of it being already tied to the EC. Three factors might point in that direction: the default of African countries on the debt obligations that may serve as a pretext for a tighter economic administration (a European version of IMF?); the deteriorating physical security of African elites who might like to have not only permanent bases from the old colonial powers (like Gabon) but also solid European police competence; and the ever-present possibility of an anti-white conflagration in South Africa that could spread to the frontline states.[28] Together these factors may lay the basis for a recolonization without the national flags and anthems of the past, but with more infrastructure than the old variety.[29]

But then there is the relation to East Asia, easily forgotten in the misleading discourse of "East-West" and "North-South." With Japan and China emerging as superpowers at the same time, the question of how all five superpowers will line up demands an answer, however tentative. This does not depend on whether the EC continues its Atlantic ties to the United States or develops a much closer relation to the Soviet Union with well-integrated, all-European cooperation. In either case there might be a white (more or less) Christian alliance against a yellow (not more or less) Confucian one when China enters the world market fully. Ominous; race and culture are powerful.

In short, big power politics as usual, expressed here as *12 o'clock = 12 o'clock*. But this time it is on a world rather than European scale, with almost half the world population involved, and with weapons that dwarf World War II into oblivion. Since it is hard to believe that human wisdom at that level of decision making has increased at the same scale in the meantime, the conclusion is that they will probably make about the same type and number of mistakes and have about the same tendency to play cards with the destinies of their peoples, in the name of their (super)national interests. And that concludes the argument with shadows of Napoleon and French leadership. France launched the process and will conclude it with the brilliance of French technocrats, "*étatiste*" rather than socialist.

Except for one rather important question: can anything be done to counteract this emergence of one more superpower? Difficult to say. But the direction in which one might look for an answer can and should be indicated.

I do not think the answer lies in trying to stop the integrative process in which the European Community is involved, with so much talent and so much energy, both where domain and scope are concerned. *The answer must be to develop the other Europes,* the alternatives, as strongly as possible. The EC12, contradiction-free, should be submerged in a contradictory ocean, not being the only lighthouse beaming messages to the outside. Alternative actors have already been spelled out. They are CSCE, E29, and all the projects in E29 such as the neutral, Nordic, Central, and Eastern European projects, and the combination of the neutral and Nordic projects in EFTA. The latter has the advantage of focusing on economic integration, leaving out political and military union. EFTA, rather than the European Community could be the core of Gorbachev's European House, adding to the present six members and Greenland the six WTO countries in Eastern Europe, as well as Yugoslavia, Albania, and Turkey, with Denmark, Greece, and the Baltic countries as associate members. And then there are the countless projects involving local governments, many of them promoted by the European Community. And the Europe of the peoples themselves, including highly dynamic minorities.[30] And the projects hinted at in the preceeding chapter, tying Western European countries to North America and Southern European countries to North Africa.

In short, there are alternatives. The European Community will probably become the European Union. But precisely for that reason, very many other things are also going to happen.

3

U.S. and Soviet World Myths:
Contradictory or Compatible?

Let us now let United States and the Soviet Union enter the stage. What are the long-term goals of the superpowers? What are, or were, they up to, in a Europe exposed to both of them, partly forced to take sides? The structure of this chapter is as follows. First, there are some general reflections on the general occidental construction of world space, on occidental world myths in general. Then a presentation of my image of the U.S. and Soviet images of the world. And finally the more topical political discussion of to what extent these images are contradictory or compatible. After having looked so contradictory for 40 years, they suddenly start looking compatible. Because superpowers have similar supermyths?

THE GOOD/EVIL DICHOTOMY

The point of departure will have to be the manichaean dichotomy between Good and Evil. Maybe one source of origin for the significance of this way of conceiving of the world is Persian, and more specifically in Zoroasterism. But there are also extremely important Western and Eastern manifestations of this way of thinking, such as the *Katars* in the West and the *Bogomils* in the East—thinking particularly of France and Russia. God and Satan are the concrete expressions as actors, even carriers of the two more general principles. Typical of the occident (as opposed to, for instance, Buddhism and Daoism) is the way in which these two principles and actors are kept separate, as diametrically opposed in cosmos as up and down, heaven and hell.

Christianity embodies this basic dichotomy and gives it flesh and blood so to speak. It is found both in the Western and Eastern churches; in the Catholic and Protestant churches in the West, and the Orthodox churches in the East. The nuances are numerous, but the basic structure still prevails. As mentioned above, maybe one expression could be as follows: there is something lighter, more optimistic about the Eastern, Orthodox churches. God loves his children, there is no doubt; there is less of Satan. In the Protestant churches in the West, to the contrary, God also loves, but the love is more conditional. Some are chosen for salvation, some are not. And those who are not, the unchosen, are in for damnation, meaning that God plays some of Satan's role if we assume that the primary sorting is done by God, Satan receiving the leftovers.[1] Maybe the Catholic churches in-between may be closer to Orthodox optimism than to the rather grueling, painful, uncertainty accompanying the puritan branches of Protestantism.

These are fundamental and collectively shared beliefs. Any social construction in general, and world construction in particular, will have to reflect such strong figures of thought. A gradient also has to be introduced in world space, sloping, even steeply, from Good to Evil. And what would be more natural than seeing one's own country as closest to God because it is Good and one's favorite enemy as closest to Satan because it is Evil? What would be more natural than invoking the figure of being Chosen by the Prince of Light and the Prince of Darkness respectively? After all, the metaphors have been worked into the population by systematic teaching of religion for centuries, even millennia; and, rather importantly, they are very easy to understand. They can be collectively shared, excluding nobody precisely because of their extreme simplicity.

Figure 3 presents world space as divided into four parts and as seen by the two superpowers, both of them within the Christian, or rather manichaean circle of metaphor production. The U.S. side of the story, the left-hand column of the table, has been spelled out elsewhere.[2] The world is divided into four parts. On top is the United States as God's own country; surrounded by a *center* of "allies," not always that reliable, meaning concretely that they may not share all U.S. assumptions about this world construction sufficiently explicitly and publicly. Next comes a *periphery* of countries that may fall either way, less reliable and consequently in need of protection from a fate worse than death. And that is the fourth and outermost circle of purely *evil* countries, chosen by Satan himself, being a manifestation of his designs, his true instruments on earth.

The question in this connection is where evil countries can be found. Searching the world's political history and geography where do we find ma-

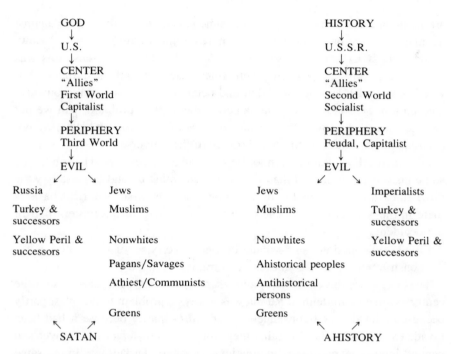

Figure 3. U.S. and the Soviet Union: World Myths Compared

terial for the construction of evil countries, or more generally evil actors, on the world scene?

I think there are four rules governing the search, limiting the choice, but also making it sufficiently broad to guarantee not only a supply, but a *fresh* supply of enemies.

First, if an enemy is needed to spur one on, the enemy has to be sufficiently strong to constitute a physical threat; and at the same time sufficiently alluring, attractive, even tempting to constitute a spiritual threat. To be Good means not only to reject Evil, but also to be able to withstand, to fight Evil. We can only know that we are Good if we are tested all the time and pass the test. And it has to be a tough test.

Second, the presence of Evil in the world also serves the important function of making us feel good even if we are not challenged. There is always the possibility of comparisons. The Evil actor provides us with the possibility of saying "we may make some mistakes but we are at least not down to that level."

Third, there should be only one Evil actor at a time. If there are more, several problems arise, such as a feeling of being encircled, overpowered by Evil forces of different kinds with the possibility that still new ones may arrive and a feeling that there may be some reason why so many are against us: maybe *we* are bad. This leads to a more complex multipolar world view, particularly if Evil forces also are Evil to each other. In a sense this was the U.S. metaphysical problem when Hitler's Germany attacked Stalin's Soviet Union in 1941; a problem that had been solved from Rapallo onward. And on top there is the more fundamental theological problem: will we not have to assume mono-Satanism as a corollary of monotheism? Have we not been taught that there is that much order in the universe?[3]

Fourth, the Evil country cannot be constructed *ex nihilo*. There must be some historical basis. And that historical basis must by and large satisfy the three rules just mentioned. The question, then, is what historical basis is there in the Western part of the occident? And then, in the Eastern part of the occident?

I think a distinction can be made between two types of raw materials for the construction of Evil countries; also relevant for the EC.

Thus there are the concrete *country actors,* sources of threat through the centuries, maybe millennia. Russia was always a problem to the West partly because of its size and consequently *capability,* partly because it had been invaded so often by the West that there might also be a *motivation* over and beyond internal expansionist inclinations: revenge. Turkey was in the same category, the capability of the Ottoman Empire since 1453 being undisputed. But a motivation, partly in terms of Islamic religious zeal, partly as a revenge for the Christian cruelty they had been exposed to during the Crusades, could also be assumed. And then there was always the Yellow Peril, probably a heritage from the Mongol tradition coming out of the steppes of Central Asia, of invasions westward, from Attila the Hun to the Great Khans. All of this could be conveniently summarized under the heading of "oriental despotism."

The second source is the *group actors,* for instance defined by some ethnic characteristic. Very important in this connection are the competitors or challengers to Christianity, in other words Judaism and Islam within the occidental religions, and then all the others, conveniently lumped together as "pagans." And that category (actually meaning the people who live in the wilderness, in the countryside, *pagani* as opposed to "civilized" people living in the cities) comes very close to the category of savages. A modern version would be the category "atheist." Behind it all lurks anti-nonwhite racism, not only ethno-centrism.

In all of this there is more than enough raw material for the construction of enemies. The Soviet Union could easily be declared an enemy, partly because of the Russian nucleus, partly because it was "atheist." The word "communist" was destined to be a new word for Satan, and the Soviet Union could be fitted into its role as Evil actor not because of anything the country does, but because of the Russian nucleus and atheism/communism. This in itself goes a long way toward explaining why the image of the Soviet Union for a long time was so inelastic, so independent of what the country did internationally, or even intranationally. The country *is* evil. Full stop.

But there is certainly more material for the construction of enemies. The "Turkey and successors" syndrome has been filled in succession by Egypt, Iraq, Syria, Libya, and Iran, singly and combined. And the "Yellow Peril" syndrome was certainly filled by "Red China" for a long period (where it could be combined with the pagan/savage/atheist/communist syndrome), a position vacated by China and now probably gradually being filled by Japan (even more fearful because they are also similar to us).

The first enemies of the "pioneers" destined to become "Americans" were the pagan/savages/nonwhite combination: the "Indians," the native Americans. The same argument can be made: it did not matter so much what they did, what matters is what they were.[4] They were the raw material out of which enemies *could* be constructed, hence enemies *were* constructed out of that material. And next in line were the Africans; treated as slaves in a way that certainly made enemies out of them, a role that they were also predestined to fill by the logic of the scheme.

But there was more to come: the Jews and the Muslims. Anti-Semitism was also predestined to become a part of the American world myth, taken over from centuries, even millennia of anti-Semitic theory and practice in the West.[5] When that changed after the holocaust, or more precisely after the TV series about the holocaust, it was probably due to three major reasons. Nazi atrocities made open anti-Semitism impossible. Israel was a part of the U.S. anti-Soviet strategy and hence not only Israel but also American Jews had to be supported. And American Jews were not only becoming mainstream Americans through vertical mobility in the social structure, and horizontal mobility politically toward the right, but also increasingly in a position to control the world myths through influence over the media.[6] One may perhaps venture the hypothesis that the present balance between an inclination toward anti-Semitism on the one hand, and "the enemy of my enemy is my friend" logic that would lead to philo-Semitism on the other, is precarious, and may be overturned any time.[7]

More reliable is the anti-Muslim sentiment. This does not derive only from the antagonism between Israel and the Palestinians living under Israeli occupation, and from the Arab states having a Jewish state with many U.S. ties and aspects in their midst. It has much older, historical roots that date back not only to the Crusades, but also to the fundamental challenge that Islam represented to Christianity as a purifying religion. The Crusades, like the many invasions of Russia, must have given to the West a sense of Muslims and Russians as very dangerous people. *One day they may come back, treating us the way we treated them.* There are, of course, also countless stories of how aggressively they defended themselves, with little or no ability to distinguish between aggressiveness brought about by Western attack, and a more permanent aggressive inclination (of which Europeans and their U.S. and Soviet offsprings seem to have more than their fair share).

In short, there is enough raw material to produce out of separate instances of terrorism conducted by Muslims a major Evil actor of sufficient magnitude to satisfy the first three requirements mentioned above. That the Palestinians were fighting for national survival does not enter the equation; one reason being that their relation to Israel was (and is!) disturbingly similar to the position of native Americans in the United States.[8]

Let us now turn to the Soviet side of the story. In the right-hand column of Figure 3, the hypothetical answers are given. The basic problem is, of course, to give sense to the fundamental dichotomy on which the whole scheme rests, between Good and Evil. The Soviet Union is officially an atheist state not believing in a world suspended between God and Satan. On the other hand, against a backdrop of a very heavy tradition of Christianity a manichaean distinction of polarity, inducing a steep gradient in the world, would not only make sense but also be expected.

The thesis is that Marxism solves the problem through the History/Ahistory distinction. History (with a very capital H) is a category that takes a position very similar to God as the organizing principle in the world, with less focus on beginning and end, on creation and destruction, and more on the process in-between. History is not only a record of events; that would be history with a lower case h. It is not only those events chained together in a process. History is the *force motrice* driving that process, more or less adequately recorded as history. A nation is under History like a Christian nation is under God; not only in the sense that History like God is above, but in the sense that the task of the nation, the best the nation can do to fulfill itself, is to be obedient to that higher force. Freedom is insight into necessity. To try to cast oneself in a role outside History is to defy higher forces, and that at one's own considerable risk. Acting against the order of nature, the nation relegates itself to a low position in the ranking of nations, or to a marginal position outside that ranking. In fact the nation becomes some kind of anti-nation, not only a-historical but anti-historical.[9]

My image of the Soviet image of the world would then run as follows:

First, there is the Soviet Union as the nation directly chosen by History, and for that reason directly under History, as the first country in the world to enter the Promised Land of socialism. Socialism being at the higher level, further ahead in the progress of peoples, this act casts the Soviet Union in the role as the First Nation. There are rights and duties in this connection; but world dominion is not among them.[10] One obvious right is a leading position among socialist nations; another right is parity relative to non-socialist nations, at the very least. The duty is to construct socialism, and to protect the gains in the USSR and the socialist countries. I think Gorbachev shares that myth with his "second revolution" after 61 years of "stagnation" between Lenin and Gorbachev (1924–85). The main duty of the Soviet Union to History is to be an example of what socialism could be; with democratic participation, individualism, modernization and market mechanisms.

Second, there is the center, surrounding the Soviet Union, of "allies," not always reliable, meaning by that not sufficiently explicitly and publicly sharing the Soviet world myths. They are like-minded countries, and once they have become socialist, which means that they have entered the higher level, they are not supposed to slide back to the level they left behind. History is irreversible; it cannot be unwilled once done.[11]

Third, the level they left behind: the Periphery that in the Soviet myth would be a mix of traditional and modern societies with feudal, precapitalist, and capitalist patterns. They are in the waiting room of History, the feudal countries waiting to become capitalist and the capitalist countries waiting to become socialist. Of course, these processes are complex. But such is, more or less, the inexorable progress of History.

Fourth, there are the Evil countries, meaning ahistorical countries. These are countries that have placed themselves outside the historical *Stufengang*.[12] A crime against history is a crime against nature. Historical laws of this magnitude are parts of the order of nature. The process, or rather progress, of History can be held up, delayed for a while, but can never be stopped, and certainly not reversed. Consequently Evil actor number one would be the major imperialist countries. Imperialism would then be defined as the last stage of capitalism where for some reason there is no evolutionary transition process taking place. History is held up through active and aggressive efforts to reverse the flow of the historical tidal waves. Lesser capitalist countries cannot afford to do this; the bigger ones can. One of them was England, and one reason why the Soviet Union under Stalin supported the emergence of a modern Jewish state, Israel, was that it was interpreted as anti-imperialist, being located on the sea route between England and its Asian "possessions." The Arabs were seen as more friendly to British imperialism than the Jews with their socialist inclinations.[13]

Then there are the two Evil actors in the East that the Soviet Union would share with the West, both the U.S. and the EC: Turkey and its successors, and the Yellow Peril and its successors. Historical experience makes them considerably more real as enemies for Russia than for the West. It was Russia that was raided by the Mongols, not the West. It was Russia and Eastern Europe that was attacked and partly conquered by the Ottoman Empire, not Western Europe. And yet it is not necessarily the case that these enemy constructions are more deeply rooted in the East than in the West. More important than empirical reality is how the image fits into the total structure of national or regional myths. And the Protestant West is perhaps even more accommodating to enemy constructions than the Orthodox East (or the Catholic South) because of excessive manichaeanism.

However this may be the Soviet Union certainly also has its share of anti-Muslim sentiment, some of it based on the Turkish experience. But then there is the idea that Muslims, like Jews, set themselves apart from history as defined by the core peoples in the occidental civilizations (according to themselves): the Christians. Jews may agree with the historical constructions of Christianity, liberalism, and marxism (after all, they were all to a large extent made by Jews!). But they may be less inclined to accept particular nation-states as carriers of these myths having themselves been forced, until recently, into the transnational existence of diaspora, with a tremendous capacity for universalist thought expressing itself in science and art, and certainly not the least in the social sciences.

And Muslims would have their own sense of history. There is an ideal society run by the *mullahs* and the *bazaari,* in other words by church and capital in Western terms. The state would just be a part of this, as something inseparable from the mullah-bazaari alliance. And the Good Society would have an agriculturally based economy with a commercial structure on top of that, with strict rules as to what constitutes honest business. In other words an idealized version of society as it was at the time of the Prophet. "Development" or "modernization" would not necessarily be against the *Qur'an,* but not necessarily in favor either. It depends.[14] Purification rather than social change would be the rule. And this Islamic rule is clearly contrary both to liberalism and to marxism, two offsprings of Christian thought on *progress,* under the eyes of a progress-oriented God.

And equally ahistorical would be people who could even be said to be *anti*historical, such as the Greens. A capitalist who believes in capitalism, and prefers to fight for it and against socialism, is performing his or her role within the *Stufengang*. A Green who believes in neither capitalism nor socialism, denying the whole logic of the *Stufengang* is committing a crime against History. And thus it is that during the German federal elections of March 1983 both the social democrats (SPD) and the conservatives (CDU/CSU) had access to Berlin with their election convoys through the German Democratic Republic, but the Greens not. An anti-historical phenomenon should not be seen rolling on the (actually somewhat antihistorical) highways of Socialist Germany, a green bus—*die Grüne Raupe auf Suche nach Kohl*.

COMPATIBLE OR CONTRADICTORY IMAGES?

That leads us to the final question: are these images compatible or contradictory? Of course, they were contradictory to the extent that the United States had the Soviet Union as enemy number one and the Soviet Union had the United States as (imperialist) enemy number one. Much of the energy of the East/West conflict derived exactly from this phenomenon.

But the content of myths are not that static; only the structure of the myths remains stable. The idea of an enemy, and the basic contours of an enemy, may not change; the precise identity of the enemy could change. The United States had the Soviet Union as enemy number one in Europe until nazi Germany replaced the Soviet Union. But that lasted only until the end of World War II, May 1945. Shortly thereafter the Soviet Union was reconstructed as enemy number one.[15] And that, in turn, lasted only until sometime in the 1960s when the détente made the Soviet Union recede into the background and "Red China" took its place as world enemy number one (having for a long time occupied that place in Asia). The country was populated not by human beings but by hordes, who were not walking but swarming. Their communism was not only red but yellow. And yet China was able to get out of that position and become something close to a center country with the predictable consequence that the Soviet Union had to take its place again as enemy number one, a place it has occupied until recently. Now the Soviet Union is depriving the United States of its major enemy, with *Muslim terrorism,* as a possible successor. With PLO and Arafat denouncing terrorism (because they discovered something much more efficient, the *intifadah*), Japan may be next in line.

Are there corresponding career patterns on the Soviet side? The United States as enemy number one was replaced by nazi Germany, which, in turn, was replaced by the United States until China took that position during the détente period, which to some extent coincided with the period of the cultural revolution in China. The basic question to be asked would be to what extent the United States—which quickly occupied the position left vacant when China was less of a threat because the cultural revolution was not only over but dead and buried—could be challenged by something corresponding to Islam and terrorism, and more particularly Muslim terrorism, in the Soviet imagery of the world?

It is difficult to say. The Soviet Union has much of Islam inside its borders, in the five Central Asian republics. However, it remains to be seen whether that will develop in the direction of the Muslim fundamentalism known in West Asia and North Africa. The demographic challenge is well known and has been pointed out very often. The terrorist threat in that connection seems to be negligible, at least so far.

But the conclusion from Figure 3 is obvious; the United States and the Soviet Union could make peace *preserving their world myths* (and that is absolutely essential since such myths change but slowly) if they *both* promote each other from the position as most Evil country to something less threatening at the same time, *and* agreed on a common enemy. The candidates have been mentioned: Muslim terrorism, the Yellow Peril and, in a minor role, the Greens. Of course, both China and Japan can be cast in the roles as Yellow Peril. Mongolia cannot possibly fill this historical role today, having been emasculated by the Soviet Union as a client country. There are also strong reasons why both the United States and the Soviet Union might like to preserve both China and Japan as friends, or at least as non-enemies. But these reasons are not so strong in connection with Islamic countries (provided oil is flowing anyhow or can be supplied from somewhere else).

So the conclusion is as follows, as a recipe for "peace-making" between the two superpowers.

First, the Soviet Union makes peace with the United States imitating the Chinese way of doing it by proclaiming that the United States is a leading country in the world, asking in return for more services from the United States in all kinds of fields, for instance, modernization of agriculture where the United States (due to the depressed nature of the U.S. agriculture) would have a lot of free-floating expertise available. In addition to that the Soviet Union confesses its sins, but also makes use of the Chinese method of claiming that whatever was bad was due to very few people. The Chinese formula was four persons, the Gang of Four. The most recent Soviet formula seems to be only three persons, Brezhnev, Andropov, and Chernenko; and mainly because they were too old when in office. On top of that the Soviet Union offers to the United States a joint fight against "fanaticism" and Muslim "terrorism," perhaps with a focus more on "Muslim" and "fanaticism" than on "terrorism." And as a reserve there is always the Yellow Peril. More or less this has been the scenario that was followed. And farther down the road there may be a reserve candidate: the coming European superpower.

Second, the United States makes peace with the Soviet Union, offering to move the Soviet Union from the number one position on the enemy list into a more comfortable position. But the United States does not have to make so much of a confession of sins, the Soviet leadership being less Christian and less demanding in that sense. However, some confession might be useful and it is quite obvious, right now, on whom evil can be blamed: the Reagan administration. Reagan may be used the way the Soviets use their three old leaders. And finally the United States would agree with the Soviet Union that the danger now is Muslim terrorism, only they would focus more on "terrorism" than on "Muslim." The Greens might also come in conveniently as disorderly movements outside the mainstream of politics; ahistorical in the East, apolitical in the West because they do not fit into the party system by making enough deals. And as a reserve there is always the Yellow Peril. And farther down the road: the coming European superpower, to be resisted by the U.S. and the Soviet Union together.

In short: the usual occidental formula, peace between two parties at the expense of one or more third parties, a formula that is wholly unacceptable as a basis for peace-building. But the rest of the formula (minus the appointment of a new enemy) could be acceptable—but hardly workable unless both parties start examining their myths more carefully. So, maybe that is our major cultural task in the years to come: to examine and reexamine our myths. And the question remains: are we courageous enough to do so?

Before leaving the waning superpowers and their myths, one afterthought. What has just been said is probably valid, but not equally valid for both the U.S. and the Soviet Union. Similarities are stressed to the point of begging the question: how do the superpowers differ? To this question the ideologists have many and well-known answers. Let me try one. The Americans believe more in their myths than the Russians in theirs. A Russian questioning the Soviet myth may have been sent to the *gulag* because his or her doubts were understood. An American questioning the U.S. myth may not even be understood.

There is a certain doubleness or subtlety in the Soviet world view as opposed to the simplicity of the U.S. world view. But this derives from a more general philosophical difference between a *nation of chess players* and *a nation of golf players*. The golf player says: there is the goal, go get it, hit, and hit again! The chess player says: if I do this, he does that but I don't want him to do that so let me make him believe that I'll not do this so that he does not do that, etc. The simplicity of action versus the contradictory complexity of interaction; in other words.

The goal of the golf player may be hard to attain, but it has the distinct advantage of not changing according to its own unknown, perhaps even unknowable, design. No empathy is required; no disturbing question like "will my way of hitting the ball make the hole move farther away or come closer or stay where it is?" The chess player has to develop empathy and ability to see himself from the other side. He has to live (at least) two lives in parallel. The golf player can do with his own.

The human condition has both golf and chess elements in it. There is room both for the technocratic golfer ("how do we get from A to B?") and the interactive chess player ("how does getting from A to B change B?"). Maybe both superpowers exaggerate their strong sides at the expense of the weak with the Americans naively believing in a technical solution to a stable problem, and the Russians becoming so subtle and tricky that both problems and solutions evade them. Their exaggerated styles may ultimately become the undoing of both of them. With the Europeans (both petanque and bridge; golf and chess) and the Japanese (both golf and go, the go-go syndrome, but also the idiotizing pachinko) already on the sidelines.

Victims of their myths, the classical superpowers are now waning superpowers. But on the way down, trying to bring their houses in order, they may develop new compatibilities in general and common enemies in particular, and redraw the geopolitical map of the world.

But we are not there yet. As it stands, the Soviet Union benefits from the freedom of the broken myths and has become very creative in the "plastic hour" before new myths imprison their minds. The U.S. is still a prisoner of theirs, and still tries to shape the world according to its myths, to retain "leadership of the free world," its title to superiority in offensive weapons and its self-imposed duty not to react to somebody else's initiative, but make the world react to the U.S. May *glasnost'* one day also bless the United States.

4

The Structure of a Myth: "Nuclear Deterrence Has Preserved Peace in Europe for 40 Years."

After this exploration of superpower myths, let us look at "the nuclear deterrent has preserved peace in Europe for 40 years"—a statement frequently made, obviously by the adherents of nuclear deterrence. How does this statement stand up in the light of data, theory, and values? There has been an East-West divide in Europe for more than 40 years, with some kind of equilibrium. But was that because of nuclear deterrence?

The statement, taken alone, is an almost classical expression of the old fallacy pointed out in any course in philosophy of science as *post hoc, ergo propter hoc;* "afterwards, hence because." Nuclear deterrence started in one sense in 1945 and in a more bilateral, symmetric sense in 1949 when the Soviet bomb was a fact. There has been peace afterward, hence because.

Obviously this type of reasoning is at best incomplete, at worst fallacious. Even if we accept that there has been such a thing as nuclear deterrence and that there has been peace in Europe, "afterwards" may not be "because." Peace could have been based on some other factors. As a matter of fact, it could even be "in spite of," because it might happen that those other factors preserving peace are strong enough to override any negative influence that may have come out of the nuclear deterrence factor. One is reminded of the data showing that patients suffering tuberculosis have a higher life expectancy than the rest of the population. Tuberculosis is a dangerous disease, but the cure of tuberculosis in a sanatorium took the patients effectively away from the other hazards of social life such as traffic accidents, accidents in the home, job and family-related stress, polution, exposure to other contagious diseases, and so on. The fact that there was no nuclear war might be due to some other factor than nuclear deterrence.

Moreover, is it that obvious that there was something to deter? Was there ever an intention to attack? But instead of just making these general points, let us look at the whole matter more systematically.

DOES PEACE EXIST?

The first question to ask is obviously whether there really was peace in Europe in this period. The answer is no. There have been five wars, even of some significance. There was the extremely bloody and disruptive war in Greece 1944–46 with Greek communists, and anti-fascists in general, fighting Greek fascists and government troops joined by the British and the Americans, and the Americans practicing such techniques as napalm bombing of villages.[1] As is well known by now, but in general not believed until recently, the Soviet Union in general, and Stalin in particular, did not support General Markos, the communist leader. Stalin stuck to the agreement between him and Churchill at the Moscow Conference dividing Europe according to the famous percentage formula.[2] It may be argued, however, that when this war nevertheless took place it was before 1949. Europe was not yet crystallized in the pattern of the two alliances. Bilateral nuclear deterrence was not established. But, however this argument would run, peace there was not.

Nor was "nuclear deterrence" able to prevent the two Soviet invasions in Europe during the 40 years' period—Hungary 1956 and Czechoslovakia 1968. It may even be argued that the causal relation flows the other way. The Soviets invaded not only to support a Moscow faithful regime and to prevent a Moscow unfaithful regime from coming into being, but also to secure geopolitically their defenses, precisely because the United States looked and indeed was so strong.[3] Nuclear deterrence would make geopolitical security regions more, not less, necessary, in a general atmosphere of threats and counterthreats.

Then there have been two other wars: over Cyprus, and over Ulster, Northern Ireland. Both of them had to do with that peculiar exercise of British statecraft: entering an area, drawing lines, resettling, then withdrawing, wholly or partly leaving the mess to the inhabitants. (Palestine, East and South Africa, Rhodesia, Gibraltar, the Falkand Islands, Fiji, and Trinidad could also be mentioned in this context.) For either case it can be argued that these bursts of violence would probably have taken place in any case, with or without nuclear deterrence. They belong to a different logic of their own.

The record is not so clearly peaceful as those who pronounce this idea would have it. But, admittedly, there has not been that big cataclysmic war, the proverbial war in which the Soviet Union unleashes its conventional forces, invades all of Western Europe, and takes some of the richest countries in the world in one gulp, if it had not been for the fact that the nuclear deterrence prevents them from doing so. But the problem with that theory is that we have no proof that the Soviet Union ever intended to do such a thing, neither before, nor after the U.S. developed nuclear arms. No proof that there ever was anything to deter. Did the medicine "work" because the patient was healthy?

At this point the methodological difficulty is obvious: we cannot rerun European post-World War II history without the presence of nuclear arms. We do not have that type of laboratory available. We do not know what would have happened *if*. But we can do something else that admittedly is a second best, but nevertheless important, in the name of intellectual honesty and as an effort to explore the structure of this myth. We can look at history and simply ask the question: What kind of experience do we have from the past of warfare in the European theater? Then, using extrapolation (admittedly a method with difficulties) we could draw some conclusions from the historical picture before 1945 about what, in general, might have been expected after 1945.

The historical picture is simple. There have been three types of war in Europe if we divide Europe into East and West, and use as a dividing line a division placing the Germanic and Latin peoples to the west and the south and the Slavic peoples to the east (we would then include, as is usually done, Finland, Albania, Hungary, and Romania in the eastern part, but not NATO Turkey nor NATO Greece; even if it differs from the division made in Chapter 1 above).

The three types of war in recent (meaning the last centuries) European history are: *intra-West, intra-East* and *West attacking East*. What we have not had is East attacking West. The Soviet army pursuing the nazi invaders in 1944–45 with the goal of routing them is no exception; nobody would say that this attack was unprovoked. The Soviet attacks on Finland, the Baltic states, and Poland 1939–40 were unprovoked, but intra-East. And then we have, going backward in time, Hitler's attack on the Soviet Union June 22, 1941; the interventionist wars after the Russian Revolution in 1917; the German attack on Russia in 1914; and, indeed, Napoléon's attack on the East, to Moscow but not beyond, in 1812. And before that a high number of Swedish and German attacks of various types. The Turks. The Mongols. The Vikings.

So what would be the relationship between nuclear deterrence on the one hand, and these three patterns of possible warfare on the other, if we take them to be indicative of inclinations in the European construction, "fault lines" in the earthquake sense of that word, so to speak?

To start with the intra-West case. It is possible that we would have had a war between Greece and Turkey, and not only over Cyprus, if it had not been for the presence of the United States in the Western European construction. These are both allies of the United States, and it is obviously not in the U.S. interest that the structure of the alliance is revealed as less than cohesive through a major war between two of its members. Hence, the argument can be made that the U.S. presence has had a dampening effect. But the argument cannot be made that this is due to nuclear deterrence. If due to anything it would be to some type of *pax americana,* exercised politically and with conventional forces, in no need of nuclear deterrence. The United States may have been afraid of escalation to nuclear war. But fear of nuclear consequences is no proof of nuclear deterrence; if anything it proves that nuclear deterrence is risky. What prevented the war was rather nonnuclear superpower control.

The same argument can be made about the intra-East possibility. A war between Romania and Hungary over the Hungarian plight inside Romania is not at all impossible. Again the same argument can be made: this was avoided, hardly because of nuclear deterrence but because the Soviet Union would not permit two of its allies to get at each other's throats. In other words, the argument would be that *pax sovietica* has been operating, and effectively so. The Soviet Union may also have been afraid of nuclear escalation, but that does not make fear of nuclear consequences proof of nuclear deterrence. What prevented the war was nonnuclear superpower control. Remove *pax sovietica* and that war may be released, like the five wars mentioned which were undeterred by nuclear arms, but stayed conventional.

At most what has been said so far could be taken to support the idea that Europeans are not good at making peace among themselves and for that reason need, in the Western part, a *big brother* and in the Eastern part a *bolshoi brat'* to keep some order. This is the hegemonial concept of peace, dear to both superpowers and to most powers capable of exercising hegemonial influence, with the obvious counterargument that even if it works it deprives the lesser powers of the right and duty to come to grips with their own predicaments. In short, no stable solution.

To this the superpowers can add an argument: "We are not so much concerned with you getting at each others' throats. The problem is not that you may do damage to yourselves, but through escalation, even if it stays conventional, to the rest of Europe, including us, the superpowers." This provides the setting for any Michael, international relations expert in the United States and Mikhail, international relations expert in the Soviet Union to congratulate each other for "keeping peace," even to the point of becoming Mike and Misha to each other. I say that with some of the bitterness of a citizen of a small European country, but also fully realizing that here are problems in Europe that any person who thinks seriously of a postsuperpower Europe will have to come to grips with, including the two conflicts mentioned. However, escalation is unlikely given how few countries are really involved. The basic point in this connection, however, is that at no point do we come to the conclusion that nuclear deterrence is a necessary or sufficient cause of peace. Rather the conclusion is that a real or imagined threat of escalation is used as a superpower domination technique.

We then come to the third possibility: West attacking East. There is only one part of the West that might conceivably have had both the capability and the motivation to do so: Western Germany. The argument can be made that even if the motivation were present in the form of revanchism (which can be disputed because it applies only to a minor part of the West German population), the capability is not present because German military power is kept within bounds, and more than balanced by Soviet conventional forces. More particularly, Germany is, by the 1954 agreement, prevented from having nuclear arms of its own (the Pershing I has a nuclear warhead administered by the United States even if the missiles to be destroyed under INF are administered by the Germans—as one example of a structure that hardly convinces the Soviet Union).

Of course, the argument may be made that if there was a sufficient German revanchist push, so strong that Western political cohesion would be insufficient to contain it, that push might nevertheless be deterred by nuclear weapons. But those nuclear weapons would in that case be Soviet nuclear arms, assuming that the United States would not have a credible deterrence since it probably would not "nuke" German revanchists. The deterrence argument would legitimize the Soviet side of the nuclear arms race. The scenario in general does not sound very convincing. It is hard to imagine the conditions under which the Germans would do this alone. In addition, just as for the famous Soviet surprise attack on Western Europe, we have no evidence that anything of the sort was ever contemplated. Neither the Western nor the Eastern nightmare has any basis in fact. The argument might be "because they were deterred." But would we not, by now, have found some traces of plans, secret build-ups, etc.? Would not some defectors have told the story?

A more convincing scenario would be that the West Germans manage to get Western allies on their side, particularly the United States, in some kind of roll-back operation, to liberate the peoples of Eastern Europe in general and, more likely, Eastern Germany in particular. But the conditions for this scenario to unfold belong more to the past than to the present. There was some kind of mutiny in 1953 in East Berlin, whatever was behind it, against their own regime rather than in favor of reunification. What we seem to know is that any effort to obtain for Germany an Austrian solution, meaning reunification in exchange for neutrality, was effectively killed June 17, 1953, not only on the Western side (where it probably had been killed already from the very beginning), but also on the Eastern side.[4] This may or may not give some hint as to the forces behind the rebellion, which took place not only in East Berlin. Regardless of how that may be, there was no effort to intervene from the Western side in general and from Western Germany/ United States in particular. Nor was there any such effort in connection with Hungary 1956 or Czechoslovakia 1968. NATO is a treaty predicting intervention in case an *ally* is attacked, and NATO as an organization tries to make that prediction credible. How credible will always remain an open question unless tested. Few people, if any, believe that the United States will risk millions of its citizens and cities to come to the rescue of some province in Eastern Turkey.

But NATO is not a prediction of intervention in case a Soviet ally is attacked, not even a prediction in case a neutral country is attacked. And the same goes for the other, WTO, side.

In fact, in Hungary and Czechoslovakia the scenario was tested. Nothing in the West deterred the Soviet Union from intervening, nor was there any reason to assume deterrence since it was totally noncredible. Nuclear deterrence, whatever that is, did not maintain peace in these cases. But that does not mean it was irrelevant. By increasing tension nuclear "deterrence" may, as mentioned, have been a contributing factor behind those tragic, and criminal, attacks.

But then the objection would be that I have left out the fourth and major scenario, that there nevertheless was/is a past, present or future Soviet plan to attack Western Europe, effectively deterred by nuclear deterrence. Even if not a part of the European belligerent tradition of the past, present and future might be different, adding this new scenario. The preceding pages are efforts to show how unlikely it is that nuclear deterrence has had any positive peace-keeping influence in connection with the other three types of war in Europe. But the fact that there has been no such Soviet attack on the West is at least compatible with the idea that Western nuclear power has had a deterring effect.[5] But we are then back to the point of departure. The absence of a Soviet attack may also be due to at least four other reasons that add up to one conclusion: the scenario does not make sense. And those four reasons are not difficult to understand.

First, there is the problem of motivation. Soviet theory is, or was, at least to some extent, marxist theory. And marxist theory takes a dim view of capitalist society and sees a coming socialist society, of which there may be many varieties, as inevitable. But that is a theory about processes inside individual European societies, not a theory of Soviet hegemony. Soviet hegemony might enter the picture as a midwife to secure the birth of a socialist society under appropriate conditions. This might constitute a factor that could trigger an invasion provided the coming of socialism was sufficiently close. A condition for that again would be a possible Communist party takeover, as in Czechoslovakia 1948 (which did not happen under Red Army cover; the Red Army came later).

However, no Western European society seems to be on the brink of a communist party takeover; and very much less so the Western European region as a whole. It may be argued that Greece once was, and that the "problem" was removed by Anglo-American interventionism precisely for that reason. If Italy ever was, this was counteracted by Stalin's insistence (to Togliatti) that Italian partisans, mainly communists, effectively fighting the nazis should be demobilized after the war—in accordance with Western wishes.[6] And France was never anywhere near takeover conditions. If anything "deterred" a Soviet intervention, it was not the nuclear weapons but welfare state practices that blunted the contradictions of capitalist society, Marshall aid, and economic growth.

A *second* motivation for Soviet hegemonical intervention would be geopolitical considerations: to secure the borders of the Soviet Union by exercising control over their neighbors so as to have a possible next world war take place outside the Soviet Union, in a security belt of countries. With the exception of Norway and Turkey, Soviet European neighbors are in Eastern Europe so interventions to secure the security belt (like Hungary and Czechoslovakia) would be cases of intra-East warfare not relevant for the theory of nuclear deterrence. Rather, they are relevant for the old theory that it is dangerous to be protected. The major danger to Eastern European countries obviously comes from their self-appointed protector, not from the West. There is something corresponding to this on the Western side: the

United States would definitely intervene one way or the other if a classical communist party came to power in Italy (plans were already drawn up for that purpose, as for Greece and for Turkey).

Then there is a *third* factor affecting the likelihood that the Soviet Union would strike westward, all the time assuming that strikes would be limited to its geopolitical security area. The country attacked may not have been capable of defending itself, which is very different from nuclear, super-power, retaliatory deterrence. Hungary and Czechoslovakia came out of World War II with a bad reputation in that regard. Other countries came out with a very positive reputation: Finland, Poland, Yugoslavia, and Albania. However much the Soviet Union has been provoked, there was never a military intervention during these 40 years of these four countries. In other words, the hypothesis would be that it was defensive defense, not nuclear weapons, that deterred.

This leads to the *fourth* factor: would the Soviet Union really have had the capability to keep several hostile Western countries occupied at the same time? To conquer a small country may be easy. But to keep, for instance, Albania under control with no observable sign of resistance would have been quite a different matter. Afghanistan is the proof of this. A major Soviet miscalculation; a typical superpower underestimation of the defensive capability of another people (although U.S./CIA arms helped a lot). Again defensive defense, not nuclear deterrence would have been operating.

Hence I am left with the conclusion that nuclear deterrence has not deterred and mainly because there was nothing to deter. The other conflicts took place either because nuclear deterrence was *irrelevant*, or *in spite of* nuclear deterrence, or simply *because of* nuclear deterrence, in order to secure buffer regions and bases, in Europe and elsewhere. When the Soviet Union has not attacked Western Europe, and probably never even really planned to do so, it may be because the motivation was not strong enough. But it may also be because the capability was insufficient throughout this period to conquer some or all of the Western European countries, and particularly to keep them occupied for social, political, and/or economic benefit/profit. This, incidentally, may also be the factor that deterred a U.S. attack on the Soviet Union in the period 1945–49. Credible occupation defense, hence, becomes crucial. And that is an important message for smaller countries. They may not be able to stave off an invasion, but could offer sufficient resistance to make an occupation a bitter and meaningless experience for the invader.

We are left with, essentially, *pax americana* in the West, *pax sovietica* in the East, and the effort to contain Western Germany in the middle. Granting that both of these superpower systems may have had some war-avoiding influence does not imply nuclear deterrence. It could also have been due to conventional deterrence combined with political influence, even to normative influence and economic incentives. It is very hard to believe that any country, in the West or in the East, with a bone to pick with its neighbor is deterred from that by the superpower on the other side threatening a nuclear war, or one's own superpower threatening something similar. It is not credible, not only because the effect would be so much bigger than the cause, but also because a nuclear attack would also hit the attacker, if in no other way than in the form of radiation.

THE CASE OF GERMANY

The case of Germany is somewhat more complicated. But here the point would be to resist revanchism as a cause, making it clear to the German people that they have no cause, that they brought their predicament upon themselves, and that neighboring countries have a very legitimate argument: *never more!* No problem with the right of all Germans to cross the intra-German border, uniting the nation so to speak. But uniting the two German states: no. Or any push eastward: no.

And this is exactly the way the issue is formulated inside Germany itself. As is well known, the parties vigorously opposing revanchism are the Greens and the Social Democrats, possibly with some exceptions on the right wing of the latter. And the parties that can never come out with clear statements against a revanchist policy are the right-wing parties, particularly CSU and the Republicans. Hence, if the real problem is to deter all wars in Europe, U.S. policy should have been to support the parties most vigorously opposed to any such adventure. But what the United States is known to do in Germany is exactly the opposite, supporting the parties that cannot be said to oppose any revanchist option. To preserve peace in Europe the factors making for war will have to be eliminated. To prevent war remove the causes of war. Revanchism is one of them; dangerous because there may be revanchists willing to take the rest of the world with them if they do not succeed.

Nevertheless, in spite of all that has been said above, there has been some type of peace in Europe since 1945. Nuclear deterrence has probably not contributed to that state of peace. *Pax americana/pax sovietica* may have contributed by putting a lid over the cauldron of conflicts, tightening the lid, maintaining the *status quo*. There is one great exception to this: the

European Community. In this area now comprising more than 320 million human beings, a peace community has been created based on a combination of diversity, symbiosis, and equity.[7] War inside that area seems today as unlikely as in the area that preceded the European Community as a peace community: the Nordic community. But neither one, nor the other, can be said to have been the results of nuclear deterrence. And the major protagonist of nuclear deterrence, the United States, cannot be said to have created the European Community, although Marshall aid was instrumental in providing some of the basis in the early years of that construction.

We may have to look elsewhere to understand better the conditions for peace in Europe today. Some people have compared the peace in Europe over the last 40 years with the peace in Europe between the Napoleonic Wars and the end of that century.[8] There is some validity to this comparison. During the nineteenth century conflicts in Europe were regulated. Seen in retrospect the countries were remarkably similar, and the similarity may have provided the basis for a deeper understanding of common interests, and for their joint pursuit.

But what were these common interests? One of them was capitalism and suppression of the working class; another colonialism and suppression of colored peoples. There was "inner peace," such as the general contentment among the European ruling elites (including the French!) when the Paris commune was suppressed, and the joyful participation in the scramble for Africa, for instance, at the conference in Berlin 1884. It is easy to maintain peace between countries when greed, including the greed for belligerence itself can be satisfied elsewhere, at the expense of the underdog, the working class within European countries, and the people in the colonies outside Europe.

Europe today also has had somewhere else to turn to: the Third World. In the first years after World War II Europeans concentrated their energies on fighting liberation movements in "their" "colonies" (Indo-China, "French" Algeria, Malaysia, Kenya; "Dutch" East Indies; "Portuguese" Africa, etc.). In the next period they were busy establishing neo-colonialism, using "development assistance" as the entry ticket. In short, the nineteenth century in a new version with more than 160 "local" and very hot wars, in the Third World, and most of them clearly related to the cold war of "peace in Europe."

Peace? Certainly not. Peace in Europe? To some extent, yes. Because of nuclear deterrence? No. Understandably, those who have held great parts of the world population hostage to nuclear extermination for more than 40 years are searching, desperately, for some legitimacy. But that legitimacy escapes them, not only because of values, but because of both theory and data.[9] Fortunately, one might add, had the thesis been valid, legitimacy would have been given to the most absurd antihuman device so far invented by humankind.

5

The Peace Movement: A Structural-Functional Exploration

ON THE SOCIO-HISTORICAL BACKGROUND OF THE PEACE MOVEMENT

When the modern state emerged out of the feudal background in Europe, the government, in the European sense of the cabinet, took over some of the functions that until then had been prerogatives of the court headed by the prince, the king, the emperor. In parliamentary democracies that cabinet was responsible to the parliament and the parliament to parties and/or to the people. In presidential democracies the president was the successor to the prince and responsible to the parliament and/or to the people. In single-party countries the chairman or secretary general of the party was more-or-less responsible to a more-or-less limited assembly, but some principle of accountability there was and is. The general idea of carrying the mantle of the feudal prince was more or less the same. However, in one important field the accountability was limited.

The feudal prince in Europe came out of a military caste, the aristocracy. He was not a cleric, not a merchant. The power he wielded was military rather than cultural or economic; the power of coercion/destruction rather than the power of ideas/instruction or the power of exchange/construction. In other words, one might certainly debate to what extent the prince should have the final say in religious/ideological matters or in economic matters. But one could not debate whether the prince should have the final say in military matters. This was his territory, his turf, the very basis of his power. Hence the theory emerged, naturally, of the modern state as an organization that might give freedom to the individuals in cultural and economic affairs, but not in military matters. The physical means of exercising power, the cannon and the gun to put it concretely, was the *ultimo ratio regis,*[1] the final argument of the king. And it became the final argument of the cabinet, the president, the general secretary.

The word "argument" is interesting here. What is said is exactly that there is a language beyond and behind the language of verbal reasoning, whether in the form of decree or in the form of dialogue: coercion, in its crude and simple form. Of course the analyst might say that there is a language even behind that level of coercion: culture in the deepest sense as the code defining when coercion can be legitimately applied and when not, thereby drawing the fine line between the king and the tyrant, a distinction inherited and enjoyed by the king's successors.

But, however that may be, there is something final in the argument coming out of a gun. In Western history movements, fighting against any monopoly held by the top in the fields of cultural and economic power have been numerous. The long tradition of struggle for religious freedom, freedom to speak one's own language, and the freedom to express almost anything one wants in that language bears clear testimony to the significance of culture; the long struggle of the emerging merchant class or bourgeois class in general for the freedom to make use of their property to make more property in one way or the other of the economy. There is also a very important coupling between these two known as the French Revolution: the bourgeois class ascends in society, gains power, and makes itself felt in two directions: economically as free entrepreneurs unimpeded by the king and his successors, and culturally as the carriers of new ideas in religion, ideology, and culture in general. The argument from above came out of a gun.

Droits de l'homme et du citoyen, of people and citizens in particular, is an expression of this coupling between economic freedom and cultural freedom. What is not mentioned in the human rights declaration is any freedom of the citizens to refuse military service or otherwise deny power to a government that wages war, leaving alone an aggressive war. To the contrary, we may even argue that what entered European history almost at the same time as the Declaration of Human Rights, general conscription into military service for able-bodied males, was the *quid pro quo* part of the new social contract. More freedom was given in the fields of culture and economy, but at the expense of less freedom relative to military power.[2] A passing observation: the human duties in connection with conscription into military service, and also taxation, were levied on men, not on women as women were not given rights as independent entrepreneurs, being subservient to their husbands. Nor were they supposed to make use of their freedom of expression. All of that was to come between one and two centuries later, as part of the struggle of the feminist movement. *Droits de la personne.*

As cultural freedom and economic freedom proliferated there were, of course, reactions. There were efforts by the state in several countries to regain cultural and economic control, or at least not to give in further to the demands of the middle classes. There were efforts lower down, in the proletariat, to defend the population against ideas they did not want to know; an authoritarianism from below that could be used by those on the top to bolster their autocratic tendencies. And there was a defense movement in the proletariat against the heavy impact of entrepreneurial dynamism, in the shape of capitalism, known as the labor movement with its trade unions, social-democratic or socialist or communist parties, and so on. In other words, the reactions against the triumph of the bourgeois forces released by the French Revolution could be brown, or they could be pink/red. Or both.[3]

Interestingly, military power monopoly went unnoticed, *grosso modo*. The focus was on political power, or the power to decide over the use and abuse of the other three power types. Political monopoly was challenged. The basis for the exercise of that power was gradually expanded through a system of concentric circles, including more and more people in the electorate of the democracies. The process was and is slow, and hardly ever went without struggle. But even so the tendency to see military power as relatively sacrosanct in the sense of not being seriously questioned or debated remained. It was assumed that in the higher levels of the state, somewhere in the deeper recesses of that organization, even in the concrete buildings referred to as ministries and so on, some unchallengeable wisdom was located. For the personal interest of the prince was substituted, not the personal interest of the successors but the "national interest," presumably encompassing leaders and led alike.

It stuck. We are still living under the spell cast by that mystique. However, the key factor here more than mystique is the awe with which exercise of violence by those "higher up" is surrounded. Seen as ultimately receiving their mandate from the Almighty, this was a new social contract. Exercise of coercive power was legitimized as a way of protecting the newly gained freedoms in the fields of cultural and economic power, perhaps even of extending them to new groups. The notion of "security" is located somewhere here: the means are military, but the ends are cultural, political, and economic, preserving the gains made.[4] Having said this, the mystique taken over from earlier periods would tend to legitimize further the exercise of ultimate, military power, within and between states, thereby definitely add-

affairs committees in parliaments and experts of various kinds as a part of the political process. There is also the possibility of doing both with trans-armament as the road to disarmament, combining the moral high stand of the latter with the political advantages of the former.

This is not the place to explore these three positions in detail. Suffice it only to say that there are many other dimensions of concern to the peace movement. Some of them are political at the domestic level and are con-cerned with the institutions that exercise political power, or should exercise political power, over the military sector. Others have political goals at the international level and are concerned with the nature of international conflict and its possible resolution, and also with the international institutions that exercise power or should exercise political power over these relations. All of that belongs to the general picture. But as this chapter is about the peace movement as such and not about the subject matter of peace in its countless ramifications, let us concentrate on the movement itself.

Rounding off this socio-historical background: maybe the essence of the peace movement goes further back, to the origins of the modern state.[7] Maybe the essence lies in challenging that vestige of feudalism, the right to exercise violence, vested in the leadership of the modern state as the successor to the feudal prince, who, in turn, exercised his power over life and death *gratia dei*. And maybe disarmament, transarmament, domestic and inter-national politics have one common denominator: to challenge the unchal-lengeable; to limit and share the *ultimo ratio regis*.

THE PEACE MOVEMENT: A GUIDED TOUR AROUND THE WORLD

Let us now make use of the mini-theory in the preceding section to arrive at some conclusions about the distribution of the peace movement in the political geography of the world, very much based on the author's own impressions, not on statistics of membership, demonstration participation, public opinion polls etc.[8] I would sometimes even tend to distrust the latter because they depend on so many circumstantial factors, and rather try to be guided by impressions and intuitions. At any rate, the differences in peace movement articulation are so considerable that the conclusions drawn are not easily shaken by what usually passes for empirical evidence.

Let us start by a division of the world into four parts, a northwestern corner of first world "advanced industrial democracies"; a northeastern cor-ner of second world state/bureaucratic socialist countries; a southwestern corner of the Third World countries in South America, the Caribbean, Africa, the Arab world, West Asia, and South Asia; and finally a southeastern corner of the countries in Southeast and East Asia. This last corner is problematic since some of the countries have first world characteristics (Australia, New Zealand), some of them have second world characteristics (Mongolia, North Korea, Vietnam, possibly also Laos and Kampuchea), and some of the countries have third world characteristics (the Philippines, Indonesia, Thailand, Malaysia, the Pacific Islands). But in this corner there is also what could be called the fourth world proper: Japan, the mini-Japans/mini-Chinas (South Korea, Taiwan, Hong Kong, and Singapore) and the People's Republic of China. Let us simply ask the question: where would we expect the peace movement to be significant, given the reasoning in the preceding section?

The basic factor would not be the level of abuse of governmental power, or potential abuse of that power, but where the country is located in sociohistorical time. More particularly, the question to be asked might be how far the country has moved away from feudalistic control at the very top of all kinds of power. The point made about European history is that cultural, economic, and political power were relinquished (but not necessarily in that order) *before* military power.[9] If there is no freedom worth mentioning in these three fields, we would not expect much popular demand for reduction or transformation, or at least effective control, of state military power either, except insofar as military power is used to block any effort to transform the patterns defining the exercise of cultural, economic, and political power.

This brings us immediately to the general conclusion: the *first world,* the northwestern corner, has the most active peace movement. Only in this corner of the world have the agenda items of cultural, economic, and political power distribution been pursued with sufficient success and perseverance for a sufficient amount of time to place military power on the agenda for popular movements, including movements that have run out of old causes and are in search of new ones, such as left-wing political parties.

We would expect the *second world* to be lagging behind not only because of strongly repressive forces emanating from the state, but also because the issue is not yet on the agenda. If we assume that the second world is now at the stage at which Western European countries were in the period of monarchic and/or state absolutism in "early modern" Europe, then the struggles fought are for cultural freedom of expression and economic freedom, meaning expansion from red (planned) and black markets via a gray zone to a blue (private) sector in full bloom, accompanying both struggles with fights for political democracy. We would not expect the peace movement to be very important. On the contrary, we would expect the human rights movement to be of primary significance, bridging as it does the struggles in the cultural and the political sectors, sometimes relating them to movements for more economic freedom. The peace movement, as Solidarność and Charta 77 insist, is for later.[10]

Correspondingly, we would expect the *third world* to be much more concerned with development in a general sense. This would cover the issues mentioned for the second world of cultural and political freedom as human rights concerns, and economic growth however arrived at, as the pivotal concerns covered by the blanket term of "development." Military power exercised openly by the state or by the strata closely linked to the state might be challenged, resisted, even with counterviolence in the form of terrorism, guerrilla, or open armies in internal wars. But that is not the same as challenging governmental monopoly over military power. An internal war of the kinds mentioned has as its goal to conquer the state, presumably for economic, political, and/or cultural reasons, *using* coercive power, not to reduce state monopoly over coercive power, but to redirect it. Consequently, we would not expect much of a peace movement here, but much movement to conquer state power monopoly, establishing "people's armies."

What has been said so far also goes for the first, second, and third world countries in the southeastern corner of the world. We would expect strong peace movements in Australia and New Zealand, but not in the second and the third world countries in that corner of the world, the political agenda items being different. But what about the real *fourth world* countries?

In Japan we would expect a peace movement. The reason is simple and in agreement with the theory. There is a fair amount of distribution of cultural, economic, and political power, all three of them to a large extent brought about recently by the defeat of Japan after World War II, to no small extent by the U.S. Occupation Forces. In short, we would expect the mystique of a state only very recently emerging from the feudalism of the Tokugawa era to have been eroded, at least shortly after 1945,[11] even if powerful forces in Japanese society now try to recover what has been lost by westernizing from above cultural and political expression. We would not expect much of a peace movement in the mini-Japans/mini-Chinas, the basic concerns of the citizens being cultural, political, and economic freedom, not military. Even though these countries are economically powerful to a level far beyond a third world country, they resemble third world countries in these regards, and the comments made above would apply accordingly.

What, then, about the biggest country in the world, the People's Republic of China? What has just been said to some extent also applies to that country, but with some additional remarks. The political freedom of the country is considerably limited. There is no provision for general elections in any meaningful sense. During the cultural revolution there was some cultural freedom in the sense of very heated debate, even dialogue within a narrow spectrum—but then the spectrum is narrow in most countries, the basic problem being whether there is a debate at all. During that period there was certainly no economic freedom. In the present period after the cultural revolution there is considerable economic freedom at least relative to the past, but practically speaking no open debate at all, no cultural freedom. Hence, the expectation would be that the focus would be on cultural and political freedom today; on economic and political freedom yesterday; and on all three tomorrow. The challenge to military power may come only later. But then it may also be argued that the position of the military in the sense of status is low in China anyhow, this being an ancient Chinese tradition. The military sector is already weak, meaning that China will not entangle itself in the kinds of foreign policy problems characteristic of the first and second worlds, and of Japan, except with some border countries.

Let us then turn to *Europe,* to the first world together with the second world, for a more detailed description. In some countries the peace movement is strong, in others weak. The general difference *between* first and second world countries is accounted for. To account for the differences *within* the first and second worlds we could make use of the factors already mentioned since there are obviously questions of degree. But we would also immediately introduce another factor: to what extent a country is involved in the major crystallization of war and peace in our time, or even of all times, the NATO/WTO alliance systems spearheaded by the two superpowers, the United States and the Soviet Union, both of them possessing incredible amounts of weapons of mass destruction. In other words, nonaligned versus aligned, and with the latter degree of alignment.

To proceed systematically let us divide the NATO/WTO system into six parts. Two of them are the superpowers on either side of Europe. Europe will then be divided into four parts (as was done in Chapters 1 and 2), using once more the compass.

In northwestern Europe we have what might be called the social democratic cluster. We place the Federal Republic of Germany in this corner, as the center of social democracy; with similar parties found in Belgium, the Netherlands, Great Britain, Iceland, Denmark, Norway, Sweden, and Finland, which obviously belongs to this part of Europe. The social democratic movement has a number of characteristics. It is usually quite large. It is both democratic in the sense of having a broad popular base and being relatively democratic on the inside, and social in the sense of solidarity and profound social concerns. It is usually slow. But when moving quite effective, although it may also be slow in reacting to new signals, slow in turning in other words. Ideologically it is usually eclectic, and not very attractive to intellectuals who might prefer much clearer contours.

The movement has been instrumental for political democracy and in making culture more accessible to the masses, but more ambiguous on economic power. On the one hand it wants to defend the workers that once constituted the bulk of the movement against economic abuse. On the other hand the movement is divided between those who see the state as the basic economic protector, and those who see the state as the basic threat to the economic freedom of the economic actor. The latter may even be the former worker, or offspring, liberated from the shackles of capitalism, now possibly entering the market as a small-scale businessperson ("petty bourgeoisie").[12] Or the present worker with more faith in the private than the public sector for economic growth. But there have been tremendous economic gains, undoubtedly, for the working class—regardless of philosophy.

In short, we would expect this to be *the* corner of Europe with the strongest peace movement, and would then include Canada on the other side of the Atlantic where the same conditions prevail. Moreover, we would expect the social democratic movements and related circles to be of key significance for the peace movement, easily placing on their agenda what is on the sociohistorical agenda of the region in general and the northwestern corner in particular. But more easily so for those who have gained some cultural and economic freedom, the educated middle classes; less easily so for people in the working classes. The rest of the commentary on the NATO/WTO region would take the form of why this should not apply equally much to the other three corners.

Let us start with some words about northeastern Europe with the three socialist countries, Poland, the German Democratic Republic, and Czechoslovakia. Everything said above about the second world in general would apply to these countries in particular. The basic concern would be civil and political human rights. Interestingly enough the strongest peace movement is found in the German Democratic Republic. To the authorities what matters in this field is less *what* is being said than *where* it is being said. The present author has witnessed very high levels of free speech and excellent debates in private apartments, in churches, and at university institutes, although in the latter case the debate very easily becomes intellectualized. The basic concern of the movement, however, would be the protection of citizens against its own military, against militarization in other words. Essentially this is also a human rights concern more than a challenge of the linkage between state, military, and war in general. As such it is only to be expected that it should be found particularly in Eastern Germany: DDR is a frontline state. Moreover, DDR is a part of divided Germany, making all these issues very tense and emotional compared to other countries.

Let us then turn to southwestern Europe, and more particularly to France, Spain, and Italy. These countries are remarkably different with regard to the peace movement, so a more differential analysis is obviously needed. We may by and large stick to the variables already used, but will have to modify the proposition that military transformation comes last.

Using that theory we would expect France to have the biggest peace movement as France tackled the problems of cultural, economic, and political freedom many years ago, even two centuries ago. Italy should be number two and Spain should have the smallest peace movement as Spain only recently, about 10 years ago, emerged from the feudal shackles of *los poderes fácticos* (clergy, landowners, military) maintained by the Franco dictatorship with very little freedom of expression, no political democracy, economic freedom only for the rich, but hardly for those not in tune with the powers in charge.[13] The problem is that empirically we find exactly the opposite! Hence, there must be some other variable at work.

Or maybe the variables are well chosen, only that time operates differently from what has been assumed here? Could it be that the French Revolution was so long ago that the French system refeudalized in the meantime, even at an early stage (Napoléon)—carefully limiting discourse, putting constraints on the operation of political democracy, and also introducing a heavy public sector and a system with state control over the private economy? And, correspondingly, could it be that the Spanish conquest of cultural and economic freedom is so recent, well into the second half of the twentieth century, that appetites for more freedom were whetted? And could it be that Italy, being in-between when it comes to having a French Revolution also is in-between when it comes to having a peace movement? Freedoms have to be reconquered; freedoms not reconquered are easily freedoms lost. They have to be put on the agenda again, and then the military issue recedes into the background, always coming last. As for France, but less so for Italy, and even less so for Spain.

We are now left with only one corner in Europe: southeastern Europe. Generally, the Balkans have second and third world aspects, but also first world characteristics found in Greece, if not in Turkey. Except for Greece— where a peace movement would be expected for the same reasons as in Spain, democracy has been reconquered—the predictions would tend to be pessimistic. And yet in this corner of Europe some kind of peace movement can be found, not at the popular level, but at the governmental level, as a revolution from above combined with nationalism. There is serious discussion about nuclear-free zones. There is a nonaggression treaty between Greece and Bulgaria. There is a significant and consistent move in Hungary toward political freedom (multicandidate elections); economic freedom (more market operation) and cultural freedom (more freedom of speech, and assembly, although far from what is needed). This sounds inconsistent with the theory, but then the theory is not about state action but about popular movements. What is found at the intergovernmental level can possibly be understood in the light of a common factor in the Balkans: the Orthodox Church, bringing together Greece, Bulgaria, and Rumania, some part of Yugoslavia excluding the rest of that country; excluding Turkey and Albania with their Muslim traditions, and catholic Hungary.

Hence, we are left with the conclusion of a popular and strong peace movement in the northwestern corner of Europe (and Greece), with the possible scenario of social democratic governments taking the lead to reorient NATO if they should come into power, *and* a governmental peace movement in southeastern Europe, held together by orthodox ties, with a completely different social dynamism. For the southwestern and northeastern corners predictions are relatively pessimistic. They will have to be dragged along, carried by any possible momentum that could come out of the other corners; singly or combined.

And this may also apply to the superpowers. A strong, popular peace movement in the Soviet Union is highly unlikely; the focus being on human rights, on cultural/political and economic freedoms for the many reasons mentioned. Moreover, it is also very clear that the repressive potential of the Soviet state is considerable, and the urgency of the matter very dramatic, given that the country is a superpower, involved at the highest level in the East-West conflict, whatever that conflict is about.

That certainly also applies to the United States. And yet one would expect a peace movement in the United States, potentially much bigger than what occasionally comes out in the open in that country. The other three domains of power have been regulated to a large extent. There is freedom of expression, there is a considerable amount of economic freedom, and there is a tradition of democracy. So why is there not also a popular challenge of the state monopoly on foreign, defense, and security policy? Or—is all of this not necessarily true?

One objection might be that the U.S. peace movement is not that small. After all, a considerable crowd filled Central Park in New York City in June

1982 on the occasion of the Second Special Session on Disarmament of the United Nations General Assembly. However, relative to the size of the U.S. population, this was still small compared to the Western European demonstrations. Moreover, it was New York City, similar to the situation in France where whatever goes on only goes on in the capital city, and even so there is not much. An objection might be that people came from far away. And one might object that the U.S. tradition of the single issue movement stands in the way of efficacy.[14] The life-cycle is too short for the movement to have an impact. The platform for a peace movement has to be so narrow that it cannot possibly lead to any basic change. But what the movement is demanding is in its consequences a rather basic change, even if the rhetoric is narrow.

Consequently, other explanations would be needed. Of course, there is the superpower element, the general calling to the very forefront of a major confrontation, a factor used above to account for the absence of a Soviet peace movement relative to, for instance, the level found in the German Democratic Republic. There is also less of a peace movement in the neutral and nonaligned nations in Europe. Sweden and Finland have a long and important tradition and so do Austria and Switzerland, but the movements are nevertheless small; in Yugoslavia very small indeed. The same could have been said about Spain. If it had not been for Spain's dramatic and recent transformation, and the leadership enrolling Spain into NATO, the level would still have been very low.

However, it is unnecessary to change one's grounds in trying to account for the sporadic nature of the U.S. movement. There is almost no *general* peace movement. There was an anti-Vietnam movement that probably would not have taken off the ground had it not been for general conscription hitting the U.S. college population of a solid middle-class background. A group capable of hitting back, if not in the interest of the Vietnamese people at least in their own self-interest. Correspondingly, the anti-ABM movement and the anti-testing movement can be seen as middle-class reactions in the Boston area. And general U.S. reaction to radioactivity in the atmosphere hitting the food chains can be seen as precisely that, rather than as a general peace movement. Why should this be the case given that the United States has this high level of cultural, economic, and political freedom?

The reason might be found in the same direction as the effort to account for the paucity of a French peace movement. The transformation was a long time ago, at the end of the eighteenth century, with no basic change since that time except for the expansion of the system of concentric circles defining the electorate in the democratic process. At that time the state also crystallized in the United States of America, exhibiting clearly feudal characteristics. The president, the successor to the king, was not president by the grace of God, but by the grace of the people. But the people were there by the grace of God; as a chosen people in a promised land. To secure those lands, even to expand them, became more than merely a question of cost-benefit analysis: asking does it pay to expand or will we have to pay too high a price? Rather, it became a sacred right, even a duty, a "manifest destiny." In U.S. eyes, to be conquered by the United States was no ordinary conquest. It was an honor—a sentiment also exhibited by the French when they moved into a country and among other things bestowed upon that people a language held by the French to be superior to any other. The sacred is not to be touched, a major reason in my view why U.S. foreign policy and the military sector will remain as it is for a long time. Untouchable, except for details.

On top of this, but not unrelated to it, comes a factor not found in France. The socio-historical logic of the United States is different. What was obtained two centuries ago was obtained by moving away from Europe, not by participating in the many and painful European transformations. Thus it is that the United States never really had a labor movement concerned with basic social transformation. That movement also became a single issue movement of trade unionism, concerned more single-mindedly with wages and working conditions. It has been pointed out above that a social and democratic working class movement, as can be found in Spain but much less in France, seems to be at least a very helpful factor in connection with the peace movement. That factor is missing in the United States. Even democracy is to a large extent missing in the United States—the parties offering too little choice and the participation rates in elections (38.5% November 1986, 50.3% November 1988) being scandalously low.

And thus it is also that the United States does not really have a Green movement. There was the explosive phenomenon of the flower children or generation for that matter, in the late sixties and early seventies, partly related to the anti-Vietnam movement. At any rate, as flowers they wilted relatively quickly, not providing a general context for a peace movement of sufficient strength. The narrowness of the debate, the discourse control, is an important factor here.

The conclusion can only be the same as for France. Maybe there is a need for a second American Revolution, this time not against some foreign power but against itself, in an effort to reconquer freedoms lost? In sufficient retrospect we might perhaps one day say that the anti-Vietnam movement was the beginning of this, later to be joined by other movements. Of course, there was a counterrevolution. The Reagan administrations of the 1980s were strong, and in line with what one would expect: the strengthening of the state in its military manifestation, legitimized by right-wing Christian fundamentalism. And, of course, they were also for capital punishment and against abortion: only the state has the right to take life; not the individual, and certainly not the woman.

PEACE MOVEMENT STRATEGY

That concludes our survey of the peace movement situation around the world. In a world perspective a small phenomenon, mainly located in the northwestern corner of Europe; Canada, Australia, and New Zealand. In a NATO/ WTO context a rather important phenomenon, threatening the solidity of these interstate alliances, particularly because the superpowers are lagging behind so much that an asynchrony is introduced, causing rifts in the system. If the superpowers were moving politically at the same pace as the leadership of lesser allies, who somehow have to reflect at least some of the popular sentiment, they could more easily find solutions together. As it is (U.S. behind, the Soviet Union ahead) there are confrontations, not only between people and their governments or leadership in general but also between the governments of the allies and superpower governments.

And inside Europe, as depicted with four quadrants, there is already a certain rift across the alliances with the northern part less reliable in the NATO alliance (to this should then be added Greece) and the southern part less reliable in the WTO system. This, in turn, is the only reflection of the impact the peace movement has had inside the countries, actually limited to the northwestern corner since the movement is mainly governmental in the southeastern corner. But the debate has been reopened all over, on military doctrines in general and deterrence in particular, questioning the unquestionable. And the basic question asked is what always should be and always ultimately becomes the question of the peace movement: *could we not abolish war as a social institution?* Could we not do the same to war as has already been done to slavery and to colonialism and to imperialism—not that we cannot find remnants of these institutions lingering on in some parts of the world, but they are no longer seen as legitimate!

For this giant task strategic linkages are necessary, and the question is in what direction. The peace movement cannot stop missiles or militarization alone, nor can the underlying peace movement abolish war alone. *Domestically* it is indispensable for the peace movement to link itself to movements in the other three domains of power. More particularly, there has to be solid cooperation with cultural power, here simply defined as religious/ideological elites and intellectuals who can formulate concrete policy alternatives. This means church and political ideologues and, nowadays, peace researchers. Equally indispensable are good links to the political domain, meaning to political carriers that can take the message and carry it into the corridors of power where decisions are made, where footnotes are written to NATO communiques, and so on. In Western democracies that means political parties, such as the social democrats and the Greens. In Eastern party states this means factions within parties, generation groups, new social strata, and so on.

But what about the economic domain of power? I think it has to be shown, convincingly, that what the peace movement stands for pays, and to all or most sectors in society. It has to be shown that the country as such, and the people more particularly, are worse off, not better off because of the arms burden; that conversion of part of the arms industry is possible; and that a world no longer ridden by armed conflict could permit an even higher level of economic prosperity for all. Today it is not so difficult to show this on paper, but difficult to convince the major actors, meaning state enterprises, private enterprise, and workers of all kinds.

Finally, it may be argued that the peace movement also has to have links to the military sector. The issues raised have also to be raised within the armed forces. The peace movement has to be a crystallizing, catalytic agent that mobilizes cultural power, political power, economic power, and military power, bringing them together in a synergistic fashion capable of transforming the social formation. And if social transformation is best done by people who themselves have undergone some kind of transformation,[15] then not only the tactic but also the strategy of the peace movement would be to provide people with a setting for that kind of personal experience. The strategy would let them be born again, to use the Christian metaphor.

All this is very important, a major reason why the peace movement is much more than a pressure group trying to change the minds and the actions of decision makers. *It is also a way of living peace,* of engendering new relations among people, of practicing the goals of the movements in its actions. In that sense it can be compared to the civil rights movement in the United States where the most convincing message was less the public goals of the movement than the fact that within the movement blacks and whites worked hand in hand. The concomitant of this is clear; since blacks and whites now work much less together than during the conflict some of the momentum has also been lost. And correspondingly, there is a limit to how much internal squabble, how much conflict a peace movement can have before the public rightly starts asking "are these people really peaceful enough, can they bring about a peaceful change when they are not even able to keep peace among themselves?"

Internationally it is equally clear that the movement has to have a very rich network of interlinkages. More concretely this means that all four corners in the quadrangle of the power domains just mentioned have to transnationalize and the same goes for the catalytic agent in the center, the movement. This is exactly what happened in the 1980s: religious and secular ideologists found each other across borders and so did peace researchers. There is cooperation, although far less than what will have to come later on among like-minded parties on peace issues across borders. There are efforts to internationalize conversion movements, but these are still weak. There are important organizations such as *Generals for Peace* across borders. And the peace movement itself, as was to be predicted given British leadership (as for the antislavery movement and the anticolonial movement) has also transnationalized in the European campaign for nuclear disarmament (END) with its international conferences in Brussels (1982), Berlin (1983), Perugia (1984), Amsterdam (1985), Paris (1986), Coventry (1987), Lund (1988), and Vitoria (1989).

But this is the small peace movement, a prelude to the big Peace Movement *qui attend son heure*. One day that time will come—hopefully not triggered by some major socio-political catastrophe.[16]

6

The Green Movement:
A Socio-Historical Exploration*

ONE PROBLEM, THREE APPROACHES

The Green Movement is still puzzling people, and particularly when it takes the form of a Green party, and most particularly in connection with the German party, the so far most important one, *Die Grünen,* with all its internal problems. Party members are said to be unpredictable and unable/unwilling to make any compromises with any other actors on the party political scene; consequently they are not really in politics, they are only political. For a party launched in 1981 to break through the 5 percent barrier (they made 5.6 percent) already in the elections March 1983, and then move on to 7, 8, 9 percent in subsequent elections, is already an achievement and leads to three obvious hypotheses about the future: it will continue its comet-like growth; it will find its natural level as a party below 10 percent but possibly still above 5 percent; it will dwindle down to zero again, which to some people is where it belongs.[1] The latter seems inconsistent with the general trend, with green or rainbow parties found in 25 countries around the world with representatives in the legislative bodies of 11 countries.

The following is an effort to explore the phenomenon, particularly directed to people used to conceiving of politics only in terms of blue and red: market forces protected by conservative parties and *étatiste* forces with planning and redistribution protected by socialist parties; both of them found in democratic and dictatorial versions. The Greens are obviously different, neither blue nor red, neither dictatorial nor democratic in the parliamentarian sense of that word. In spite of participating in parliamentary elections, mass

77

action, direct democracy, local autonomy, self-reliance, and so on are obviously closer to the green heart.

Hence, what do they stand for, where do they come from, who are they? Without in any sense claiming to have valid or novel answers to these questions, three analytical approaches are tried here: *ideological, historical,* and *sociological;* not necessarily compatible, not necessarily contradictory, but well suited to shed some light on the Green phenomenon.

THE GREEN MOVEMENT: AN IDEOLOGICAL CHARACTERIZATION

"A Survey of Green Policies" that follows is divided into 20 points, organized in five packages with four points in each. Mainstream characteristics of first world societies are confronted with their counterpoint Green policies and movements. The list is self-explanatory; suffice it here only to add some remarks about how it came into being[2] (see pp. 80–81).

The point of departure is a simple model of mainstream society with an economic basis, military basis, and structural basis. The latter is particularly important for this is where the pillars of the Western social formation are found: the state with its bureaucracy and its plans, capital with its corporations and its markets, and the intelligentsia with its research, serving both of them. The BCI complex, for Bureaucracy, Corporation, and Intelligentsia. Then there is a biased recruitment of people into these institutions: Middle-Aged Males with University education (MAMUs) from the dominant racial/ethnic group being preponderant almost everywhere. It is this structure, then, and composed in that particular manner that organizes the economic and military basis of society. And all of this is done, manifestly, in order to achieve what is here called the "Bourgeois Way of Life" with its four characteristics. This way of life seems to carry in its wake a "Chemical Way of Life" with addiction and *panem et circenses,* in ways known to everybody in the first world. The BWL/CWL complex.[3]

Let us now formulate two propositions about the Green Movement:

1. The Green Movement is an umbrella movement for a number of partial movements, each attacking one or more elements on this list.
2. The Green Movement differs from many other social movements in denying that basic social problems can be solved attacking one single factor; advocating a much more wholistic approach.

Thus the Green Movement is a federation of constituent movements and aims at an alternative society roughly characterized by the right-hand column in the survey of the policies. Many other lists can be made, not necessarily better or worse than this one, and usually somewhat less comprehensive. To be a "green" one does not have to subscribe to all of these ideas, but probably has to agree with more than just one of them. There is a correlation in the ideological universe and not only because ideas happen to be held by the same people. There is some kind of internal consistency. The list conjures up for one's inner eye the vision of a decentralized society, probably some kind of federation, with strongly autonomous units using the local bases in a self-reliant manner, trying not to become dependent on the outside, including for military purposes. Inside this social formation an Alternative Way of Life is supposed to come into being, more or less as described here.[4]

There is no doubt that ideologically the Green Movement is in neither the liberal/conservative/capitalist nor the marxist/socialist traditions, but more in the anarchist tradition, and more particularly in the nonviolent part of that tradition. Two great names from the Third World in this century, Gandhi and Mao Zedong, have overshadowed the great French and Russian thinkers of the nineteenth century, St. Simon and Proudhon, Bakunin and Kropotkin. There is much to draw upon. But this is not necessarily a philosophically deeply reflective movement. It is rather, as pointed out above, a more or less tightly knit federation of single-issue movements, some of them with relatively low life expectancy, but then possibly to be revived within a more general Green setting. Thus I doubt that there is much to learn about the ideology of this movement from the study of the six names mentioned and I doubt that the members of these movements themselves have been much inspired by those books. Rather, *the Green Movement is a general reaction to the malfunctioning of the Western social formation.* It is a reaction to the generally lamented "crisis," and purports to bring into society a number of initiatives that, when realized on a large enough scale, would constitute a solution, in the usual sense of giving rise to new types of problems.

THE GREEN MOVEMENT: A HISTORICAL CHARACTERIZATION

However, this ideological approach is a much too rational way of looking at a phenomenon like the Green Movement. The movement is a part of a socio-historical dialectic, like any other social movement, and should be understood in the light of that dialectic. There are many opinions about the basic dialectic of the Western social formation. My perspective runs about as follows.[5]

Let us take as point of departure the classical European social formation, often referred to as "feudal," which is acceptable if that concept is understood to transcend the Middle Ages. In that formation the clergy was on top, then came the aristocracy, then the merchants (and some artisans), then

A Survey of Green Policies

	MAINSTREAM CHARACTERISTICS	GREEN POLICIES, MOVEMENTS
ECONOMIC BASIS	1. Exploitation of *internal proletariat*	cooperative enterprises, movements, labor buyer/seller difference abolished, customers directly involved
	2. Exploitation of *external sector*	co-existence with the Third World; only equitable exchange relations; liberation movements
	3. Exploitation of *nature*	ecological balance Person-Nature; building diversity, symbiosis; complete or partial vegetarianism
	4. Exploitation of *self*	more labor- and creativity-intensity; decreasing productivity some fields; alternative technologies
MILITARY BASIS	1. Dependency on *external sector*	self-reliance; self-sufficiency in food, health, energy and defense
	2. Dependency on *formal sector*, BCI complex	local self-reliance, decreasing urbanization, intermediate technology
	3. *Offensive* defense policies, destructive defense technology	defensive defense policies, with less destructive technology; also non-military, nonviolent defense
	4. *Alignment with superpowers*	non-alignment, even neutralism; decoupling from superpowers

(A Survey of Green Policies *continued*)

STRUCTURAL BASIS	1. *Bureaucracy,* state [plan] strong and centralized	citizen's initiatives (*Bürges initiatives*); recentralization of local level; building federations of local units
	2. *Corporation,* capital [market] strong and centralized	building informal, green economy; production for self-consumption, production for non-monetary exchange, production for local cycles
	3. *Intelligentsia,* research strong and centralized	high-level non-formal education building own forms of understanding
	4. MAMU factor; BCI peopled by middle-aged males with university education (and from dominant race/ethnic group)	feminist movements, justice/equality; new culture and structure; movements of the young and the old; movements for racial/ethnic equality
BOURGEOIS WAY OF LIFE	1. *Non-manual work,* eliminating heavy, dirty, dangerous work	keeping the gains when healthy, mixing manual and non-manual
	2. *Material comfort,* dampening fluctuations of nature	keeping the gains when healthy, living closer to nature
	3. *Privatism,* withdrawal into family and peer groups	communal life in bigger units, collective production/consumption
	4. *Security,* the probability that this will last	keeping security when healthy, making lifestyle less predictable
CHEMICAL CIRCUS WAY OF LIFE	1. Alcohol, tranquilizers, drugs	*moderation,* experiments with non-addictive, life-enhancing things
	2. Tobacco, sugar, salt, tea/coffee	*moderation,* enhancing the body's capacity for joy, e.g. through sex
	3. Chemically treated food, *panem* natural fibers removed	bio-organic cultivation, health food, balanced food, *moderation*
	4. *Circenses,* TV, sport, spectatorism	generating own enrichment *moderate* exercise, particularly as manual work, walking, bicycling

the peasants (and some workers), and at the bottom were the marginalized groups: gypsies, Jews and Arabs, women.[6]

Let us now see each of these five groups as the carrier of successive social transformations. *First,* the revolt of the aristocracy against the clergy, secularizing the social order, separating state and church, gradually marginalizing the latter. *Second,* the revolt of the merchants against the top two, claiming a place in society that could be legitimized neither as God's servants nor by noble birth, invoking such instruments as human rights to promote social and geographical mobility. *Third,* the revolt of the fourth layer, workers of all kinds, basically men, in order to have a better share in the social product that the workers themselves were largely responsible for bringing into being, and in order to benefit from the social mobility channels opened by the bourgeoisie. Socialist parties, social democrats, trade unions—and communists.[7]

And then, *fourth,* the transformation spearheaded by the bottom layer, by what today would be the foreign workers, by the women, by ethnic groups marginalized by the social order set up by the other four, with the clergy transformed into intellectuals, the aristocrats into bureaucrats/capitalists, and the commercial people; the capitalists remaining capitalists so that the three together constitute the BCI complex, populated by MAMUs, many of them coming from the working classes. Logically, socio-logically, and socio-historically, there is not the slightest reason why they should not also claim their right to come into the society created by the other four, opening that society for foreign workers and women alike, thus constituting a pressure on the patriarchal, ethnocentric Western social formation.[8]

However, no social movement wants only to fill positions in the existing structure. It also wants to change that structure. If this is not the case, the movement is no longer social. It is just a number of parallel individual activities to promote their own social careers, on an individual basis, into slots already prepared in the structure. Social change is used to legitimize striving for individual careers; individual careers may then be used "inside the system" to promote social change—either approach may be more or less successful. The third social transformation, by the working class, probably changed the workers more than the social order they wanted to transform, but in so doing also changed that social order. Neither the fifth nor the fourth group in this image of the classical Western society was alone in what it was doing; it was always aided by enlightened/disgruntled individuals from the other groups. Nor did everybody in the group participate in the transformation, Social history is never that neat.[9]

Let us try to translate this into the concrete terms of party politics. Let us assume that the first two groups, the clergy and the aristocracy with their institutions, church and university, land, military, and law constitute the backbone of conservative society. They are the basic carriers of conservative parties. Of course, they have many more followers than their own numbers should indicate, among other reasons because they command institutions that reach deep down in society, to its very end, the outcasts (particularly true of church and military), serving as vacuum cleaners to scoop up even the social debris at the very bottom, putting them at the disposal of the top, at least as believers, soldiers, and voters.[10]

Given that image, it is clear that the *conservative parties* have received three basic challenges, corresponding to transformations nos. two, three, and four, respectively.

The first challenge came from the second transformation, from a strongly individualistic, human rights-oriented bourgeoise in favor of free circulation of production factors, goods and services, of labor skilled and unskilled, of capital and nature. In other words: the *liberal parties*.

The second challenge came from the third transformation: the mass movements of the working classes, backed up by their strong institution, trade unions; in other words the *socialist/labor parties*.

And then the third challenge corresponding to the fourth transformation: the Green Wave, ultimately, and necessarily also organized as one or more political parties, the *Green parties*.

The basic hypothesis in this connection would be that the conservative parties tend to remain, although they transform their content. *Their task is always and invariably to resist the social transformation demanded by those challenging the social order*. The first challenge, the liberals, came, broke through the conservative barrier, formed their own governments, declined, and are now by and large disappearing from the scene.[11] On the way down the liberals made electoral alliances in many countries with the next party on the way up, the working class parties. The socialists, in turn, were able to liberate themselves from the liberals, broke through the conservative barrier (of which the liberals may now have become a part), made their own governments, started declining, and are now in all likelihood on their way out. One basic reason for that, incidentally, is that the trade unions are also on their way out as major social forces, simply because they do not muster adequate numbers of sufficiently exploited workers who think collective action with major strikes will bring more benefit than the skillful use of individual career opportunities.[12]

Working class parties on their way down would then be coalition material for Green Wave parties on their way up in spite of everything that is now so often being said about their ineptitude as political partners. We shall enter a period of *red-green alliances* and see the Green parties break through the conservative barrier with the help of such alliances (later on perhaps alone), until they reach their climax, start declining, and ultimately disappear. In other words, the idea is not that the Green party is the end of the political history of the Western social formation, nor that that social formation is doomed in advance to a lasting Green future.[13]

Everything is an episode, including the Green Wave. What is claimed, however, is that the phenomenon will increase in importance, that working class parties will decrease, and that they will form alliances so that for some period they may break through the basic conservative pattern and constitute something new. That prediction, like any prediction, may be right or wrong. I would tend to believe in it because it seems to fit the logic of Western social history quite well.[14] The Green parties belong in that history.

However, there is another danger with this kind of perspective. The focus is on the Green party rather than the Green Movement, simply because the Green party is more in the mass media, in the public eye. Yet, the Green party can only make politics (as opposed to politicking) when supported by a Green Movement, made like their predecessor, the labor parties/movements (missing in the United States). Both are needed.

THE GREEN MOVEMENT: A SOCIOLOGICAL CHARACTERIZATION

Who, then, will tend to join the Green Movement? Above three categories have been mentioned: foreign workers, the whole "ethnic" complex within any country, marginalized because of their ethnicity, and women—certainly not all members of these groups, but sufficient numbers to make the movement grow. But many of them would tend to vote with the parties that represent preceding social transformations, having no need at all for new social transformation, only for stability and security and possibly some advancement within the *status quo*.

However, there are many other groups that might be interested in the Green Movement according to the type of analysis made above. They can be seen by looking at the list of Green policies presented above, especially if one makes use of two simple criteria: is the subjective *motivation* to feel concerned, strong enough? And is the subjective sense of *capability* strong enough to make the person feel that it matters if he or she joins? Or would an individual solution be preferable?

Thus, take the issue of *cooperative enterprises*. To be interested in this, today a major aspect of the Green Movement, one definitely has to be interested in some kind of production, but basically in doing things together, in closeness, overcoming feelings of isolation, alienation. And this immediately concerns a considerable number of the citizens of the contemporary Western social formation. Work as therapy becomes a major slogan, work together as group therapy even better.[15]

When we move on to *solidarity with the Third World,* the members of the Green Movement would be sympathizers with those in the Third World suffering the consequences of "modernization" and those in the liberation movements suffering the consequences of continued or renewed repression. But they would be relatively few and relatively ideological. The people really hit are found outside any first world society[16] (with the possible exception of the United States where there are also major groups inside) and will act politically in the Third World, including in green movements.

This is not the case with the *ecological movement* as a part of the Green Movement, however—the one that has given rise to the name of their movement, "Green." At this particular point in world history the motivation can only increase all over the world, with the growing perception of impending disaster, right now particularly in connection with the dying of forests, the ozone hole and global warming. At the same time, there is increasing frustration in people feeling that there is very little they can do individually. The matter is in the hands of big corporations and big bureaucracies. Individuals may cut down on electric consumption and save water in their private households; chances are that the big will spend what individuals save. Individuals may also change their dietary habits, but they feel helpless facing such macro-phenomena, and that helplessness will increasingly be translated into demonstrations and mass movements and be the kind of material of which political party formations can be made.[17]

New work styles, however, are more a question of capability than motivation. Many people engage in artisanal modes of production simply because they are capable of doing so; others may sense a strong motivation but feel totally incapable. The search for alternative technologies will continue. But it may also be that the momentum of the 1970s is no longer there, or at least not so forcefully. There may be a new cycle, however.[18]

On the other hand, there are all the points associated with another major component in the Green Movement: the *peace movement*. This is a broad movement not only concerned with such military matters as decreasing dependence on offensive weaponry, particularly nuclear arms; and transarmament in the direction of social defense or defensive defense in general (including conventional military defense and paramilitary defense).[19] The peace movement is also concerned with such issues as nonalignment/neutrality, various forms of decoupling from superpowers, at least in the sense of denying them bases, particularly with nuclear "tasks," and of withdrawing from their command structure in times of war. Some parts of the peace movement are concerned with both local and national self-reliance, with making countries stronger so that they can resist economic blackmail, and making local communities stronger, more capable of defending themselves, less dependent on the center of the country.

In short, the peace movement does not only stand for international transformations with transarmament and transformation of the alliance system; the peace movement also stands for changes at the national level to make national and local societies stronger. The peace movement will probably continue growing, in depth and quality if not always in street demonstrations and quantity—the latter was more typical of the antimissile movement, which no doubt has played a considerable role for consciousness formation, political mobilization, and even confrontation. Neither the blue, nor the red, nor the pink were capable of solving these problems alone. The motivation behind the peace movement will still be there, although frustration and a feeling of being cheated may also have a paralyzing impact.[20]

Then there are the structural changes envisaged by the Green Movement, such as decentralization with more power to the local level and transformations from centralized to more (con)federate structures; the building up of informal, Green economies (more locally based, less monetary, more for quality of life and less for money); decentralization of knowledge production to very many and much smaller universities. I think the motivation will continue to be there, also the capability, particularly in the form of cooperative Green economy and nonformal Green education. When it comes to changes in the heavier structures, the state formation itself, central and local government, ministries, political parties have to operate through parliaments. Individual capability is negligible against such forces, all indispensable in a democracy, and the motivation is not so strong as it was in the 1970s.

But a major component of the Green Movement, the *feminist movement*, has had considerable success. It is obviously split into two: the "fifty-per-centers" wanting social positions to be gender blind, meaning 50 percent women in positions so far dominated by men and 50 percent men in positions so far dominated by women (including family roles); and on the other hand those who think and act in terms of a specific feminist culture that could serve as a model for social relations at large.[21] It is useful to conceive of the feminist movement in terms of *both—and,* and not *either-or.* Both types of momentum are terribly important in the ongoing social transformation.

Of activist women there are many. Many men will join them and many women will not, but it is hard to believe that motivation and capability will not increase rather than decrease in the years to come. It may also be that the movement for the older generation, the *troisième cycle* of retired people, will be of significance as movements for racial/ethnic equality in hetero-geneous countries (and that means, increasingly, all countries today). In principle, the Green Movement will be an umbrella for all of them, de-pending on the extent to which it is capable of articulating their demands in a politically relevant direction.

Finally, there are the two "ways of life"-packages, very relevant individ-ually. Again it may be that the big wave of the 1970s with communes, kitchen gardens, health food, and such has flattened out to some extent, in some quarters even decreased. But on the other hand, it may also be that the days of fundamentalism are over, with new life styles penetrating all sections of society (with very expensive health food for those who only feel well when they spend a lot of money), in smaller packages, less densely packed, more pragmatic. The transformation of individual ways of life may also have an impact on the political outlook, although it is not at all certain that this will lead to votes for Green parties. It could also lead to the greening of red, pink, and blue parties. Like the feminist movement, these may be signs of successful social transformations, changing the essence of what it means to be a first world inhabitant during the last decade of the twentieth century.[22] Just think of what happened to smoking!

The net conclusion of what has been said is that the Green parties will continue to grow. The reasons are simple. There are so many critical issues generated by the present Western social formation and so much frustration around at the same time as there is so little capability in the blue, red, and pink parties to bear upon these issues in a forceful manner. Many people are hit by the problems. The motivation is high at the same time as capability in rich and educated societies is high. Individual level solutions are insuf-ficient; group action is needed. Obviously, to feel motivated by a social evil not directly hitting oneself, both social knowledge and social compassion are indispensable, together with the sense of individual frustration: "there is nothing I and my family can do for ourselves to solve the problem."

These conditions taken together point in the direction of middle and upper class people with a certain level of education, but at the same time away from upper class people who because of their resources usually will be able to find a solution for themselves and their families—like moving out of polluted cities to nonpolluted countrysides, combining work and leisure, affording the transportation/communication expenses involved. At the same time, any transformation movement would appeal more to the young and the middle-aged, than to the old. Some old might say, why bother, we shall not be around very long anyhow. Finally, the movement will appeal more to women than to men, both because women are worst hit by the system, because the feminist movement is an important component of the total Green Movement, and because women are, presumably, more capable of wholistic thinking. So much for the sociological portrait.

But wholistic thought is almost a condition for Green Movement behavior in general, and Green party behavior in particular. Look again at the issue catalogue: there is no simple, all-encompassing formula like "the interests of the entrepreneurs/employers" or "the interests of the workers/employees." If society is a layer cake, the issues do not necessarily mobilize one layer against the other. Rather, the metaphor would be a layer cake with some poisoned almonds, raisins, and what not distributed all over, visible only to those who have a vision of the cake as a whole. Unfortunately, they have to be removed, something has to be done about it, otherwise all layers will be poisoned, those on the top, those in the middle, and those at the bottom. The happy message is that the poisoned items do not all have to be removed at the same time. Removal of one of them already makes sense for the local environment. The sad message is that there is no method by which one can remove all at the same time, nor does removal of one guarantee that all the others will disappear. Well-coordinated, synchronous work is recommended, as mentioned above.[23]

It may be objected that we have now come a long way from the theory of the bottom layer in the preceding section. But that is a historical theory of social dynamism, of major social forces that may carry on their shoulder much of the movement. It is like the preceding movement of the working class. There were the obvious interests of the working class. But the socialist wave contained considerably more than that. There was also "socialist humanism," an international peace movement, and so on. As a matter of fact, many of the tasks taken on today by the Green Movement are problems of the socialist program, the preceding wave of social energy, left unsolved.[24]

And that gives us an important additional perspective on the Green Movement in general and the party in particular: as a meeting ground for frustrated people from blue parties (conservatives, recycled nationalists, even with a nazi past) and from the red parties (recycled from the 1968 generation), finding nowhere else to go. Strange bedfellows these: the Green party seems to have some transformative capacity, making Green people out of the most diverse raw material. How lasting these transformations are; and how lasting the cohabitation will prove to be, is another matter.

CONCLUSION: THE GREEN MOVEMENT HAS COME TO STAY

I think it is very difficult to arrive at any other conclusion but that the Green Movement will stay. Like any political movement, it will have ups and downs, and although it is a child of the Western social formation, the geographical variation will be considerable, also inside the West. But the movement is here to stay.

Take the case of the Federal Republic of Germany. Why is the movement so strong there? The problems of one-half of humanity, the women, are not particularly worse in that country than in other western countries. The peace problems are more acute, the ecological problems about the same with the exception of the dying forests. The major reason is probably historical: the Green Movement is also a rupture with the nazi past that encompassed almost all of German society, leaving the communists relatively alone as a nucleus of solid resistance. But anti-nazism cannot be built on communism in western Europe in general, or in West Germany in particular. Marxism was tried, from the mid-1960s to the mid-1970s, the student revolt, and terrorism (RAF) as an extreme form of expression. The Green Movement with its focus on nonviolence and wholism is also a rejection of terrorism and single factor, Marxist determinism.[25]

Take France as another example. The Green Movement is growing, but the ecological party made only 0.5 percent in the cantonal elections in spring 1985 (but 2.5 percent on the average where they had candidates). Why is that?—given that in 1977 Green candidates got an average of 10 percent in Paris, Lyon, Lille, and other cities, then declined, picking up spring 1989.

One reason, very conspicuous in the eyes of a foreign observer like this author, would be the sharp distinction in France between a *classe politique* with not only decision monopoly but also, practically speaking, knowledge monopoly and, for that reason, interest monopoly. The population at large is uninterested in a wide range of political phenomena, and uninformed. It is not like West Germany (and the DDR, for that matter) where one can travel to almost any little town or village and find people deeply concerned, well-read, and articulate about the points on the Green agenda. In France disinterest is the rule.[26] The Green Movement tries to fight that.

But this, of course, is also begging the question: why is that so? Maybe one reason is to be found in an extremely strong French individualism. The French love of "freedom," meaning the right of the individual with his/her nuclear family to do exactly what they want to do, a right also expressed in the somewhat particular French way of driving and parking cars. In the Green Movement there are strong collectivist elements, togetherness beyond the confines of the nuclear family and very much concern for the world and the society as a whole and for collective solutions. French individualism would point in the direction of interest parties rather than interested (or for that matter interesting) parties. The layer cake model with one layer against the other, not a greening cake but cake expansion to counteract the poisoned cake model![27] Besides, many French probably prefer carefully groomed parks and gardens to wild nature. Not polluted parks and fields, however!

Still, another difference relative to Germany would be the shared feeling in France, right or wrong, that there is no past to reject, no sins to atone for. The old parties may not be perfect, but they can do the job. They have been with us for a long time. If the left doesn't make it, then the solution will by definition have to be with the right and *vice versa*. This may be totally irrational reasoning. Economic problems may depend on changes in the world system and be totally beyond the reach of left or right. The many problems of contemporary French society may also be outside the paradigms for political action shared by left and right. In either case, the Green formulas may be relevant, but if they are not seen as such in a French setting, then that does not help much.

Still another reason may be the strong reaction against the undeniably puritan elements in the Green Movement. The French are very tied to their cuisine. The cuisine is meatist rather than vegetarian; as such it is, of course, excellent, one of the two best in the world, the other being Chinese. To challenge meatism is to challenge French cuisine. Not to go in for the bourgeois style of life, including some elements of elegance in dressing, is un-French activity and can probably only be legitimized if one is aesthetically elegant in some other field, for instance, by being an artist. The Germans do not have much cuisine to defend, hence there is no problem of that kind. And although the ordinary German looks very bourgeois, there is no *haute couture* to defend either. National pride is not at stake, only bourgeois feelings. The Green Movement is more of a challenge in France.

Finally, Germany is a neighbor, watched relatively closely by French politicians. The inroads made by the Green Movements in German politics must have given the French a shock: this must not happen here. The calumnies coming out of the French press against the peace movement and the ecological movement are telling signs of irrational fear, not the invitation to reasoned debate that should characterize democratic society. On the other hand, the French feminist movement is strong and relatively successful, although it has a very long way to go with the remnants of feudalism. But then, *la femme française* is also a part of the national pride. She is not un-French activity, she is French. And yet France will probably sooner or later have to follow suit with the other countries in this regard as well.

The countries of southern Europe do not have these French problems and will not follow suit, Italy even being ahead. They are still in the throes of the third social transformation, even the second, even the first for that matter (Spain, Italy). But precisely for that reason, as argued in connection with the peace movement, there is no illusion that problems are solved. In the countries of northern Europe one may even talk of a general greening of all political parties with conservative parties picking up ecological and feminist issues, but certainly not peace issues.

So, the picture is mixed, as it should be. But there are green points all over that picture. Anyone wanting to understand the first world today would do better not pretending that the Green parties are not there. They may commit all kinds of mistakes, and like others have all kinds of internal quarrels. But the problems of the Western social formation do not disappear even if Green parties or movements should decline. The historical forces are undeniable. And individual as well as collective motivation and capability will produce sufficient mobilization in sufficiently many corners of Western society. In short, the Green phenomenon is here to stay, making its contribution to much needed transformations of the Western social formation. It is one more way in which Europe is in the making.

7

Gorbachev—A Second Socialist Revolution?*

We are living in the Gorbachev era, the era of *glasnost'* /*perestroika*. Again, the Russians have contributed words to the international vocabulary; words of pride before the war (*petiletka,* five-year plan) and words of shame after the war (*gulag,* the concentration camp archipelago). Not only the Russians but all Soviet citizens; not only they but also the people living in the Soviet sphere of influence; and not only they but peoples all over the world are relishing the signals of change. And the questions to be asked are, of course, many. Why did it happen? What is happening right now? And what is the likely future of this new trend, will it come to fruition or be aborted?

I do not think any explanation in terms of *external* factors, and particularly pressure from the United States, would carry us very far in this connection. The pressure brought on the Soviet Union from the Cold War is nothing particularly new in Soviet history. From the very birth of the first socialist republic, the external world has been hostile. An extreme expression of that hostility was the nazi onslaught. There was no excessive hurry among the Western allies to launch a second front. To have hitlerism and stalinism eliminating each other was the preferred course of action. A modernizing China to the south, blending capitalism and socialism, may have constituted more of a pressure. But that theory presupposes that the Soviet Union in general, and Soviet Russia in particular, is receptive to a challenge from China. Americans proclaiming that theory should contemplate to what extent the United States is willing to learn from Latin America. Learning from Japan has been more than hard enough and in a sense has not yet come off the ground. Nor is it very likely that Japan will learn much from Korea. Or Korea from Indonesia. Or Indonesia from Papua New Guinea. International stratification is a hard reality.

On the other hand, the Gorbachev era is quite easily explained in terms of *internal* changes. More particularly, one could imagine two explanatory hypotheses, one "liberal" and one "Marxist" that do not exclude each other and together offer a relatively rich basis for understanding the Gorbachev phenomenon. The transition from Rule by Partocracy (party-military-police) to Rule by Technocracy (bureaucracy-state corporations-intelligentsia) has been in the coming for a long time in the Soviet Union. In Moscow, in 1967 in connection with the fiftieth anniversary of the Revolution triumphant social science colleagues told me that "our time has now come." They were quoting the amazing achievements in Soviet higher education[1] and were convinced that the sheer pressure from the university graduates would bring about a new social formation. They were probably right in principle, only that they still had to wait almost 20 years. And if ever a single person had a role in history it was probably Brezhnev, a true representative of partocracy, blocking change by offering technocrats, individually and materially, satisfactory career patterns without any social transformation. In other words, a pattern not too dissimilar from what could be found under reaganism in the United States, not only underlining similarities between Brezhnev and Reagan, but also raising the question of whether Reagan's successor, who made less of a jump downward in age,[2] will be able to bring about *glasnost'* and *perestroika* in the United States. Probably not.

Leaving that aside, an important difference between a system run by partocracy and one run by technocracy should be pointed out. In the former the basic criterion of excellence would be *tested loyalty;* in the latter the basic criterion of excellence would be *tested professionalism*. The two differ in a very important sense. Tested loyalty increases with age simply because the test period is longer; whereas the quality of professionalism may decrease with age because of limited human absorption capacity of new professional paradigms after the original gestalt has been formed in the first period of professional training. Simply put: partocracy leads to gerontocracy, technocracy to the rule of the middle-aged.

There is another major difference. Partocracy can deliver only the two forms of power within its expertise. The party produces ideology, and the military-police machinery, on which single party power rests, produces coercion, force. The power of the idea and the power of the stick, in short. But if loyalty is the criterion of excellence, a renewal of ideological stock will be difficult. Ideas will fade in color and wane in significance as their increasing irrelevance becomes apparent. And coercion is not the way to win friends and influence people. In the longer run, moreover, neither ideas nor coercion is sufficient to produce and deliver the goods and the services.

This has been a major dilemma of the Soviet Union not only in its relation to its own citizens but also in its relations to other countries. The country has tried to relate to others in terms of what was held to be a superior ideology, Marxism/Leninism, and a socialist formation with a promise of communism "on the horizon." If this was not convincing enough, there was always the Red Army for military pressure, including intervention. What the Soviet Union demanded was the acceptance of the Soviet Union as a model country on the road via socialism to communism; one implication being that no other country in the Soviet orbit was permitted to be ahead of the Soviet Union in the difficult transitions from capitalism to socialism and socialism to communism. What is obvious to everybody, that there are similarities between *glasnost'/perestroika* and the Prague spring 1968, misses the point. There is a basic difference: 19 years. And more precisely: 19 years in the wrong direction, the chicken being ahead of the hen, and not *vice versa*. A crime against History, in other words.

The consequence of this has been a very poor offering in foreign relations. The Soviet Union has not been able to add to *ideas* and *threats* the very powerful medium of communication known as *goods* and *services*. What has been offered commercially may be cheap in price, but then also often cheap in quality. People draw their conclusions. The system does not work.

On what grounds can technocracy promise to deliver goods and services more efficiently with less rather than more partocratic supervision and leadership? At this point Marxist formulas may be quite useful. If we assume a basic Marxist hypothesis to be that the driving force of history is the contradiction between means and modes of production, then all we have to do is to point to the increasing irrelevance, even counterproductivity, of the heavy state planning mode of production. This critical look will not necessarily lead to a wholesale rejection of centralized planning. Centralized planning may be adequate for giant tasks of mass production like state farming of vast areas with simple products that do not require much individual attention such as potatoes and grains (major staples in Russian diets) and large-scale industrial production patterns related to coal, iron and steel, and energy. Planning may also stimulate military production—under considerable pressure from a formidable enemy abroad—to render the utmost both in quantity and quality, not only to be able to defend, to retaliate or even to attack, but also in order to have sufficient cards on the table to back up the claim for superpower status.

But heavily centralized, often crude and unimaginative mass production from above is totally inadequate for more refined consumer goods, for vegetables, possibly for anything dealing with animals; in short, for major necessities in daily life. As a consequence the Soviets may have enough bread but not vegetables and meat. Of course, alternative means of production in these fields have been known in the Soviet Union for a very long time, in the private sector, including the possibility of producing goods and services in small units, independently managed, in a decentralized manner. It should be remembered that centralized planning presupposes the ideology of "economy of scale," not necessarily for strictly economic reasons but for socio-political reasons. The big is easier to plan and control than the small, or at least so the planners think. Thus the mode of production, once chosen, also limits the choice of means of production, which in turn limits the quality and quantity of the products.

Where in all of this will a profit motive be built into individual Soviet citizens? The famous differential incentive that would make for differential achievements that would make for higher productivity and better products that would make for a better society to live in? I am not so sure that these are the basic concerns even if U.S. analysts tend to see it that way. There is certainly a concern with the bad quality and quantity in consumers' goods of all kinds, and that concern has been there for a long time. There is also a concern with heavy centralized planning structures that stand in the way, making it impossible for elements in the production chain to tie up directly with each other and coordinate their activities. The chain of communication via the two ministries coordinating two factories had to be short-circuited. And the perception and reality of a mode of production standing in the way of what is technically possible, impeding satisfaction of even basic needs for the vast masses of the population, is more than sufficient to motivate a basic transformation.

At this point the professionals, the "technocrats," might enter the scene and say: look, we have the new means of production, computers, smaller machine tools, potentially better means of transportation/communication; all we have to do is to change the mode of production. The hypothesis of a basic profit motive underlying it all may be useful as a projection from the motivation structure of U.S. analysts, but is probably a much too one-dimensional perspective on the situation. What might develop in the future, even in the near term, is another question. Cooperatives, definitely.

A major implication of what has been said so far is obvious: a shift of power from the old to the middle aged; from loyal partocrats to professional technocrats; a general pattern of decentralization structurally; and ability to talk about much of this culturally. But that is only the beginning of the story, there is much more to be said. Hence, let us enter the analysis with some basic queries now that an effort has been made to clarify the past, *why* this did happen.

First, there is Amalrik's basic point in his analysis.[3] If everybody in the

Soviet Union has only one employer, the state, where does one find the independent basis for a revolutionary transformation? And we should note that we are here dealing with a transformation of such a magnitude that the word "revolution" could be used; not in the sense of a second Russian revolution (it may be argued that what happened in November 1917 was already the third Russian revolution, after 1905 and March 1917) but as a second socialist revolution, in the Soviet Union and not Russia this time. Amalrik was probably right in his basic point, but forgetful of one possibility: *the revolution might come from above.* As a matter of fact it was only from the top it could come, not necessarily because of the partocratic coercion machinery (which is a very good reason in its own right), but also because of the more basic Orwellian mechanism for controlling the proletariat: scarcity. In a situation of scarcity, with no alternatives for satisfying basic needs, people become scared and do not rock the boat unnecessarily.

So the second socialist revolution came from the top, and precisely from where one would expect: from "rank disequilibrated" elites,[4] people high on knowledge and professional competence, yet low on political power. One of them, a young tractor driver from far out in the periphery, later party secretary in Stavropol, became their leader. Mikhail Sergeyevich Gorbachev already showed his aggressiveness as a young student of law when he pointed out to a visiting *apparatchik* that everybody at the university was able to read and write, so there was no need to read a document aloud; what was needed was a discussion.[5] Professional criteria were pitted against the loyalty expressed not only in reading a party script, but in obediently listening to somebody reading a party script. And those cosmopolitan criteria make Gorbachev (and his PhD wife) so much more internationally adequate than his inward, party loyal predecessors. Were the Gorbachevs the first intellectual (in the sense of ability to question assumptions) couple the Reagans ever met?

No doubt Gorbachev is a political genius, one of those rare phenomena whose time had come and understood it. He also understood clearly that there was no question of overthrowing the party. The point was to imbue the party with a new ethos, with more professionalism and less loyalism. Being at home in both worlds he was able to bridge the gap and survive doing so. He gave the signal from the top knowing that the number of followers would be considerable. And the followers hesitatingly followed suit, not quite knowing what to do when granted that much freedom, having to decide for themselves what the new course of action should be within extremely general, but one might also say generous, guidelines.

Second, in any political transformation there are winners and losers. The winners can be counted upon to support the transformation. The losers have to be taken more seriously. As long as they are scattered in separate groups unable to cooperate, there is no problem. The difficulty comes the moment they can join forces and topple the budding new regime before it has crystallized and set roots, reversing the process.

Roughly speaking, who would be the winners and who the losers? This, of course, depends on the concrete content of *glasnost'/perestroika*. But the following list might give some indication:

1. *Party members*. They have for a long time been more profession-oriented and less loyalty-oriented in the sense of loyalty to old ideas. Much of the problem has been age as many point out, combined with inability of the old to listen to and understand what is happening among the young. As the old retire socially and even biologically, this problem may be solved, favoring technocracy over partocracy. In other words, the party will increasingly become a party of professionals as is the case in many other countries in the world only that in democratic countries we are not dealing with one party only, but with a coalition of two or more ruling parties. Except for some isolated but admittedly important persons, the transformation that has already taken place inside the party has been a major force behind *glasnost'/perestroika*, one reason why the party may not be the basic source of opposition.

2. *Military/police*. This is a formidable power machinery. However, there is an old Soviet tradition against "bonapartism," meaning the military taking ultimate power in the society. A phenomenon like Oliver North, meaning a military operating with that much latitude, not alone but together with strong military and police elements from the outside (retired Pentagon and retired CIA officers, to be more precise) and out of the very center of executive power, would be almost inconceivable in the Soviet Union. One reason for this is not necessarily any superior control pattern in the Soviet Union against power abuse but perhaps a basic dislike for the type of entrepreneurial talent that North no doubt displayed. But there is also another factor at work here: an old Soviet theory of division of power to the effect that among the three, party, military and police, two of them should not be able to gang up against the third. In other words, an alliance of military and police against the party is not inconceivable but unlikely. More likely would be strong sabotage, even a takeover from within the KGB itself. It is not obvious that the forces Gorbachev

has unleashed with his professionalism would be strong enough to
stem a tidal wave of that kind. Nor is it likely that anything like that
will ever happen. A "revolution from above" does not threaten those
already above. But if the party should not succeed, but start disin-
tegrating before a multiparty system is installed, the military/police
may fill the power vacuum.

3. *Bureaucracy*. This would be a more likely source of origin for basic
resistance. Bureaucrats do not like basic changes in bureaucratic rou-
tines, particularly not changes that make them less relevant. Restructuring carries exactly that in its wake. The whole *glasnost'/pere-
stroika* package is a blow to bureaucracy. They increasingly hear evil
things said about themselves and see themselves as a part of the problem, not as they believed as a part of the solution. But then the same
question as in connection with the party: Is this not to a large extent
an age problem? Would it not be possible for the Gorbachev forces
to put into the bureaucratic machineries a sufficient number of younger
people to try to counteract resistance by the old who see their rele-
vance in Soviet society decrease, and even in an accelerating manner?

4. *State corporations*. In principle these should be the people who have
much to gain from restructuring. There will be management inertia
to overcome, but the incentives are many. A new type of accountability and decentralization would generate more pride in one's own
achievements, more possibility of being heard and seen and read about,
a broader range of individual careers for the person and collective
careers for the state corporation. On the other hand, some of them
would also have to swallow decentralization to the point of seeing
their corporation dismantled and scattered in many small groups operating according to a pattern more similar to "free enterprise" in the
West, and guided by market principles. The question is to what extent
the system will be able to promise transition opportunities for people
from one mode of production to the other. Direct sales to other firms,
direct export abroad, focus on quality are very positive new aspects
of the situation; the institution of bankruptcy possibility less so.

5. *Intelligentsia*. This is the group that has most to gain: artists and scientists of all kinds, professionals. Not only are their professional criteria raised to the status of being social criteria; they also experience
freedom of expression, and freedom of impression from foreign literature and other media of communication, from trips abroad, from
foreign visitors. Not that such things did not happen before, but these
privileges were reserved for the old and the loyal, for the partocracy.

Increasingly younger people are given access to these freedoms, implanting new ways of thinking at expanding and key places in the social structure, letting the old wilt, contract, and ultimately fade away. Blossoming of cultural life is taking place, some kind of permanent spring that could catapult the Soviet Union into a position as a major cultural producer by the end of this century, in a period where so much of Western creativity has been destroyed by excessive commercialism.

6. *Workers*. Some workers will gain, some will lose. The old interpretation of socialism as a system where everybody has guaranteed employment and there is no incentive coupled to achievement because everybody is basically guaranteed the same in terms of basic needs satisfaction, is probably up for revision. More particularly, many Soviet workers will have to get used to the idea of *working* during working hours, subject to quality standards that have not been lived up to before. Professionalism, and increasingly demanding consumers, including foreign consumers, will hit the worker in addition to separate accountability for the companies. In the choice between secure and inefficient socialism and insecure and efficient capitalism, many workers may prefer the former, with a fixed salary.

7. *Peasants*. We are talking here essentially of the people working on the *sovkhozi* (state farms) and the *kolkhozi* (collective farms). The peasants have been treated very badly under socialism, not meaning by that that they were not also treated badly before. They have been exposed to the direct violence of expulsion and extermination, and to the structural violence of abject exploitation. The obvious solution has been the famous private plots, trying to adjust the mode of production to the labor intensive means of production needed for delicate agricultural products. Expansion of this sector, combined with adequate marketing facilities should benefit producers and consumers alike and bring about something close to a general euphoria. It might also serve to reintroduce skills in a heavily deskilled agricultural population and to reinvigorate a countryside desperately lagging behind in cultural and political isolation. In short, privatization, perhaps leasing rather than owning the land.

8. *Non-Russian nationalities*. It is not easily seen that *glasnost'/perestroika* immediately means any advantage for these nationalities relative to their situation today; nor is it obvious that they are underprivileged except in terms of a political autonomy that may not necessarily be pursued by all of them. If increased autonomy is a

goal, one would imagine that *glasnost'* conditions would make it easier to articulate that goal, as has been seen clearly in the Baltic states,
and in some of the Trans-Caucasian republics. Whether there will be
any *perestroika* in that connection in the sense of new political structures remains to be seen. Total independence from what the leadership sees as an indivisible union is as unlikely as increased internal
autonomy is likely.

9. *Periphery countries in the second, socialist world.* With the green
   light being given for *glasnost'/perestroika* in the mother country of
   socialism, the green light is also given to the periphery socialist countries in Eastern Europe, the Caribbean, and Asia. To what extent they
   will act accordingly depends on the local power structure. More particularly, it probably depends more on the articulation of the technocratic sector relative to the partocratic than on the means/mode contradiction that can be assumed to be present in all of them. Consequently
   we would imagine the pressure for reform to be highest where the
   technocratic sector is most developed. On the other hand, that sector
   is relatively well developed in all of them, so it may also be that this
   particular factor does not discriminate well enough to account for the
   differences. And the differences are significant. Under Gorbachev the
   Soviet Union has even managed the incredible feat of becoming close
   to popular in Romania. After 1968 the joke had it that the Romanians
   were putting posters all over the borders to the Soviet Union: "we
   want words not deeds!" Today it may be the other way around.

10. *Communist parties outside the socialist world.* What some years ago
    was called Euro-communism, and actually was Latin-European com-
    munism, will today probably be the world model for communist par-
    ties, with increased autonomy and attempts to produce their own po-
    litical programs. General abdication of the Soviet party from the
    leadership position in the communist world will make that particular
    world look more like the British Commonwealth of Nations, except
    for the absence of a common language. Outspokenness by foreign
    party leaders will be the rule rather than the exception; obedience
    being the exception rather than the rule.

Looking at this list in order to arrive at a simple summary, the general
conclusion would be that there is much more for most actors in the socialist
world to gain than to lose. But there are some glaring exceptions. A hard
nucleus at the top of society, including bureaucrats accustomed to the old
way of doing things, might build an alliance with elements from the party

cadres, the military and the police, and some of the state corporate and intelligentsia people. One would expect this group to be above average age, and much above average power. Workers losing more than they gain in a more competitive atmosphere for attractive but scarce incentives, one of them being guaranteed full employment, might provide a popular and populist basis.

Ideologically an alliance between these two groups would probably be nationalistic, anti-socialist, possibly also anti-capitalist, and in general anti-Western. In other words, it might reveal similarities to the type of ideological position identified in the West with Alexandr Solzhenytsin. The mystique of the Russian *mir* in the sense of "village" rather than "peace," "world." The West seems to believe that underneath repressive communism is liberal democracy waiting to be liberated, whereas what comes out is more like *Pamyat* (remember) in the Russian republic, and anti-Russian nationalism in the non-Russian republics. And they use *glasnost'* to criticize Gorbachev, not his predecessors.

However, the general gains to the whole society from *glasnost'/perestroika* could be of such a magnitude in social, economic, cultural, and political terms that they would outweigh the costs even for disgruntled strata and segments of the population. The release of creative energy in so many parts of the population should in principle show up in new skills, techniques, and technologies, and in new management practices. If these had been the missing elements in the Soviet economic equation, given that there are plenty of natural resources and labor available, the only additional factor missing to make the machinery function economically would be capital. If that capital is made available from decreasing, or at least not increasing, military expenditures and foreign investment (under a 51 percent Soviet control clause), then one possible prediction, and a quite dramatic one, would be: *the Soviet Union is in for spectacular economic growth,* in the longer, if not in the shorter run.

The basis for this assumption is essentially that the Soviet Union is a highly *under*developed country, meaning that there is something to develop. Seventy years of socialism have brought advantages to the country in terms of liberating, in principle, all natural resources for collective purposes. Socialism has also mobilized human resources, although more successfully in the field of education than in the field of health. The shackles of socialism show up in the rigidities connected with capital formation and capital flow, in the failure to bring new technologies or means of production to bear on the production of consumers goods, and in management rigidities; in other words in the modes of production. Precisely because these are identifiable shackles, breaking them should in principle entail a substantial release of new productive forces.

This will have important implications also for Soviet relations to other countries. The Soviet Union will suddenly have products to offer that might be competitive, if not with the best from countries like Japan and the Federal Republic of Germany, at least with more average countries like the United States where quality and price are concerned. And more particularly where the quality/price ratio is concerned.[6]

But there are also cultural, military, and political implications of *glasnost'/perestroika*. I am thinking of the release of cultural creativity that might even come in an accelerated manner. One consequence of this increased creativity may also be more ability to follow and even be ahead of the unfortunate U.S. effort to develop successor weapon systems to nuclear weapons: Star Wars. *Glasnost'/perestroika* as such do not eliminate military "development"; for that to happen the entire military-bureaucratic-state corporate-intelligentsia complex would have to be dismantled. And this is not much more likely to happen in the Soviet Union than in the United States.

In conclusion, what are the implications of all of this for international politics?

As mentioned above, the Soviet Union will have a richer spectrum of power components to play on, and consequently a more subtle foreign policy. There will be less isolationism accompanied by threats and use of arms; more economic bridge-building through trade, and above all a rekindling of the socialist dream around the world that went sour under stalinism and even more so in its aftermath when the horrors became known. It may not be that difficult to bring the socialist dream to life again. The Soviet Union will probably be host to a large number of political tourists who will come out of curiosity, ideological attachment, and romantic dreams to watch socialism again, and judge whether the future works. A modified socialism using some capitalist techniques, yet guaranteeing basic needs and rights may be highly attractive to Third World countries.

It is not at all obvious that the West is headed for a similar ideological renaissance. Thus there is hardly anything in the Reagan/Bush-Thatcher type of "revolution" that kindles frozen hearts and stimulates underutilized brains. The only thing that could make the West look ideologically interesting again would probably be a green revolution, but for that to happen there are very powerful obstacles to be overcome. Moreover, in the future a second socialist revolution in the Soviet Union might increasingly incorporate some green policies in addition to the light blue, capitalist policies that evidently are being introduced. Green movements are very active all over Eastern Europe.

However, there are deeper aspects of Soviet politics that may remain, according to the French adage "plus ça change, plus c'est la même chose." Thus there is hardly any reason to believe that the basic socialist mystique is not still intact. Socialism and communism would still be the goals, not "world domination" (if it ever was). But the concrete features are changing, as indicated. The much more basic idea, however, that the Soviet Union is a country chosen by History to carry out the epoch-making mission of showing the world by example what socialism is, has hardly changed. It is also under present conditions hardly changeable. There is no reason to assume that Gorbachev believes less in his fantasy than Reagan/Bush in theirs. Gorbachev's point is that what happened in the period of stagnation was to betray the mission rather than to fulfill it, not to doubt the missionary command.

Thinking along such lines, his support in the Russian populace will probably remain considerable. Seeing themselves as a chosen people, badly treated by history and misunderstood by all, any sense of a new mission will have a redeeming quality; be it capitalism, socialism, or communism. What matters is that the Russians can remain convinced that they still have a mission in the world as a model for others. The euphoria of that nation, and the brightening not only of collective and individual lives in the Soviet Union under *glasnost'/perestroika* conditions, does not only derive from the promise of socialism with a human face, and—even more importantly—a socialism that works economically. It may also derive from the idea that Russia might again become a center of major attraction, true to its mission in history.

However, the present leadership seems to have discovered the old daoist wisdom that he who rules least rules best. In other words, it is through relaxing the grip on the "satellites" that the probability of influencing them may increase in the longer run; not by tightening the grip. Again, the West should not assume that the only thing the "satellites" want when that grip is relaxed is to run away from the Soviet Union and throw themselves into the arms of the democratic West. To the contrary, the West may wake up one day and discover that the relations among the socialist countries are better than before and not only at the government but also at the popular level. Some kind of Eastern European Community may still become a reality. Much to the benefit of Eastern Europe, the Soviet Union, Western Europe, and peace in general.

8

The INF Agreement—and Then What?

WHY A ZERO-ZERO INF AGREEMENT?

The official Western line in connection with the rightly celebrated INF agreement—the nucleus around which the Washington December 7–10, 1987 summit meeting was built—was essentially that it was all due to Western show of strength, and cohesion in the alliance.[1] The Soviet Union had deployed intermediate-range, land-based missiles of the SS-20 variety. The West responded with the "double-track decision" of December 12, 1979 to deploy land-based Cruise (464 in number) and Pershing II (108 in number) unless an agreement could be arrived at.

This theory hardly holds up against the facts. First of all, land-based intermediate-range missiles possessed by the Soviet Union, possibly pointing at Western Europe, were nothing new. SS-4 and SS-5 were already in that category. Second, the decision to deploy Cruise and Pershing II was taken before SS-20 had become a relevant factor in the decision making and was probably independent of the SS-20.[2] Third, the NATO decision was originally, from the U.S. side, not thought of as a double-track decision at all but was simply a decision to deploy Cruise and Pershing II. The allies, and particularly Western Germany, insisted on the second "track," according to Egon Bahr, the disarmament specialist of the Social Democratic party of the Federal Republic, in order to get the Americans to the negotiation table.[3] And then, finally, there is nothing new in the Western side arguing from a position of strength as they have been stronger than the Soviet Union in most weapons systems and theaters after World War II. Nor has this prevented the two parties from arriving at agreements, although these agreements have been about limitation rather than reduction or elimination of a category of nuclear weapons.

Nevertheless, the INF agreement is something new to be explained in terms of new factors, not in terms of such old factors as Western superiority and "alliance cohesion" (if not in the population, among the political parties in general or not among the countries then at the level of final decision making in NATO itself.[4]) The interesting point is that the INF decision arrived at was the zero-zero solution, in other words that the Soviet Union came down to the U.S. level before deployment. There were also the other three possibilities: the United States could come up to the Soviet level and stay there; they could meet somewhere in-between (for instance, at the level of "75" in the Kvitzinski-Nitze "walk in the woods" formula), or both could meet at a higher level, such as 1,000 land-based intermediate nuclear-tipped missiles for each, a "solution" that would be more reminiscent of SALT I or SALT II. The "zero-zero" is what has to be explained, not that there was an agreement. The explanatory factors to be used should, if possible, be specific to this point, not to just any agreement that might have been made. It should also be noted that the agreement is only about the missiles, not the warheads; only about land-based, not air-based and sea-based missiles; and only about U.S./Germany and the Soviet Union, not about France and England. A genuine INF agreement would have covered the whole field. Only then would the propoganda about "elimination of a complete category of nuclear weapons" be true. Had the peace movement "won" in 1983, we might have been there today.

TWELVE REASONS FOR THE ZERO-ZERO AGREEMENT

The following is a list of 12 efforts to explain the zero-zero agreement, pointing to factors and theories that certainly do not exclude each other.

1. *Both parties had particular reasons to eliminate this category of weapons on the other side.* The point may certainly be made that the Russians were particularly upset about land-based nuclear systems stationed in Europe, capable of hitting the Soviet Union. For a country so many times attacked from Europe, this attitude should not lead to any accusation of paranoia. Symbolism is important, and although an incoming missile with a warhead would not necessarily be more destructive because it is land-launched, as opposed to air-launched and sea-launched, there is an implication in terms of hostile territory used for launching, like territories used for launching invasions. Symbolically important in Russian history in this regard would be Turkish and German territory, and for that matter also French, although this is more remote and there was only one and rather short-lasting

invasion of significance (Napoléon). The Turkish and German threats were both long-lasting and devastating. The Soviet Union got rid of U.S. intermediate missiles, also capable of hitting the Soviet Union, in Turkey in 1962 as a part of the Cuba deal (which actually should be seen as a Cuba-Turkey deal)[5] with the Russians not deploying missiles capable of hitting the United States in return for the Americans withdrawing the Jupiter missiles from Turkey. But what would be the U.S. motivation for arriving at a similar deal, the removal of the Soviet missiles capable of hitting Western Europe in return for U.S. nondeployment? The United States does not have a similar war experience emanating from the Soviet Union, nor does Western Europe, for that matter, except for the German trauma of being partitioned after the nazi onslaught on the East.[6]

There is, possibly, another factor working in this case: a U.S. desire to be superior in all weapon systems in all theaters. In sea-based and air-based intermediate nuclear missiles in the European theater, one might argue that the United States was and is superior, at least together with the major allies, United Kingdom and France.[7] But in land-based missiles the United States was clearly inferior, having zero in that category. A situation of that kind was intolerable to a country that interprets the word "balance" in "balance of power" as positive balance, not as equality: in other words as superiority rather than parity.

Consequently two superpowers, the Soviet Union and the United States of America, could agree on a zero-zero solution simply because it was in the interests of both parties. Both of them had to give up something to obtain something; both of them saw the benefits as higher than the costs. The United States gave up superiority and got parity at the zero level in land-based nuclear missiles in Europe. In the particular calculus done by the Soviet Union in this connection, the emphasis must have been not only on land-based missiles in a European territory defined as particularly hostile: the successor state to nazi Germany. The emphasis was also on the United States, otherwise they would have continued insisting on the removal of U.K. and French missiles, that now constitute land-based superiority relative to the Soviet Union. But of U.S. land-based superiority there will be none. Maybe "defeating" both Germany and the United States was worth a very unbalanced sacrifice of missiles?

2. *Land-based missiles serve as foci for demonstrations.* For a demonstration to take place, space and time coordinates are needed. How else can people meet? For the demonstration to have high pedagogical value and hence political value, at least potentially, space and time should preferably carry a message. A deployed, land-based missile certainly carries a message,

so does the date or period of deployment. Demonstrations do not even have to take place on the exact site of deployment, but should be in the geographical neighborhood so as to carry a message, and at a symbolic point in time such as the anniversary of arrival of new missiles. Much less ideal would be air-launched and sea-launched missiles. The aircraft, the aircraft carriers, the submarines, and other ships that serve as platforms are less available as rallying points for demonstrations, particularly when in the air or in the ocean. The environmentalist organization Greenpeace has been able to stage very imaginative and successful demonstrations on sea. But even that organization has not been able to get demonstrations up into the air (except with unmanned balloons), or deep down into the oceans—so far.

Of course, there is always the possibility of demonstrating at and around airfields and ports where aircraft land and ships call. But it is not so symbolically powerful as demonstrations around a base, on land, against missiles that are physically there. One might object that a counterstrategy for those who deploy land-based missiles would be to make them mobile. But then a counter-counter strategy would be to demonstrate against the vehicles carrying the missiles, as indeed has been done. In short, there are strong political arguments in favor of air-based and sea-based intermediate nuclear forces if the goal is to make their presence less felt. And a strong hint as to what is going to happen next. But then the counterargument that land-based missiles serve to share risks, not only costs, inside the alliance should not be forgotten. As long as there are land-based missiles in the United States, their removal in western Europe means less sharing of risks. Consequently their removal in western Europe will probably sooner or later lead to their removal in the United States (and the Soviet Union too).

3. *The political costs of deployment to the European allies in East and West were considerable.* In the light of the preceding point the political costs to the government of the deployment countries became quite high, a point not only driven home by public demonstrations in the streets in the West, but also by less public demonstrations, and not necessarily in the streets, in the East.[8] If the superpowers wanted to exercise alliance management, even control by forcing allies to do something they were reluctant to do, the costs were already there. But the total costs were even higher.

The client governments found themselves in the middle, between a demand from the superpowers to share costs and risks and a demand from the population to reduce both costs and risks, particularly the latter. The conflict must have been agonizing to governments in both parts of Europe. The demands put on the superpowers to find ways of reversing the decision in favor of other forms of deployment must have been considerable. And again it should be pointed out that this demand did not necessarily apply to air- and sea-based missiles, nor to land-based missiles outside European countries. As a matter of fact one outcome might have been land-based missiles in Israel since the government is in less of a position to put demands on the U.S. government, having no alternative to U.S. protection. Israel is also in less of a position to make a separate peace with the Arab neighbors in the same way that western Europeans easily could do with eastern European countries in general and the Soviet Union in particular if they so wanted.[9]

4. *Land-based nuclear missiles are vulnerable.* They are easily discovered and easily targeted. If they are made mobile their elimination would call for fusion bombs rather than fission bombs, assuming that even a rather indirect hit is sufficient to immobilize a missile on a moving vehicle. Once again simple cost-benefit analysis is in favor of air- and sea-based missiles and space-based systems, and against the land-based variety.

5. *Land-based nuclear missiles are destabilizing.* One particular reason often pointed out is that in any war there will be a tendency to use secret, expensive, and efficient missiles rather than to lose them. If the war takes the shape of an invasion on land, and evacuation of the missiles is difficult or even impossible, then the temptation to use them before they are lost to adversary intelligence rather than having to destroy them might be considerable, leading to an escalation of several orders of magnitude. If the attack is from the air, this might be even more true, given the short time factor for rational decision making. For sea-based and air-based missiles this would be a less important factor as a high level of mobility and concealment is already built into the deployment pattern.

The five arguments presented so far are arguments against land-based nuclear forces in Europe. However, the current spate of arms control negotiations also includes strategic nuclear forces (START), meaning that there are important arguments against nuclear forces in general. Four of them are fairly obvious and follow in the next point.

6. *Nuclear forces are not good as arms.* The arguments against nuclear forces are simple and also powerful. So much radioactivity is released that the sender, not only the receiver of nuclear arms may be seriously hit. A further development of this factor would include the nuclear winter, leading to the conclusion that nuclear weapons are like an unpractical gun firing a bullet in the direction of the target and at the same time a smaller bullet in the direction of the person holding the gun. In other words, in political terms: nuclear weapons may be deterring, but also self-deterring. And if one adds to this the wanton destructiveness of nuclear arms as well as the extended warning time given to the adversary because of the time needed for the

missile to cross intercontinental and regional distances, the impracticality of nuclear arms as weapon systems becomes even more obvious. The conclusion, consequently, would be to look for other arms that would be less self-destructive, less destructive of the environment, more politically useful, and give less warning to the other side. Chemical, possibly also biological arms may satisfy some of these criteria, and they already exist. And "Star Wars" may be interpreted in this direction.[10]

7. *New and "better" weapons systems are being developed.* I am not only thinking of the big family of systems under the name of Star Wars, particularly microwave and reflected laser beams, but also of other possibilities. The Soviet Union has indicated that this time it may not follow the United States on the road, imitating U.S. qualitative changes in weapons systems, but may go its own way. Genetic engineering has been mentioned.[11] Needless to say all of this is shrouded in secrecy, and we should also be open to the possibility that we are already entering a new generation of secrecy, *meta-secrecy*. In the old days, still with us, we had at least some indication of what kind of thing was considered secret. Today and in the future we may have to face the possibility that secrecy also includes what is secret. In other words, weapon systems may be researched and developed, deployed and even used, hitting us without people knowing that a war is in fact taking place. The suspicion that AIDS may in fact be a weapon is not so crazy as it may sound, and the same may apply to meteorological phenomena such as drought and excessive precipitation.[12] A circumstantial factor contributing to this type of thinking: if it is true that 400,000 researchers are working for the military around the world then we would assume that they would come up with something once in a while and not be stuck with, for instance, nuclear systems all the time. We would also assume that new weapons would be in need of testing, which may or may not explain the random nature of the biological and ecological damage incurred.

8. *The arms race has become very costly.* I do not find this a very convincing argument. Of course it is true, but that does not mean that the factor constitutes a major motivation to abolish the land-based INF. If the destruction of the INF missiles went unaccompanied by any further "modernization," not to mention "compensation" for the missiles "lost" in the agreement, then the argument might look more convincing. As it stands it is not obvious that there are savings involved, nor that there will be savings in the future. On the contrary, to destroy very expensive missiles in what looks like a rather irreversible way (as opposed to the preservation of the warheads that can easily be put into similar missiles more conveniently deployed) is a considerable sacrifice. In other words, there are probably more

costs than benefits from a purely economic point of view. This, however, does not mean that the two leaders might not like to make it look as if they are paying attention to the economic costs of the arms race. The ultimate test will be in the military budgets, but even if they should decrease it is not obvious that the INF agreement as such is the cause. Much more can be saved by eliminating foreign bases or withdrawing from foreign wars, not to mention reducing the payroll. A general decrease in tension may be the cause of such major changes, and also the cause of the INF agreement.

9. *Both Reagan and Gorbachev needed a good agreement.* This may be true. A besieged president seen as responsible both for the Iran-contra scandal and the U.S. economic decline may be in need of at least one foreign policy victory, particularly as any contra victory in Nicaragua seemed to elude him. Similarly, a secretary general surrounded by promises and new ideas and initiatives may have to prove that his policies can bring results and also give him a free hand domestically because there is no particular global threat facing him. On the other hand, there are few periods in the lives of top politicians where similar things cannot be said. They are always in need of some victory. The question may also be raised about who was more in need of a victory, Reagan or Gorbachev? Who can tell since the inner workings of the Soviet Union are not well known at this point. But it is not obvious that Gorbachev was the one most in need of an important foreign policy agreement. He may still have the upper hand since he can more easily threaten to withdraw from the process.

10. *A superpower agreement is a way of reinstating superpower hegemony.* The two superpowers that have been holding the world population hostage to their deals and conflicts, with occasional spates of cooperation, have looked out of touch with reality in recent years. It is difficult to maintain faith in the Cold War as a really serious conflict given all the other things that happen in the world. For instance, the Cold War looks insignificant relative to the conflict between the United States and poor people in the Third World (some of them using terrorist techniques); and between the United States and the powerful new economic actors in East Asia, particularly Japan.

Superpower conflict has been backstage for a long period already relative to recent developments on the world arena. One interesting way for the superpowers of bringing it centerstage is precisely an INF agreement. If you look powerful when the arms race is going upward, you may also look powerful when it goes downward. In either case much is at stake. The world is watching. We have witnessed destruction of missiles on television, catapulting superpowers into the forefront of world consciousness. And even more important: in doing so they have also demonstrated their power over their allies, even the power to make them reject the very same weapons they had barely become reconciled to accepting. Actually, it may even be rather difficult for a government functionary in Europe West or East to de-learn arguments it took so much time to internalize as to exactly why land-based INF was indispensable: not only to counter the SS-20, but to balance alleged Soviet conventional superiority and to function as a tripwire guaranteeing U.S. involvement. Were those arguments all false?

11. *Gorbachev, glasnost' and perestroika: the three new factors.* In order to explain an event such as a new agreement, it is not strictly speaking true that the cause has to be found in an other and recent but antecedent event. There could also have been a gradual build-up of some causal factor that suddenly led to a quantum jump on the effect side, the INF agreement that suddenly got the green light.[13] The Soviet side might have become increasingly frustrated by their inferiority in strength as well as U.S. intransigence and NATO cohesion, and been forced to give up their own hard line.

And yet, as indicated in the beginning: this is hardly the major reason. Those who believe that the factor that eventually caused an agreement was U.S. strength and NATO cohesion should ask themselves a simple question: would that have changed the minds of Brezhnev, Andropov, or Chernenko? Hardly. Gorbachev was a necessary if not sufficient factor; probably because his world view is different. The other factors were old. Hence Gorbachev is the key factor. And Gorbachev is more than one person.

More particularly, he represents a new educated, more technocratically oriented class that for a long time has been gradually substituting for the partocratic class in power. As argued in the preceding chapter the Soviet Union is now turning away from its old reliance on ideology and force as the major forms of power in foreign affairs. Trade, exchange, and friendly relations based on give-and-take will be more attractive to others, but also more demanding because the Soviet Union has to have things to offer and has to know the people with whom they deal. An intellectual, cosmopolitan leader like Gorbachev would be a much better leader for that type of policy than his predecessors, any one of them, including Khrushchev.

If this is the case, then a disarmament agreement would be only one part of Gorbachev's approach. The other part would be a consistent effort to try to establish friendly relations with as many countries in the world as possible, including all 12 land neighbors[14] and the United States and Japan, and more often than not based on trade relations, not on ideology and force. And for that to happen the Soviet Union has to have something new worth offering on the world market. Even 70 years after the revolution it is remarkable how little the Soviet Union has to offer beyond raw materials like oil and gas, some other commodities, a Soviet-built Fiat, and some tractors. Obviously an economically ambitious program is now on, and the INF agreement was an effort to get rid of particularly obnoxious, provocative weapons in order to pave the way for more positive relations.

12. *The INF agreement symbolizes that the Cold War is over.* One may discuss exactly when the Cold War actually was brought to an end. Some people might say it was never on; it was a misunderstanding needed by both or at least one of the parties. Others might say that it died if not with Stalin, at least with Stalin's political death after Khrushchev's denunciation at the 20th Party Congress in Moscow in February 1956. This author would argue that the Final Act of the Conference on Security and Cooperation in Europe in Helsinki almost 20 years later, in 1975, was also the final act in the Cold War. It was a brilliant piece of peace-making, exchanging one basket (borders) for the other (human rights), splitting the third (economic co-operation). The conflict residues after Helsinki were details.

However, it is not so easy to *declare* an end to the Cold War. A hot war is very well defined in terms of open, hostile, and destructive activities. A cold war is more loosely defined, in terms of conflicts over value (ideological conflicts) and over interests (economic conflicts). They certainly are still there. Who can declare an end to the conflict between capitalism and socialism? Between liberalism/conservatism and marxism? Who is entitled to declare an end to West-East rivalry as to who shall have the upper hand in Eastern Europe?

And nevertheless there is probably a strong feeling that these conflicts have outlived themselves and are toward the end of their life cycles, partly because nothing much will change by one party trying to impose its will on the other, and partly because other conflicts have come in their place, dominating the world scene. However that may be, the East-West conflict today engenders a sense of fatigue, even a yawn in addition to enormous frustration in people who have spent most of their adult life in the shadow of the Cold War. The INF agreement makes it possible for the two leaders to express a corresponding sentiment in a language they fully understand, that of weaponry. If one cannot eliminate all hostile feelings, one can at least eliminate some of the weapons. Hence, the symbolic significance of the agreement is tremendous and by far its most positive aspect. The arms situation becomes a projection screen for the underlying conflict; this time in reverse.

Given all of this, what should we now hope for in the wake of the INF? Where are the new lines of political initiatives, which are the things to watch out for? One way of being systematic about this would be to have a second look at the 12 factors noted above as contributing causes to the elimination of the intermediate land-based nuclear forces in Europe.

TWELVE FACTORS, TWELVE WARNINGS, TWELVE TASKS

First, the United States and the Soviet Union may have had good reasons for eliminating this category of weapons on the other side, but could it be that two other countries in Europe would not have corresponding reasons? Both the United Kingdom and France have vehemently opposed any participation in the deal, having neither the Soviet nor the U.S. motivation. Of these two, France is probably the more critical case. One distinct possibility following the removal of land-based, intermediate nuclear forces on the continent of western Europe would be a corresponding build-up in the other two countries, including legitimation (in the eyes of some western Europeans) of the French land-based missiles. This might or might not be related to the current tendency toward French-German military cooperation, bordering on military integration. Another consequence might be a French effort to integrate the "Latin brother countries," particularly Spain, Portugal, and Italy under a French nuclear "umbrella," and then try to have other members of the European Community join, under the umbrella of the Western European Union. Obviously this would be a long-term project, but also a project entirely in line with what seems to be long term French policy, as argued in Chapter 2. Watch out, peace/green movements!

Second, if land-based missiles serve as foci for demonstrations, then the obvious response is to have sea-based and air-based missiles instead. Since the agreement only covers missiles and not the warheads, there is no mutual commitment to reduce the number of warheads, only the stationing mode. This tendency should be watched and the peace movement should develop new strategies for demonstrations, perhaps focused on ports and airports.

Third, if internal political costs to the European allies were a factor, then this situation was brought about by the peace movement. Consequently, the major danger that might occur in the wake of the INF agreement would be for the peace movement to retreat into the background and declare that victory has been won. A maximum of a couple of hours or days for celebration since the peace movement definitely was a contributing cause; after that work, and even harder work is resumed. The basic formula would be to make the costs of a pro-nuclear policy, or in favor of weapons of mass destruction in general, ever higher for the politicians.

Fourth, if land-based nuclear missiles are vulnerable, then we might watch out not only for other modes of basing the missiles, but also for new and less vulnerable ways of deploying land-based missiles. One possibility would be deep-lying bunkers, use of underground tunnels not declared in the process of negotiation, and so on. The process uncovered so many discrepancies between the publicly acknowledged number of missiles and what they finally declared they had, once they got in negotiation distance of each other, that continued skepticism would certainly be appropriate.[15]

Fifth, if land-based nuclear missiles are destabilizing, then one military approach would be to make them less destabilizing. The solution hinted at in the preceding paragraph is one possibility: underground, secret stationing, possibly even warheads behind enemy lines. Anyone feeling that this is stretching the logic too far should ask him- or herself the question: has that logic not already been stretched rather far? In other words, watch out, or rather *down.*

Sixth, if nuclear forces are not good as arms, then the basic approach would be to find something better, but not the way the military in general seems to be thinking right now. At this point it becomes even more important that the peace movement does not satisfy itself with the answer "conventional weapon systems," but intensifies the effort to work for alternative security systems, including nonprovocative, defensive defense based on short-range conventional weapons, para-military defense, and nonmilitary defense.

Seventh, new and "better" weapon systems should meet with continuous and massive protests. The obvious candidate is Star Wars. Getting out of the intellectual-political trap of defining the debate over Star Wars in terms of whether or not it is effective as a defensive measure is essential. Unmasking the offensive potentials of Star Wars should be an everyday task for the peace movement. The same can be said for other possible alternatives to nuclear arms such as genetic engineering.

Eighth, if the costs of the arms race are a factor, then that point should be brought home to decision makers as often as possible. One way of doing this would be by showing opportunity costs; another in terms of conversion possibilities and not only from military to civilian but also from offensive military to defensive military systems. And then there is the third possibility that is increasingly becoming obvious: not only the Soviet Union and its allies but also the United States and its allies, at least some of them, can no longer bear the costs. Cutting or at least freezing the military budget becomes a necessity. The size of the deficit of the U.S. federal budget, the military budget, and Japanese investment in U.S. stocks and bonds are of the same order of magnitude, indicating not only that the United States can barely afford what it does, but also that this is underwritten by a country with which the United States has a far from unproblematic relationship. In other words, the economic costs may very quickly become rather basic political costs as people become less convinced that they serve any useful purpose.

Ninth, if both Reagan and Gorbachev needed a good agreement, then the world should see to it that the agreement is really a good one, in other words that it is not only for window-dressing, to be circumvented, side-stepped in all the ways indicated. The world should hold them not so much to the letter as to the spirit of the agreement, including the many flowery words they both pronounced in connection with the summit meeting.[16] In other words, no "compensation," and no further "modernization" of other systems.

Tenth, if the superpower agreement is a way of reinstating superpower hegemony, then it should be counteracted. The superpowers should not be unnecessarily praised for abolishing an evil just as there are limits to how much a drug dealer promising no longer to poison youth deserves praise, regardless of his protestation that he pushed drugs to help the economy of his country.[17] Rather, other countries should go ahead and point to other ways of building security, for instance as mentioned through alternative security systems, including nonprovocative defense. Time is long overdue to build down superpower hegemony rather than to have it reconfirmed, even celebrated.

Eleventh, if Gorbachev, *glasnost'*, and *perestroika* have had a positive impact on the stalemate, then these factors should be upheld and maintained. In other words, the rest of the world in general and the European peace movement in particular should do their best to maintain the momentum of this second socialist revolution (if that is what it is) in the Soviet Union. At the same time there should be a consistent call for *glasnost'* and *perestroika* in the United States, for a reexamination of the foundations of U.S. politics in general and foreign policy in particular. This will hurt not less, perhaps even more than in the Soviet Union, and is a necessary condition for further progress in the general arena of peace politics.

Twelfth, if the INF agreement symbolizes that the Cold War is over, then steps have to be taken to ensure that political consequences are drawn. One such political consequence would be what might be termed an Arias Plan for Eastern Europe, similar to the plan for Central America. Gorbachev has already indicated a certain autonomy for Eastern Europe in foreign policy as being in the cards.[18] Eastern Europe should design its own future, much like Central America did. The Eastern European leaders should come together and train themselves in resolving their own internal and external conflicts (particularly difficult is the relationship inside Rumania and between Rumania and Hungary), without any dictate from the Eastern European superpower. This would also come as a part of the general training of superpowers in relinquishing power and getting used to accept the rightful autonomy of their former clients.

And then we need a second Arias Plan for the two Germanys, detached from their superpowers, over the theme of uniting the German nation, but not the two German states. An implication is obvious: *West Germany gives up its claim as successor state in return for East Germany giving up the wall and the fence.* And, needless to say, the Soviet Union gets out of Afghanistan (with the United States) and the United States gets out of Central America (with the Soviet Union).

So far, so good. But then comes the ultimate warning. When they no longer have each other as enemy, will they cooperate in finding a joint enemy, as argued in Chapter 3? The Muslim world? Japan? The Greens? Or—can the rest of the world help them getting out of the idea that they are anointed for a special mission that inevitably does create enemies?

CONCLUSION

In short, there is more than enough to do. And it is sad to contemplate how few in the world, including peace research institutes and the peace movement, were ready to face an occasion such as the INF agreement with a concrete political agenda for the future. The outcome was to be expected. The militarily inclined governments in East and West, particularly the latter, immediately started talking about continuation of their "modernization program" and added to the vocabulary that formula of "compensation."[19] In short, the 400,000 war researchers are already at work, as they have always been. And what becomes very clear is the tremendous world deficit in peace researchers (400?) who could stand up against them and provide the world with a positive agenda, much more attractive and compelling than the new war instruments and scenarios produced by their colleagues in the war field.[20]

The alternative? Not necessarily a major war in the NATO/WTO system; as argued in Chapter 5 not likely.[21] But let us assume that the peace movement of the 1980s grew out of the gap between a high level arms race and a low level objective conflict. People in general probably want balance between the two, and (again, probably) want to see the arms level moving in the direction of the conflict level. If once again it turns out that the arms level shoots up without any objective change to the worse in the conflict situation, people will feel cheated and the peace movement will (this time) hopefully be in the streets again. Hopefully the cybernetic mechanism of extra-parliamentarian democracy is not needed; hopefully parliamentary democracy will be able to handle the challenge next time.

9

Alternative Security Policies in Europe*

MILITARY DOCTRINES: A LAYMAN'S GUIDE

Alternative security policies have to spell out alternatives in two fields: *military policy* and *foreign policy*. The two together constitute the external posture of a country, divided into military and political (including economic and cultural) postures. That this division is far from sharp is in the nature of the problem we are discussing. Military posture is an expression of foreign policy; political postures (and this is less obvious) have to be in agreement with the military policy chosen. If military policy is based on possible retaliation with weapons of mass destruction in general, and on nuclear arms (and possibly particle and laser beams)[1] in particular, in other words on superweapons, then the political posture has to correspond to this. A military doctrine based on superweapons can make sense only if the other side is not only a superpower but a superenemy. The construction of the enemy as "focus of evil in the modern world" or as "imperialist in the last phases of capitalism" is a concomitant of the weapons chosen, and *vice versa*. We are political prisoners of our military doctrines and—military prisoners of our political doctrines. To get out of that vicious circle is not going to be easy. What follows is an exploration of what can be done at the military end, given that with Gorbachev political opinings have been made.

The next pages offer a layperson's guide to alternative military doctrines. The assumption is that we are dealing with nonaggressive doctrines; aggressive doctrines justifying unprovoked attack are not included. The basic distinction made comes in the very beginning, between *offensive* and *defensive* military doctrines. It should be noted that the distinction is based on *capability*, not on intention. What matters is what is *possible*, not political declarations about the "mission" of weapons systems. Capability can change only slowly; motivations from one moment to the other. As indicated in the preceding paragraph: motivations also have a tendency to follow capability, not only *vice versa*.

The distinction in Figure 4 is made on the basis of the *range of the weapons systems* and the *size of the impact area*. The typical *offensive* doctrine to the left combines long-range capability with vast impact area, exemplified by intercontinental and intermediate range aircraft, submarines and ballistic and cruise missiles whether land-based, air-based, sea-based, or space-based. The warheads delivered by these weapons carriers often have very vast impact areas. If they should be highly precise, not only in the sense of hitting the target (low CEP) but also in the sense of very limited destruction, then such systems might be characterized as interdiction systems and be located in the gray territory between offensive and defensive systems.

To the right in Figure 4 are the *defensive* weapons systems based on short-range capability and limited impact. Just as weapons systems with the offensive configuration obviously are intended for enemy territory, defensive weapons are intended for territorial self-defense—as expressed in Figure 4. Both of them can be used as systems of deterrence in the sense of deterring enemy attack. But there is a question mark for the offensive systems—*how can the other side know?* Offensive capability *can* be used for retaliation as a second strike, but it *can* also be used aggressively, for a first strike. Weapons systems that are only short range can by definition be used only for self-defense and not for attack, *that* is the crucial point. A defensive doctrine would be based on that kind of system, and would obviously rule out weapons of mass destruction as too destructive.

As mentioned, there is a gray zone inbetween defensive and offensive systems. Antiaircraft guns, or antimissile systems, when shooting upward, are clearly defensive of the part of the territory known as air space (and, possibly, protecting land space from the bombs/warheads carried by aircraft/missiles). But when the angle is lowered and the gun is mounted on a long-range carrier (a train, a ship), the same gun can become an offensive weapon. This gray zone, however, is nothing compared to the negative window between first strike and second strike weapons systems in the offensive category, where nobody really has come up with clear criteria as to what constitutes one and what constitutes the other. The same systems may be part of both first and second strike packages. This discrimination problem lies at the root of the arms race.

Another point in connection with defensive military doctrines is the missing fourth category: a weapons system with short-range capability but vast impact area, such as nuclear land mines. Or scorched earth tactics in general.

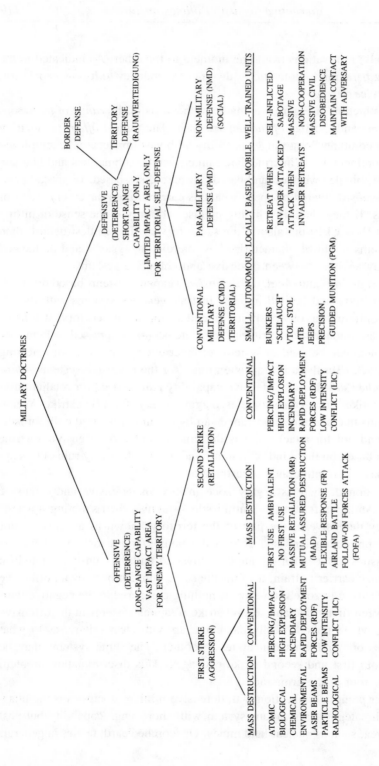

Figure 4. A Layman's Guide to Alternative Military Doctrines

These could be seen as defensive weapons in the case of despair. However, another way of looking at them would be as intellectual errors, inflicting so much damage on own territory that they in fact constitute a case of self-deterrence (deterring oneself from using them). To withdraw such systems is not a disarmament measure but error-correction.

Still another point should be made clear before proceeding. There is the distinction made to the right[2] in Figure 4 between border defense and territory defense. The former is an effort to stop the enemy already at the border. As a military doctrine this approach died with the Maginot Line for the defense of France against the German attack in 1940. Hitler's armies went around it, and had they not done so parachutists and/or the German navy could have done the same. But even if the whole perimeter of France had been sealed off, including antiaircraft defense for air space, the military doctrine would be irrational in addition to overly expensive. An enemy wants more than crossing the border. The enemy wants to occupy and use the country, after military occupation, for economic, political, social, and cultural reasons imposing his own values! A much more rational defensive doctrine would take this as a point of departure and not only make occupation hard to obtain, or at least difficult to maintain, but also deprive the enemy of any economic, political, social, and cultural benefits. And that calls for defense in depth, *Raumverteidigung,* to obtain the kind of protracted warfare most big powers try to avoid.

Continuing down Figure 4 on the offensive left-hand side, we come to the distinction between first strike and second strike doctrines, the former being a case of aggression, the latter of retaliation. One might say that no country today admits to having an aggressive first strike offensive military doctrine. They are all at least presenting their military capability in the name of defense. But even so, a first strike offensive doctrine makes sense. There is the old adage that "attack is the best defense," and the contemporary presentation of that doctrine as a "preemptive strike." Launch-on-warning and launch-on-suspicion, "use'm or lose'm" are expressions of the same basic idea. In fact, there is a continuum between first strike and second strike not only in terms of capability but also in terms of motivation behind the capability. It is not only those on the other side, the enemy, who will have great difficulties knowing whether a capability is intended for a first strike of aggression or a second strike of retaliation. The owners of that capability may also have the same difficulty, and deliberately keep the posture ambiguous.

The classical subdivision for both first strike and second strike capabilities would be between weapons of mass destruction and conventional weapons.

The listing in Figure 4 is traditional, except that laser and particle beams have been added as offensive weapons of mass destruction. Two examples of first strike offensive systems that still may be conventional have also been added: "rapid deployment forces" and "low intensity conflict."[3]

However, the military doctrines usually discussed under the offensive heading are *second* strike doctrines, triggered by verifiable enemy aggression. The subdivision for own *use* of weapons of mass destruction in "first use," "ambivalence," and "no first use" reflects a very important dimension in military doctrine analysis. As is well known the official Soviet position is "no first use" (of weapons of mass destruction in general and nuclear weapons in particular), whereas the U.S./NATO position is "neither first use nor no first use, but ambivalence." We may or we may not—*we* decide, keeping the option open. No self-imposed restraint, no contract with the enemy, like "if you only attack conventionally, we shall only respond conventionally."

Under that heading four major military doctrines are listed, all containing nuclear components:[4] *massive retaliation* and *mutual assured destruction* based on weapons of mass destruction; then *flexible response,* which is more conventional since the flexibility consists in answering with weapons of mass destruction or conventional weapons, depending on the nature of the attack; and last but not least, *Airland Battle,*[5] which integrates air force and army with chemical/nuclear and conventional systems, seizing initiative from the aggressor and is offensive in the sense of bringing the battle outside own territory.[6] The last point, "follow on forces attack," is not necessarily nuclear as a concept.

If we move back again, reading downward on the right-hand side of Figure 4, more flesh is put on the bones of defensive military doctrines. There is the classical subdivision into *conventional military defense, para-military defense,* and *nonmilitary defense.*[7] All three operate all over the national territory in small, autonomous, locally based, mobile, and very well trained units. The national border is less essential. Security is defined not only as territory geographically empty of enemies but in terms of the capacity to withstand any effort to use the territory, including the inhabitants, for purposes imposed from the outside. In this task there is a division of labor between conventional military forces that would be more geographically oriented, and nonmilitary defense that would be more socially oriented, denying the antagonist any social gains through not only self-inflicted sabotage of physical objects (carried out at the minimum level, not as scorched earth tactics) but through massive noncooperation and civil disobedience, yet

maintaining contact and engaging in constructive action to maintain the social formation as much as possible.

Nonmilitary defense would be bolstered by conventional defense using
bunkers scattered over the territory, vertical or short takeoff and landing
aircraft, motor torpedo boats, jeeps—all of this as platforms for precision
guided munition such as short-range but very smart rockets with passive
and/or active homing devices. No doubt recent technological innovations
in this field have made this particular type of defense more meaningful.

Inbetween is para-military defense according to the well-known doctrine
of retreating when the enemy attacks and attacking when the enemy retreats.
It should be noted, however, that para-military forces may not be that different from conventional military defense, and also have a social function
when really embedded in the local society not that different from nonmilitary
defense.

A difference in the structure of the two wings of the military doctrines
can be pointed out. The two subdivisions under offensive doctrines, first
strike and second strike, exclude each other. Through a first strike a second
strike posture has already been excluded, and *vice versa:* a credible, viable,
and honestly pursued second strike posture excludes a first strike posture.
But the subdivision on the defensive side in conventional, para-military, and
nonmilitary defense is not mutually exclusive. There are efforts to conceive
of them as such. Many, both pacifists and antipacifists, see nonmilitary defense as excluding the other two, otherwise the socio-psychological mechanisms of nonviolence cannot work. This is not necessarily the case, as
brought out to a large extent in the Vietnam war where the Vietnamese
fought with all three types of defense, including the self-immolation of
Buddhist monks as an extreme case of nonmilitary defense. Rather, one
could think in terms of a mix[8] with the three types supplementing each other
at different points in space, different phases in time after the attack, and for
different social functions.

Then, there is also the distinction between the conventional military forces
and para-military forces, the former being "legal" according to the laws of
war, the second illegal. If the criteria are wearing a uniform and carrying
the weapons openly, para-military forces can do this. They might still, like
conventional military forces, prefer not to expose themselves openly to enemy attack, in other words hide, and hide well. The dichotomy is artificial
and essentially brought into the laws of war to protect occupying forces, in
other words big powers.[9] It might be in the interest of the smaller powers
to overcome that distinction since the weak can defend themselves only by

being dispersed and unpredictable. And it is only by building this type of defense in advance that defensive defense can deter by being credible.

The important point about Figure 4 and the chart of military doctrines can now be made: *with the elaboration of defensive defense, which has taken place during the last years, the entire discourse about military matters has become much richer.*[10] Not long time ago there were only two positions. There was a mainstream position clearly based on *offensive nuclear systems,* with a majority inside that majority with a clear second strike orientation, and a minority that was no stranger to the preemptive attack idea. And there was countertrend, deeply opposed to the arms race in general and nuclear arms in particular, in favor of *unilateral nuclear disarmament.* The problem with that position always became rather clear when they were asked "and then, what?" Focusing so much on the distinction between nuclear and conventional weapons had, perhaps, blinded the antinuclear weapons groups to the much more fundamental distinction between offensive and defensive weapons systems in general, and military doctrines in particular. To try to balance long-range missiles with long-range conventional bombers does not seem to make much sense. Hence, the nuclear unilateralists were driven back to the last position of intellectual, political, and in a sense also military defense: *nonmilitary defense.* Of course, this was not only due to the lack of elaboration of defensive defense, but also to the circumstance that antinuclearism often was a position derived from general antimilitarism.

And antimilitarism is not a majority position in European countries. The majority is in favor of military defense and the NATO alliance in Western Europe, but not in favor of nuclear arms in general and more particularly not in favor of U.S. military policy in connection with nuclear arms, at least not by the recent administrations in Washington.[11]

Defensive defense fills the gap between the extreme positions of nuclearism and disarmamentism, and opens for a number of different combinations. Taking the pacifist position as a point of departure, the adherent of nonmilitary defense can now add para-military and conventional military defense, because they are nonprovocative, yet acceptable to a majority not convinced about the pacifist option of nonmilitary defense only. Hence new political alliances become possible.[12] And from the position of conventional military defense one might extend the options in the other direction so as to include para-military defense, and nonmilitary defense, as occupation defense by civilians. In fact, it would be difficult not to open for that possibility as an additional element in a defensive defense posture. Reasons for not doing so would probably mainly be expressions of intellectual conservatism and military resistance against occupation defense by the civilian sector (and even by conscientious objectors!).[13]

But then the adherents of conventional defense could also expand in the other direction, even if at the risk of losing the purity of nonprovocative, defensive defense. An argument could be made for conventional defense in general, with no weapons of mass destruction but a range far outside the national perimeter, building on the notion of an interdiction defense, which admittedly is on the borderline between offensive and defensive systems. Some of those interested in that kind of military systems might also be interested in building further in the same direction and include weapons of mass destruction and postures that would be compatible with a first strike capability.

In other words, the range of options is now considerable, with a number of different doctrines available as well as their combinations. The old military/antimilitary distinction has been bridged and is probably missed by extremists on both sides.

But the key question, which doctrine is better than the others, remains. As usual this is a question of weighing the consequences. By and large I think the key arguments in favor and against defensive and offensive defense can be summarized as follows, leaving out in this connection the most obvious argument: that a war fought with offensive systems might become omnicidal.[14]

In favor of defensive military doctrines speaks of one very important factor: *defensive defense is nonprovocative.*[15] The country cannot attack, it is "structurally impossible" to give a somewhat simplified translation into English of the expression used by the German Social Democratic party.[16] Hence, whatever tension there is in international relations would not derive from the offensive potential of the country. If there is offensive armament it would be stimulated by internal forces, which may be strong enough, not by mimicking what the other country, the defensive defense country, is doing. "*Die Schweiz provoziert niemanden*" (Switzerland provokes nobody).[17]

Another strong argument *in favor* of the defensive defense doctrine is its *capacity for real defense if an attack should ever come.* A country of that type would offer an enemy trying to occupy and change it a considerable challenge. The argument in Chapter 4 was that when the Soviet Union did not attack Yugoslavia in 1948, Albania in 1960, and Poland in 1980–81, this was at least to a large extent because of the reputation all three countries had gained during World War II as countries capable of offering effective resistance. In fact Yugoslavia and Albania were the only European countries apart from the Soviet Union capable of liberating themselves; and Poland would probably have done so had it not been for Stalin's treason outside Warsaw in 1944. It belongs to the story that two other countries that were invaded by the Soviet Union, Hungary in 1956 and Czechoslovakia in 1968, both came out of World War II with a reputation for not defending themselves, contributing very little to their own liberation from nazi occupation.[18] Maybe the Soviet Union drew the conclusion: we can invade.

The argument *against* defensive defense is the *incapacity for retaliation*. The country could be exposed to blackmail, threats, by the country possessing offensive weapons systems, mass destruction or conventional. This is an important argument. The best rebuttal is probably not in terms of denying that this could happen, but rather in pointing out that this may also happen if that country has an offensive military doctrine and capability. The blackmail weapons may have been installed inside the country as warheads smuggled in, to be exploded by remote ignition without anybody ever knowing who placed them there. This is the type of age in which we live, unfortunately; my guess being that such weapons are already deployed.

The argument *in favor* of offensive military doctrines would take exactly this as the point of departure and promise *retaliation, a second strike, in case of transgression*. As already indicated this might work in case the transgressor is known. It might be considerably more difficult if the transgressor could be anybody in possession of nuclear warheads (for instance), or any terrorist, national or international. The number of nuclear actors is already quite high with Israel, South Africa and India added to the classical nuclear Club of Five.

Against offensive military doctrines the argument that it *offers no alternative to an allout war* should weigh heavily. The type of military systems under an offensive doctrine would not be good for occupation defense. In fact, if that military system is successfully beaten, there might not be any second line defense, and the country would have to capitulate. The pattern is just the opposite of a country with defensive defense where it might take very little to break through the first line of defense, the border—but after that the resistance would become stiffer and stiffer. Hence the temptation to break down that first line of military capability through a first strike might be considerable, knowing that there would be rewards after the first risk if the country has only border defense (or mainly offensive systems—like the United States).

And then, there is certainly the argument against, that *offensive military capability provokes*. As there is no clear criterion that can be used to distinguish between first and second strike capability, any present or future adversary might be in doubt about the intentions, and for that reason prefer to err on the "safe" side, meaning at least acquiring a second strike offensive capability for retaliatory purposes. The result is an arms race, or to be more precise, one of the mechanisms underlying an arms race.[19]

To this could be added that the offensive system is more expensive than defensive systems, and also, because it is more capital-intensive, less capable of providing jobs in a period of unemployment. Defensive military resistance would be based on much simpler military installations that by their very nature would be labor intensive, based more on domestic production capacity, and above all less expensive.[20]

What about the level of militarization of the population? The argument can be made that offensive doctrines do not presuppose much in terms of militarization of the country. The systems are capital- and research-intensive, demanding highly qualified personnel that might be isolated from the rest of the society but for that reason also constitute a danger because they may have their own vested interests. Defensive military systems are more based on civilian-soldiers not very different from the rest of society, particularly if para-military and nonmilitary defense are included. A spirit of resistance would have to be engendered. Some of this might become chauvinistic, even militaristic. Switzerland is perhaps an example of this, but Yugoslavia and Finland much less so, and Sweden and Austria—in the view of this author—not at all.

The conclusion here is in favor of defensive military doctrines. When I draw that conclusion it is because of the risk that the military systems themselves become a factor causing tension, even war, not because I disregard the difficulties in connection with the blackmail argument. Rather, I would tend to think that everything has to be done to provide an international atmosphere that would reduce tension in general, thereby making it possible for low key, nonaggressive foreign policies to be operative. For this to happen a defensive military doctrine may not be a sufficient condition but it is close to a necessary one. Under the atmosphere prevailing when major powers have offensive military doctrines, we get exactly what we used to have: fear, anxiety, efforts to justify the weaponry developed by one's own side by constructing the enemy in such a way that he merits that type of weapon, frustrations when disarmament negotiations break down. But why should they not break down when the logic of the whole game given the nature of offensive military doctrine would work against disarmament and in favor of a continued arms race?

The relative weight of these arguments in favor of or against defensive and offensive doctrines would depend on a number of factors. Some countries are more predisposed for offensive, some countries more for defensive military doctrines. The next section spells out some of these conditions as hypotheses. This is important because it gives us some cues as to where the real, as opposed to the professed, difficulties may be located.

FACTORS CONDITIONING CHOICE OF MILITARY DOCTRINE

In a sense the title of this section is misleading. Military doctrines are not necessarily chosen consciously, after long and rational deliberations. They may also grow out of a historical situation, being built into the social structure one way or the other; or imposed from the outside by very threatening or very helpful big neighbors, for instance.

The following is a list of factors that should be taken into consideration when a country's military doctrine is evaluated.

First, *how credible is it that a country can be invaded,* for economic, political, social, and cultural gains, not only in order to destroy military capability? For instance, it is not very credible that the United States could be invaded with these goals in view. The United States has four major means of defensive defense: the Atlantic Ocean, the Pacific Ocean, Mexico made relatively innocuous after the United States took approximately half of the territory 1846–48, and Canada made innocuous through U.S. control of the Canadian economy. The only possibility would be through air (via space or not), but then for military purposes rather than for the other four. The effort to make a Soviet invasion credible in the TV series *Amerika* did not carry much conviction, and the scenario with the United Nations as the agent through which the invasion/occupation took place, was not very credible either. The series was a flop.

On the other hand, the Soviet Union has repeatedly been invaded in its history, in 1941 through Operation Barbarossa. Invasion is a highly credible scenario. Thinking in terms of defensive defense, for that reason, would come more easily to the Soviet Union than to the United States. Historical experience does matter in shaping their positions today.

On the other hand, take a small country like Switzerland. Being surrounded by four of the major powers in Europe (Germany, France, Italy, and the Austro-Hungarian Empire) up to 1918 attack, invasion, and occupation were certainly credible. Since Switzerland itself is composed essentially of German-speaking, French-speaking, and Italian-speaking people, the four surrounding big powers already had parts of themselves inside the country. Neutrality became the obvious solution to that problem as any position in favor of one or two of the neighbors would have split that little nation.[21] Moreover, it was certainly not the tradition in European history that the four would ever be on the same side. Only the Cold War crystallized Western Europe in such a way that (West) Germany, France, and Italy became members of the same alliance. At the same time it was obviously in Switzerland's interest not to have any provocative weapons systems that could be used as a pretext for a preemptive attack.[22] From this a choice in favor of defensive defense flows readily. The pattern that emerged, the famous Swiss Army, carried a high level of social mobilization even to the point of militarization. For that reason it was not to be expected that nonmilitary defense would play any prominent role in the military doctrine (but militia does). But defensive deterrence has worked, or the Swiss experience is at least compatible with that hypothesis.[23]

Second, *is it credible that the country could use its military forces aggressively, to attack others?* Obviously, to the extent this is credible, military thinking would tend to favor the offensive branch of the tree of military doctrines. A history of offensive use of the military, if "successful," will tend to be a part of the national tradition, even an honorable one. A change in military doctrine from offensive to defensive will tend to be interpreted as some kind of self-emasculation. At the same time the country may have a "warrior caste" of considerable magnitude and influence to whom war is far from the worst evil.

Switzerland has that "caste," but not a tradition of expansion through aggression. Of the other NN (neutral and nonaligned) countries in the center of Europe, from north to south, Finland and Yugoslavia cannot be said to have any tradition of expansion either. But Sweden and Austria have that tradition, and also what might be referred to as a "warrior caste," meaning families with a long-standing military tradition. Consequently, when Sweden and Austria opt for a defensive military doctrine, they are placing more constraints on themselves than the other three to which this comes more naturally. And they should be watched for any extension of the range of their weapons systems.[24]

The United States and the Soviet Union both have traditions of aggression, readily recognized by comparing the series of maps of the 200 years history of the United States and the 1,000 years history of Russia, over time. Both of them will justify the expansion as a "civilizing mission" and for defensive reasons, to consolidate behind defensible borders against hostile forces. Others might see these as pretexts in justifying expansion for economic and political gains. However, regardless of how that may be, one might take note that the United States, given the two factors explored so far, has an unambiguous tradition favoring offensive military doctrines, whereas the Soviet Union has a more ambiguous tradition. One possible prediction given this difference would be a higher level of readiness in the Soviet Union at least to discuss defensive military doctrines than in the United States.[25]

But how about the other countries in Europe? In Eastern Europe Poland is perhaps the only country with an expansionist, aggressive inclination after World War I. But Western Europe is full of such countries: Germany, France, Italy as already mentioned, Great Britain, and—if we stretch the historical perspective—Spain, Portugal, Belgium, and the Netherlands that all were colonial powers until recently (if we stretch the historical perspective further back it would be hard to find any country without an aggressive tradition somewhere in the past). Thus, again we come to the conclusion that it is easier for Eastern than Western European countries to adapt a more defensive military doctrine. The latter would have to overcome more of their own historical traditions, particularly France and Great Britain—as evidenced by their insistence on keeping an "independent deterrent" that certainly is offensive even if it is not aggressive.

However, it is also clear that this would present no major problem for smaller countries such as Norway and Denmark (and indeed Iceland), the Netherlands, Belgium and Luxemburg, Ireland, Spain, and Portugal. It is the "hard core," the four big Western European countries, Germany, France, Italy, and Great Britain that have major problems to overcome. On the other hand, it should also be noticed that in two of these countries (West Germany and Great Britain) the largest opposition parties have on their programs both the reduction of offensive weapons systems and steps toward the creation of a more credible defensive defense (SPD in West Germany[26] and the Labour Party in Great Britain).[27] Given the novelty of such propositions, the historical traditions of the countries, and insufficient training in thinking and discussing from the point of view of defensive military doctrine, there will still be some time before the electorate would be willing to accept the idea.[28]

The factor of ethnic pluralism was mentioned above in connection with the credibility of being attacked. Switzerland was seen as driven into a defensive posture, and more particularly into nonalignment, even neutrality, through ethnic identification with all neighbors. How about the United States and the Soviet Union in this connection, both being ethnically very diverse?

Any analysis of this problem shows how ambiguous the factor turns out to be. In the United States the most numerous categories of Caucasians populating the country are Germans, Italians, British, Polish, Irish, and Russians (particularly Jews), in that order. The argument can be made that there is no case in history where all these nationalities were on the same side, which the United States then could favor or be against with no risk of splitting the population. The argument is strengthened if we go further down the list, passing the Scandinavians toward the Asian and Hispanic elements; and particularly if the Africans forced into the country and the native Americans forced into reservation ghettos are taken into consideration. Total alignment would have a close to zero probability.

Hence, there should be a tendency in the United States toward neutralism, withdrawing into itself precisely in order not to split the nation. But there could also be a tendency in the opposite direction being "a nation of nations," above other nations, supranational, with not only the right but a duty to intervene and set matters straight. Thus the ethnic diversity of the United States would, in a sense, be compatible with the two major patterns of U.S. foreign policy behavior, "isolationism" and "global responsibility."[29]

How about the Soviet Union? Historically the Soviet Union has intervened abroad considerably less often than the United States. But then there is a major difference: the minorities in the Soviet Union of the same nationality as the neighbors are small and powerless, both nationally and internationally. There are Tadzhiks/Uzbeks both in the Soviet Union and in Afghanistan. But this does not prevent the Soviet Union from attacking Afghanistan and may also have been a contributing factor. The Soviet Union might have been afraid of "political contamination" from Afghanistan into the Soviet Union precisely because of ethnic similarity, not too different from the U.S. fear of Japanese-Americans in World War II, leading to the internment of 130,000 of them. And they were afraid of the Americans coming in, but the possibility of Tadzhik/Uzbek resentment did not prevent the 1979 invasion.

In other words, the small country would certainly have to take ethnic divisions into account. The bigger countries can afford not to do so, and might even see them as factors favoring aggressive responses to international situations.

Third, *the internal situation of the country.* Offensive military doctrines are based on long-range weapons not very useful for crushing internal revolts, as experienced by the Shah of Iran when he was facing precisely this phenomenon and had long-range aircraft at his disposal. Defensive weapon systems are short-range systems and are also very useful for internal warfare against dissident elements in the population. The way Switzerland has been able to accommodate this factor is admirable: by creating unity out of diversity through a federal system uniting different religions and languages, and by trusting the population so much that the Swiss soldiers literally have their army guns at home and are reputed not to use them for criminal assault against their compatriots.

In other words, one might argue that only a country that has overcome major internal social contradictions is ready for defensive military doctrines. This situation already obtains in a substantial number of European countries. It is hard to believe that the military institution would be abused in most of these countries, so far advanced not only in terms of the first generation of human rights (civil and political rights) but also the second generation (social and economic and cultural rights). The point made is simply that this is a factor that has to be taken into consideration.

Fourth, if the preceding factor was social costs, the next would be *the factor of economic costs*. The argument can be made that offensive weapon systems are more expensive than the defensive ones. This should not be confused with the costs of nuclear weapons. The warheads are inexpensive, but not the weapon carriers and the whole infrastructure that goes with it. A considerable national and international machinery will have to be constructed to make that type of weapon system credible. The defensive weapon systems mentioned above are much more modest.[30] Being more locally based local resources can be drawn upon as done by most countries when they construct their militia systems. A military doctrine based on conventional but offensive weapon systems might be as, or even more, expensive than a military doctrine based on nuclear weapons. But the argument made here is that we should compare defensive and offensive systems, not conventional weapons with weapons of mass destruction. Substantial savings can be made through transarmament toward defensive defense, or—in Soviet terminology—sufficient defense.

And substantial savings are needed for both superpowers. The Soviet Union has colossal tasks within its own borders constructing a viable and attractive socialist society as conceived of by the new leadership of the Soviet Union. *Perestroika* is incompatible with a war economy, an arms race, and hostile relations with most of the neighbors of the Soviet Union. There is also the challenge from present and former communist countries diversifying their economy considerably, not giving up planning but modifying it with an expanding market sector (Hungary, Yugoslavia, China). The corresponding peace theory would not be based on *convergence* as there is hardly any basis for assuming that countries similar to each other necessarily are peaceful to each other; they could also be more competitive. The basis would be *interdependence* theory. Neither ideology in particular nor culture in general, nor military postures—offensive or defensive—are so productive in making countries interdependent as economic relations. What has to be watched, however, is that those economic interdependencies do not become too asymmetric, with one of the parties exploiting the other, which then starts accumulating resentment until the whole situation becomes a source of peacelessness rather than peace. Europe still has too much of that, both North-South and West-East.

If the Soviet Union needs a less expensive defense, so does the biggest debtor nation in the world, the United States. A change toward defensive defense might be the answer also in this case. With no doctrinal transformation taking place the legitimation probably has to be in terms of "rationalization," closing "useless" facilities, cracking down on overcharging, corruption, graft, etc. A U.S. *perestroika* is also incompatible with a wartime economy. But the readiness to admit this is lower than for the Soviet Union.

POLITICAL CONSIDERATIONS

Soon 45 years after World War II, the peoples of Europe—and of the NATO-WTO system in general, from the United States to the Soviet Union via Western Europe, the NN countries, and Eastern Europe—should be entitled to live without the threat of an impending nuclear war. At the same time anybody who knows European history also knows that Europe is a dangerous place to live. Given this, one possible way of "squaring the circle" is to eliminate the offensive component in military systems in order to take the threat away, yet develop a defensive component in order to be prepared lest something should happen. The question is whether the conditions are ripe for the transformation, known as transarmament. The basis for the following reflections was presented in the preceding section. Let me only point to some additional factors.

It is natural for Western Europeans to ask that question first of all of the Soviet Union. The Soviet Union is now in a major transformation in its history associated in the West with the name of one particular person, Gorbachev. It is probably a major mistake to discuss the politics of a major country in the name of one person; we should concentrate on the social factors underlying the Gorbachev phenomenon. They are, in my view, as follows.

From being a country run by the triad *party-KGB-Soviet army,* we are now witnessing the breakthrough for the Soviet *technocracy,* a triad of *bureaucracy-big state monopolies-intelligentsia/professionals*. The usual commentary on the Soviet Union, that the economy is not functioning very well (although not entirely badly, misery has been abolished and the country is capable of matching the United States in the arms race) obscures the rather basic factor that education is functioning extremely well. There are millions and millions of people with higher education in the group described above as "technocracy," and this is the class behind the Gorbachev transformation. Not that Gorbachev is not also supported by many people in the party, the KGB, and the army, and opposed by many people in bureaucracy, and among the professionals. The basic point is that a new logic is entering Soviet society, more familiar to countries in the West: the primacy of technocratic rather than ideological adequacy and efficiency.

As a result the Soviet Union has become much more amenable to negotiations. This does not necessarily mean that disagreements will disappear. But they will be expressed in the idiom—if not in the language—familiar to people in the West, less ideology, less threat—more trade and exchange in general. More freedom.

The old Soviet Union, ruled by the *partocracy,* had essentially military power and cultural—meaning ideological—power to fall back upon. The new Soviet Union, increasingly ruled by the logic of technocracy, will base itself more on economic power, knowing that any ideological message will fail unless the Soviet Union is viable economically, both domestically and in foreign trade. The new elites want to show what they are capable of doing, untrammeled by partocracy constraints. They want a materially better life for their own citizens as well as a better trade posture. Trade is also seen as an act of communication. Like the United States they are overspending on armies—to the point of killing their economies—by putting so much of their creativity into the military sector. A defensive defense posture, hence, may be very attractive.

How does this apply to the Eastern European countries? Most of them would be ready for transformations permitting them to become politically more pluralistic societies by having a system of election with a real choice of candidates (in the future perhaps also parties, although it is not obvious that party choices are more democratic than candidate choices). This development has already taken place in Hungary. When realized in the Soviet Union, it will definitely be repeated elsewhere in Eastern Europe.[31]

The general model for a positive relationship between an Eastern European country and the Soviet Union would be Finland. Characteristically this model includes not only pluralism, in other words democracy, but also a social profile to that democracy. In addition there are two basic rules in the relationship to the Soviet Union: *armed neutrality* with a guaranteed readiness to defend the country in case the Soviet Union is attacked through that country ("by Germany or a country allied with Germany"), and *economic exchange.*[32]

There are reasons to believe that the Soviet Union today is much more satisfied with its arrangement with Finland than with other countries in Eastern Europe. The problem the Soviet Union has had with the socialist countries in Eastern Europe can perhaps be summarized as follows: either the population is also in favor of socialism in which case the whole country might like to establish its own national variety, independent of the Soviet Union (Yugoslavia, Albania, to some extent Romania), or the population in general is against socialism in which case the Soviet Union (for security reasons? for "historical reasons"?) will have to maintain an unpopular government at considerable economic and political expense to itself, to that country, and to the rest of the world. Finland offers both security to a Soviet Union badly in need of that commodity, and economic opportunities.

Obviously, the Finnish solution is not only compatible with but indeed demands a defensive, nonprovocative defense. How would that work in other countries in Eastern Europe? Armed neutrality has to be two-sided (at least), not only for defense of the country against an attack from the West, but also from the East—meaning rather unambiguously from the Soviet Union. Post-World War II history seems to indicate that the Soviet Union would prefer that type of arrangement, as it is embedded in the *Staatsvertrag* with Austria in 1955, to almost any other relations short of what might be ideal: unswerving loyalty to the building of socialism and to the Soviet Union (the Bulgarian solution?). Hence, if this solution at the same time is acceptable to the peoples in Eastern Europe and to the Soviet Union, then the solution should certainly also be acceptable to the West.

How about Western Europe in this connection? Western Europe is economically strong but has relied on the United States for its military security. Whether there ever was a credible Soviet threat to Western Europe or not is not discussed here; whether the arrangement with the United States was a rational reaction to that kind of threat or had other goals (possibly in addition) is not taken up either. The basic point, as argued above, is that defensive defense on the average would provide a higher level of security than offensive, provocative defense. Neither socially nor mentally would the Western European populations in general be prepared for general and complete disarmament. There is a whole military-bureaucratic-corporate-research complex that certainly will not disappear overnight and would demand some type of military establishment. They might, conceivably, be persuaded in favor of a defensive rather than offensive military doctrine, but not in favor of no military doctrine at all. Nor would the Western European populations, accustomed not only to a military establishment in their midst, but also to the idea of a threat, be sufficiently convinced about the virtues of 100% disarmament, as argued by one wing of the peace movement.

But the historical opportunity for a great compromise in favor of turning to defensive defense in Europe both East and West, imitating the nonaligned countries has perhaps never been so good as now. There are also good reasons to assume that the Soviet Union might be interested in the same type of arrangement. And if it is acceptable both to the Soviet Union, Eastern Europe and Western Europe (with the possible exclusion of France, which is building its security policy around a *force de frappe* for which no disarmament plans seem to exist), then it should also be acceptable to the United States. In fact, both superpowers could insist on maintaining the two alliances as arrangements for collective bargaining as long as the military doctrines of the alliances could be revised. The superpowers could help each other develop defensive defense. And the alliances could, ideally, serve as a peaceful setting for like-minded countries to cooperate in the implementation of defensive defense, and then wither away.

And that leads to the final conclusion: *time has now come to discuss military doctrine*. We have for much too long been discussing separate weapon systems, sometimes singly, sometimes combined, and only insufficiently the underlying rationale. We would take a great step forward if somebody could call a conference for a multilateral discussion of military doctrine, preferably under United Nations auspices. All countries would benefit from this, particularly the countries squeezed inbetween the two superpowers in Europe, east and west, north and south.

10

Active Peaceful Coexistence:
Is a New Departure Possible?

It sounds like an eternity ago, but it is actually only since 1967. Major things had happened in the East-West conflict process. The French president Charles DeGaulle had disinvited NATO from France and with it a number of military installations, and taken France out of the integrated military command of the North Atlantic Treaty Organization. At the same time there was clearly the beginning of something new called "cooperation." *Détente* had started, although it took some time before there was general and shared awareness that such a thing was around, not only in plans and speeches, but in reality. NATO even produced a policy paper, under the name of the Belgian Foreign Minister Pierre Harmel, a document from which there is still a lot to learn.[1]

In Strasbourg the Council of Europe was interested in exploring, in general terms, possible new patterns of East-West cooperation and asked the newly founded International Peace Research Association whether such a study could be made. The task fell on this author and the document was produced the same year.[2] In that document there are some elements of a theory of peace, or more precisely, a list of conditions under which cooperation is seen as conducive to peace.[3] Five such conditions are singled out for special attention: *symmetry* or some degree of equity between the partners; *homology* or some degree of structural similarity between the partners; *symbiosis* in the sense that cooperation is really important for both partners; *institution building* at the supranational level; and *entropy,* meaning that the cooperation has to take place in all kinds of channels, well distributed, not only government to government and between the superpowers, for instance.

It is easily seen in retrospect that the critical condition among these five is the first one, the condition of symmetry. European countries are relatively homologous, being developed countries in the northern hemisphere, modern and industrialized with bureaucratic and corporate institutions, with professions, intellectuals, and urbanization. They differ as to whether capital should dominate over state, state over capital, or some kind of balance, and with respect to pluralism and the extent to which rulers should be accountable to the population in elections. There was no doubt that the cooperation was symbiotic and still is. East needs technology, West needs raw materials and energy, so there is at least that basis to build on, as very clearly illustrated in the famous gas pipeline from East to West.[4] But it has been equally clear all the time that supranational institution building has not been on the agenda beyond the very limited functions provided by the Economic Commission for Europe under the United Nations Economic and Social Council, located in Geneva. The level of entropy has also been low. Cooperation has been mainly governmental, although certainly not only between the superpowers,[5] given the skepticism about popular links.

The crucial condition is that of symmetry, and here five more specific points were mentioned. The gains should be about equal, the inputs should be about equal, the level of dependency on the cooperation about equal, participation about equal, and the change caused by the cooperation about equal.[6] The rationale underlying such conditions becomes very clear when one considers situations where they do not obtain. Imagine that one party puts very much into it because it means so much, depends on it, participates with great eagerness, and as a result exposes itself to the risk of change. It would also have to gain a lot in order to feel that the pattern of cooperation is reasonable. On the other hand, imagine a party that does not put very much into the cooperation, neither depends on it nor participates very much, and changes nothing. In that case, small gains do not matter much, but if it gains a lot it has certainly made an advantageous deal. However, since this is politics, not simply a question of trade, it is not sufficient that gains are seen as off-setting inputs. It is not sufficient that they both gain.

It is also important that the *net balance* should be relatively equal for both parties, that participation in joint enterprises of all kinds should be relatively equal and that changes should balance out. For if they do not, then one party can use cooperation or co-existence as a lever in order to, for example, make the other party more "capitalist." And that certainly is politics. Either party may feel that the other *needs* change and is consequently justified in using any leverage. But such feelings are not very helpful in this connection. We are dealing with parties that both are tremendously self-righteous, at least at the higher levels of power. Both see themselves as carriers of some message and cause that will ultimately prevail. Neither is willing to be subject to or submit to the other. Change may be wanted; they may even agree with the other side. But they would like the change to come from the inside, not from the outside. If cooperation brings about change, then it should be balanced. I may need change, but so do you!

Conditions such as these, or similar conditions, have to be taken seriously if peace is to be a by-product of cooperation. The frequently quoted expression to the effect that cooperation should be of "mutual benefit" is a general formulation in that direction, but excludes nothing since both parties seek some benefit. "Mutual and equal benefit" would be better. It is also relatively easy, on the background of such conditions, to see what went wrong in East-West cooperation. Take the case of Poland as an example, extreme but also fairly typical. Trade relations were set up, basically exchanging raw material, semimanufactures, and agricultural products, and some finished products from the earlier phases of the industrial revolution from the East, with much more advanced technology and products from later phases of industrialism from the West.[7] In a sense this pattern is normal. This is what East-West trade has been about for centuries, as has been the case for North-South trade, only even more so. And that makes the results quite predictable.

More particularly, there are three basic changes that will take place in the eastern country (or the southern country): the people will get accustomed, even addicted to the type of consumer goods that become available under the deal; the elites will become addicted to the luxury goods and resources in general that become available through them, since it will enhance their power, at least in their own eyes,[8] and the deal will in general be decreasingly favorable to the East (South). This is so because of the tendency of terms of trade between the processed and the unprocessed to develop in disfavor of the latter, with the notable (but obvious) exception of oil since 1973. But this is not true for all types of energy resources. Poland did not benefit from improved or equal terms of trade over time with its export of coal; Soviet Union did benefit because the export was gas and oil. Deteriorating terms will generally apply to agricultural products: to pay for technology with agricultural produce will tend to become an uphill fight.

Hence the options available to the eastern (southern) country in the deal become increasingly limited. One measure would be to compensate for deteriorating terms of trade through increasing output, by increasing the productivity and/or the input of work in number of workers, number of hours— the latter possibly disguised as a "voluntary contribution." Another possibility is to fill the gap between imports and exports with loans that then will have to be serviced. Engaging in both at the same time, the net result will be a tendency to exploit workers more and more while the country sinks into debt burdens that tend to consume closer and closer to (or even above) 100 percent of the income from exports,[9] meaning that the policy is self-defeating. In this kind of situation the addiction of the people to the life-style of the West, combined with increasing exploitation of them in order to pay for it as well as the considerably higher life-styles of their own elites, not to mention for the waste in the whole process, cannot but lead to revolts, even attempts at revolution. Or, alternatively, to frustration and apathy. Or to both. In short: both Solidarność visions and general depression and cynicism.

When an addicted system has managed to paint itself into the corner, the room for maneuver for the governing elites is very limited. Whatever it grants to the population in general, and the workers in particular, in terms of consumers goods or improved working conditions (including decreased hours of work) will have to be more than compensated for by increased productivity. It is not at all obvious that this would come high on the agenda of those who want a system change. The rest of the story, again given the case of Poland, is rather well known.

This is not to say that the system would have reacted differently had East-West trade been differently structured. There were certainly also overriding political causes for the Polish débacle. Some were located inside Poland in the struggle between the Polish people and the power elite fighting for survival, some outside Poland in the Soviet fear of losing a client country or even having it turn against the Soviet Union, and some in the interest of the United States in having all of this happen. The non-symmetric way in which East-West trade was structured was certainly one important factor. Basic changes were being wrought inside the Polish social formation without any corresponding changes taking place in the West as a result of the pattern of exchange. Dependency was very high, inputs equally so, the net gains more and more dubious. If the purpose was to promote security through cooperation, not only through the highly dangerous means of deterrence, even balance of terror, then that purpose was not obtained. It was simply a bad piece of social engineering at the international level. If the purpose was to wreak havoc inside Poland, then the purpose was obtained, but in that case it does not belong under the heading of "active peaceful coexistence." Hence, and that is the net conclusion of this exploration so far, cooperation has to be done in a different way if we are to attempt it again.

But before we try to say something about that, it should once more be remembered how epoch-making the changes at the end of the 1960s were as a phase in East-West history. A new paradigm was being ushered in.

There was to be less concern with the military, even with the military balance, and more with cooperative relations between East and West; less concern with moralism and political conflicts in general, more with factors that could unite or at least serve as a basis of cooperation. After all, this was the type of politics that had been started in Western Europe in the 1950s and formalized in the Treaty of Rome, eventually leading to the European Community in which two arch-enemies, Germany and France, were brought under a common roof in a pattern of symmetric, homologous, symbiotic, supranational, and highly entropic cooperation.[10] Even though the situation was different, could one not try what seemed to work in the case of the European Community also at the East-West level?

Today, some 20 years later, the question sounds totally misplaced. The United States has had administrations bent on trying to bring the Soviet Union down on its knees through military threats, political action, and economic pressures beyond what the United States thinks the Soviet Union can stand.[11] That policy did not succeed. The Soviet Union was not blackmailed into capitulation—this may be one of the few things elite and people in that enormous country might agree totally on. But it certainly meant that the atmosphere has not been as good as it could have been. The five rules mentioned above are traffic rules for a gentler international climate, rules of behavior for *associative* politics, building peace by coming closer to one another, yet not so close that the identity of the systems is threatened. They are rules that presuppose that both parties see their own security as predicated upon the other party feeling secure, not insecure, as "common security" (Palme Commission) in other words. Here it should again be remembered that if security is the probability of keeping one's own systems intact so that possible changes are truly endogenous changes, then cooperation *may* threaten security. It *does* involve the risk of change, one reason why both parties will probably prefer to keep cooperation below certain limits. A good example here is television cooperation by beaming TV programs from satellites even when this is not wanted by the ruling elites.[12] An unnecessary provocation. Rather, have daily "TV-bridge" debates!

Singling out the U.S. administration during most of the 1980s for critical attention in no way means that there is not a constant underlayer of efforts by both camps to subvert the other. No doubt this is most pronounced in the superpowers. But there has been an explicitness, a directness, and something viciously aggressive about U.S. behavior in this regard in the first Reagan administration possibly to be continued by the Bush administration. May we hope for a new departure after that?

NEW DEPARTURES

What would be some new departures if we should try again? In other words, if once more we should try to build security on cooperation rather than deterrence (and in addition to that build deterrence on defense rather than retaliation), then precisely what should we do?

Assuming that there is something to the principles listed in the beginning of this chapter, the *first* conclusion to be drawn from the past 15–20 years would be: *Do not give to economic relations, whether in the form of trade or joint ventures, such a dominant position in the whole cooperation picture.* Of course, there are exceptions to this rule. Between countries at a relatively similar level of technical-economic development, there should be no objection; relations between Bulgaria and Greece possibly being an example, and there are others. With the terms of trade developing the way they tend to do, and adding to this the very asymmetric spin-off effects, inegalitarian deals are doomed to be destabilizing, not only inside the Eastern countries, but also for the East-West relationship as a whole.[13]

The *second* major conclusion to be drawn would be something like this: *Do not give to intergovernmental relations, whether in the field of economics, politics, cultural or military matters, such a dominant position in the whole cooperation picture.* That good, even cooperative intergovernmental relations are a necessary condition for good international relations in the contemporary world goes without saying. But they are not sufficient as a condition. Much more has to be done at the nongovernmental level, and it is possible to do so. I can give a small-scale testimony to this myself, having been more than 20 times to the Soviet Union during the 35 years from 1953 to 1988. On most occasions it was for meetings and conferences, usually in the context of some type of cooperation between an organization in the Soviet Union and an organization in the West. All occasions were instructive. But visit number 20, in the summer of 1982 was by far the best: a camping trip with the other members of the family, by car through the western part of the Soviet Union from north to south, entering from Finland, exiting to Romania weeks later. And number 22, by train Budapest-Moscow-Beijing in 1988, was also very provocative.

Very many people have done this. The exchanges of information and opinion at night, at the camping sites, in the train corridors, almost always pointed in the same direction. Once inside the Soviet Union the freedom to move around in a car appears unrestricted, except that one should show up at night at the place where overnight facilities have been booked. The Soviet people in general are as warm, charming, and interested in talking and discussing with foreigners as humanly possible. That there are material shortcomings relative to the affluence prevailing in the West is well known. But the one single headline that can be written on top of all such experiences of direct contact remains that *the Soviet people wants peace, not war*. It sounds like a platitude. But if so it is a rather important platitude and one that, unfortunately, cannot be said of all peoples in the world.

Travels of that type should be reciprocal. Western individualistic tourism cannot be fully engaged in when traveling in the Soviet Union but to a considerably extent in Eastern Europe. Millions make use of this opportunity every year if we include Yugoslavia. Most travelers would be surprised by the amount of latitude there is for individualistic tourism also in the Soviet Union as long as some planning is done in advance, and as long as one is not limited by group travel. Groups have a tendency to be "processed," with political overtones substituting for the economic overtones in the corresponding type of processing in the West. There is stupid propaganda in both places; political in the East, economic in the West. But escape is possible.

Whether the Soviet Union will give the opportunity of individualistic tourism to its own citizens in the near future remains to be seen. But group travel is also a possibility and should be encouraged. Given the state of tension still existing between East and West, tourism as such becomes a luxury. A political dimension should be added, discussions, dialogues should be encouraged. Informed or uninformed, critical or constructive, or all four does not matter much. What matters is that as many people as possible try to explore together the problems that divide European countries and groups of countries, and what are the possible solutions.

Tourism should, whenever possible, be politically conscious tourism. Imagine thousands of such encounters, not necessarily so spectacular as when Scandinavian women were marching to Minsk in the summer of 1982, but involving many more people. Does it not stand to reason that this could increase the level of mutual concern, the number of people who would start thinking constructively of how negative stereotypes could be counteracted, not merely by changing images of the other side but by doing something about our own side so that the other side has reasons for changing its images?

Add to this the dimension of people meeting their opposite numbers; physicians meeting physicians (as they have done effectively, warning against any faith in the health care system being able to handle the consequences of a nuclear war), retired people meeting retired people, young people, students, women's organizations—whatever. I am thinking in terms of Europe as one great peace seminar, for people in general and for people that are somewhat similar one way or the other; if possible reporting their findings to the population at large so more people could have more material to consider. As is always the case it might very well be that the process is more important than the goal, that discussions of how to achieve peace may themselves lead to, even be more peace than the proposals that come out of the discussions.

But in addition to the Europe of the people just described there is also the Europe of local government, and more concretely the idea of municipalities becoming peace municipalities with an active foreign policy. Before spelling out in more detail what being a peace municipality could mean, let me give three general arguments for demonopolizing foreign policy.

First, wherever there is a monopoly some people get an enormous challenge to do something, and others get none. The challenge of organizing relations to other countries is not always that pleasant, and it is certainly not always easy. However, may it not also be that others would like to have more of that challenge? Why should the central authorities have a monopoly on doing such things as recognizing or not recognizing a foreign government? Maybe they would decide according to one logic; maybe a local authority or a "nongovernmental" organization sees it all differently and would vote and act according to a different logic? Who is to say that one logic covers 100 percent of the truth and the other 0 percent?

Second, it is true that more independence in foreign policy for municipalities will make it more difficult for a country to speak with one voice. The situation becomes more anarchic. But, since when did "speaking with one voice" become such a positive criterion? Is it not rather clear that this is a totalitarian criterion, reminiscent even of some recent decades we would rather like to leave totally behind us, the mid-1920s to the mid-1940s? Is not, in general, pluralism, variety, something more worth believing in?

Third, there is no guarantee that foreign policy at the local level will necessarily be better from, for instance, a peace point of view than foreign policy at the national level. Ultimate wisdom is not necessarily found only at the local level. Nor do I think the foreign policy motives will be worse than at the national level, and I have two arguments why they may be better.

Thus the local level is closer to people. It is more difficult for local decision makers to conceal, to retreat in solitude, in hidden think tanks, protected by veils of secrecy. People are too close and can contribute new ideas. But then comes the basic argument: even if the motives should be bad, oppressive, exploitative, aggressive or what not, whatever bad decision comes out of one municipality matters less than what comes out of an entire country. Even if the motivation should leave something to be desired, municipal capability is limited. A small country, not to mention a commune will generally do less harm than a big one, if for no other reason than because of limited resources, including the military. Small is not necessarily always beautiful. Small can also be rather ugly. But it is usually more harmless, like individual medication as opposed to medication administered to the whole population. And that is what foreign policy monopoly does.

PEACE PLANS

Concretely what could municipalities do if they want to be active components in a policy transcending national borders, for peace?

First, and obviously: continue the excellent policy of finding twin, brother and sister, municipalities. This is an old idea and practice and served a major function in bringing together Axis and Allies countries within Western Europe after World War II. Time has now come to extend the pattern to twinning with municipalities in the other worlds; the socialist countries, the third world and the fourth, the world of Southeast Asia, Japan, China, and the mini-Japans/Chinas. In the search for the brother and sister municipalities maybe priority should be given to denuclearized municipalities to build a network of municipalities for peace. They are concrete peace forces.

Second, a municipality should think of itself as having a foreign trade policy and develop not only profitable but also peace-building trade relations. Local business should be encouraged to think of brother and sister municipalities all over the world first, helping them develop as members of the family, so to speak.

Third, a municipality or city for peace could organize symposia and conferences to discuss the problems of the world, not accepting that this can only be done in the nation's capital, nor that the only thing municipalities can do is to organize flower festivals. Just to the contrary, the capital may be the place this cannot be done because of the overriding concern for national dogma, often couched in terms of national, elite interests.

Fourth, by discussing, inside the municipality, how to defend the municipality if a war should come. Would we really like central authorities to destroy the municipality if that fits into their plans for "national" defense, for instance, by using nuclear weapons? Do we accept the right of central authorities to use the local level as a pawn in some big strategic game? Or would a more local approach be more likely to have good results: a combination of militia/guerrilla based on a superior knowledge of local conditions on the one hand and a mobilization of the civilian population for nonmilitary, nonviolent defense on the other? But then it has to be thought through, because national authorities tend not to think along such lines. Rather, they tend to see this type of thinking as subversive, being afraid that the local level becomes too independent and not sufficiently grateful to the national level for protection.

Nothing in this has to be in opposition to the authorities in the nation's capital but could take place in an atmosphere of cooperation. The municipality offers local initiatives as a part of the total contact surface the nation has with the outside world. The municipality can even offer totally nonaggressive defense proposals as a part of the total national defense plan. What is new is the idea of initiatives from below and more, not total, local autonomy in matters literally of life and death, peace and war.

However, in order to implement such ideas a minimum infrastructure is needed inside the municipality. A municipal foreign policy does not come just by itself. More particularly, the municipality would need something like a think tank, and something like an executive branch for peace matters. Policies have to be drafted, the municipal council has to take decisions, decisions have to be executed.

Let us start with the executive side. The proposal is very simple: all municipalities and not only the denuclearized ones, should as a matter of routine add to their list of councilors a *peace councilor*. The more advanced ones already have a councilor for culture (and they certainly have one for garbage disposal); so why not also a councilor for peace? Why capitulate in advance, saying this is the exclusive concern of the foreign ministry in the nation's capital only? Why be so modest? Constitutions have been changed before.

What would be her tasks, assuming that this particular mission will often be better carried out by women than by men, given the role divisions so deeply ingrained in our societies? Examples of items in a job description for a peace councilor: To organize a good library on peace matters. To keep the files on relations to sister municipalities, in fact, to be in charge of that particular sector. To encourage business contacts and, of course, contacts between schools and all kinds of voluntary associations, for people exchanges, sport, etc.

But in addition to that there could also be the more touchy matters like alternative defense policies at the local level. For this to happen some good groundwork would have to be carried out. At the level of the militia there is less of a problem as the military might like to see more local initiative. The difficulty is nonmilitary, civilian (some would say civilized) defense.

And this is the point where the think tank enters. Who said there could only be peace research institutes attached to universities and to the big units, such as major cities, particularly in the capital, and even more particularly to the university in the nation's capital? Why not have such institutes everywhere, as a major part of our search for a better society? For what is peace but the struggle, with peaceful means, for a less violent society in a less violent world? As such it explores the conditions for all kinds of violence, direct, structural, cultural, including such issues as stereotypes against outsiders, with a view to finding adequate remedies, concrete policies that can be implemented here and now.

Time is overdue to challenge the old division of labor inside the territory of a "modern" state that foreign trade, foreign relations in general, and matters of defense are the prerogative of the center, leaving to the periphery of the country, to the local level, such matters as local roads and schools, health and culture. Maybe that social contract, if there ever was any, should now be regarded as an "unequal treaty" and be rewritten, in favor of the local level.

But the people and local government levels in no way exclude the governmental level. Countries as such have to relate to each other. The *third* conclusion is this: *the basis for a cooperative approach to peace and security is deep symbiosis; that countries are really useful to each other.* The security of a system is a function not only of its usefulness to its own citizens, so that they remain relatively satisfied, but also of its usefulness to the outside. This can only come about through interaction. Much of this mutual usefulness will have to be economic, but it can also be political, humanitarian, ecological, cultural, to mention some. Switzerland has been mentioned, using its banking services, its conference services, and its Red Cross organizations as examples of how to be useful to the world community along the first three of these dimensions. The invulnerability of France relative to any adversary may consist not so much in excellent French technology that can be made by anybody, but in the ever-lasting significance of French culture. The security of Norway, on the other hand, may rest more on the humanitarian factor: the image of Norway as a country that comes to the rescue of others in distress, including Armenians after World War I. In short, there are many formulas beyond economic interaction, and each country may develop its own.

But above all of them, the following has to be written. They only contribute to security if it can be convincingly shown that they are better available when the country is free and intact than when it is conquered and destroyed. In short, peace must be more beneficial to all parties than war. Whenever a country has something to offer to the world community in general, and adversary countries in particular, the latter might think: "This looks nice, I would like to possess it completely, forever. A war has its risks but might be worth it if total possession could be the outcome." The outer usefulness of a country, hence, depends on its ability to show that the usefulness is available only under conditions of peace and freedom; if not, those things will either be destroyed by the warfare itself, or by self-inflicted sabotage. Any country with important raw materials is useful to others when these commodities are floated on the world market, and this fact may add to its security. But it may also add to its insecurity by tempting others into conquest. To counteract that, *usefulness in peace should somehow be accompanied by uselessness in war*—for instance, by finding a process whereby raw materials, even ores, would self-destruct in the war process. To take an example: if it is really true that the ice-free harbors in Norway constitute a temptation to the Soviet navy, then some way of making these harbors useless in war, if not blocking them on a permanent basis by artificial ice, then by some other method, should be found and be communicated.

However, all of this is a rather negative approach. The basic approach would have to be positive and be based on national self-reliance. Concretely this would combine inner strength with outer usefulness in a carefully worked out balance. On the one hand there would have to be sufficient mobilization of economic factors inside a country to guarantee self-sufficiency in times of crisis, so that the country cannot be blackmailed into surrender just because essential products are not produced within the borders of a country. Beyond that level, however, the country would reach out for partners all over the world, also—indeed—with potential adversaries, in the search for symmetric (equitable) trade structures.

To concretize: the gas pipeline from the Soviet Union to Western Europe constitutes a linkage between East and West of a highly symbiotic nature. That linkage, however, should never constitute the only answer to the energy supply problem of the countries in Western Europe. It should come on top of a program of energy self-sufficiency by means of the many methods that now are known in the field of energy conversion, including isolation and fight against waste. Only in that way can the needs of people and the interests of countries be turned into the raw material out of which peace and security can be constructed, partly through inner strength ("independence"), partly through outer usefulness ("interdependence"). It is on top of an infrastructure of national self-reliance, combining a minimum of self-sufficiency with equitable trade at the international level, that much deeper webs of human interrelations can be spun, ultimately based on millions of person to person contacts.

And in that connection an important point cannot be made often enough.

Eastern Europeans are so much more competent in Western European languages and culture than vice versa. As a very minimum the level of knowledge of that beautiful (although unnecessarily difficult) Russian language should increase. There were good attempts in many countries in the early years after World War II that should be taken up again. The suffering caused by the intricacies of Russian grammar are considerable, but more than compensated for by the beauties of the language and the culture to which the language is the key. And the Soviet Union could contribute greatly to this by organizing summer schools in Russian (like so many Western European countries do for their languages) in their many resort areas, thereby also opening their country for more meaningful tourism. Summer language institutes for many languages, east and west, north and south, could be a wonderful and safe basis for building international peace. They should be heavily subsidized, with only a very small fraction of national defense budgets. A little money goes a far way here.

In short, there is more than enough to do. Let us get started!

Conclusion: Toward a
New European Peace Order

For peace politics to happen, at least three conditions have to be fulfilled. There has to be a broad political consensus backed by *people's movements;* there have to be *political carriers;* and there has to be a *program.* I would say that by and large the first two conditions are now better met than ever since the Cold War started. There are the millions in the peace movement, not to mention the hundreds of millions who do not support the "deterrence" policy of the governments, and in Eastern Europe the countless study groups, churches, discussion groups, and even demonstrations. The Western peace movement is no longer in the streets. But their thinking is everywhere. Then, there are the peace parties/ecological/green parties that are getting into parliament, including the European Parliament. There are the parties already there, social democrat and liberal, in the process of becoming nonpacifist peace parties. And, in Western Europe the United States sometimes has to adjust itself to NATO countries not following the line, such as Spain, Denmark, the Netherlands, even the Federal Republic of Germany, Greece. The Soviet Union has had to do the same in Eastern Europe.[1]

The picture is different from what it was even a few years ago. There is, in latent form, a mass movement that will not tolerate reversal of the trend. There are political carriers. But what about the program? What is happening in this field? There are very concrete plans for *Europa minor.* But how about *Europa major?* Only Europe I, CSCE Europe, reflects some of the aspirations of so many people in Europe V who see all of Europe (perhaps particularly Central Europe) as their home. Very weak relative to EC12.

The concrete content of a New European Peace Order (NEPO) can be, is being, and will have to be discussed, under two headings:

1. *Alternative Alliance Systems.*
2. *Alternative Defense Systems.*

They are, of course, related to each other. For each of them a division of the range of possibilities into four alternatives may be useful.[2]

Thus there seem to be four positions on the alliance issue in the West, meaning on NATO:

1a. *Status quo, meaning a U.S.-dominated NATO,* today hardly a majority view in any NATO country because the United States is seen as domineering, sometimes reckless, and lagging behind in understanding what is going on. To get a war out of the present situation one needs an irreconcilable conflict posture; an arms race that goes on unabated (with nuclear disarmament talks that may or may not serve as a cloak for new weapons systems such as Star Wars); confrontations around the world; a military posture *as if* a first strike is being contemplated—with decapitating capability (7,500 cruise missiles, sea-and air-based, around the Soviet Union against 2,500 targets?), with effective antisubmarine warfare to eliminate the other side's second strike capability; with laser defense to eliminate surviving missiles; with civil defense to offer residual protection; with preparation of the population for sacrifice in case all of this proves insufficient. The United States has been seen as combining all these elements, the major reason why people in Europe were more afraid of a war coming from the Reagan United States than from the Soviet Union. Washington had difficulties understanding this and has not denounced its own policies of some years ago. On the other hand, the United States is also seen as withdrawing, if for no other reason because of its deteriorating economy. But not as "Leader of the Free World."

1b. *U.S.-Western Europe partnership, two pillars NATO.* One basic problem with this concept is the uncertainty about the future role of France, seen by increasingly many as "Napoleonic" in its ambitions, wanting a *l'Europe de Paris*. The five deployment countries constituted a forward Maginot Line, a missile fence. The refusal of France to be counted in disarmament talks leaves it free to continue nuclear armament (e.g., by 7-mirving of the 18 + 80 missiles). A Western European defense concept would be France-dominated through French continental nuclear monopoly, administered alone, jointly with Germany (in a junior role) or within a European Defense Community, based on the Western European Union, as a way of activating a two-speed European Community. As mentioned in Chapter 2, this will not reassure Moscow, which will hardly ever remove all missiles as

long as France does not. Mitterand was wrong: *France* has missiles,
and (almost) no peace movement.

1c. *An egalitarian NATO with a clearly defensive military doctrine,* which
is probably what the Western European people want even if their
governments do not reflect it. NATO could be a political association
with most of the defense effort carried out individually by the countries—with the transition possibility of countries leaving the military
integrated command if a defensive, nonprovocative strategy is not
accepted in a first phase. NATO would continue as a defense of political democracy and WTO as a defense of an increasingly democratic socialism, with Finlandization of Eastern Europe as a possible
goal.

1d. *Dissolution of the alliances, neutral status all over.* This should be
the clearly defined long-term goal; the problems right now being (1)
there have to be steps in-between, (2) as a short-term goal it is believed in by very few. About as many (2/3) believe in NATO as
there were people against the "double-track" decision, which, of course,
from the beginning was a single-track decision (except to the very
naive). That there later was a change in the Soviet Union, mainly for
internal reasons, and pressure from the peace movement that together
brought about the seriously flawed INF agreement, does not change
this.

Then there is the parallel discussion of the defense issue, also with four
major positions:

2a. *Status quo,* including the possibility of first use of weapons of mass
destruction, and more particularly of nuclear arms. This is the strategy people are dead against, and not only those who identify themselves with the peace movement but increasingly the majority of the
population, important political parties, and the governments of some
countries. As a very minimum they would request freeze/zoning/no-
first-use. The problem is what kind of alternative defense system they
would envisage. That question is usually left unanswered. In the
meantime work to compensate for the "lost" INF missiles continues.

2b. *Conventional, offensive arms.* This is what many top military, including Rogers, the former NATO commander, have been arguing in
favor of. The highly offensive Airland Battle (2,000) strategy is a
good example, fighting the battle in Eastern Europe (Germany) and
not in Western Europe (Germany). These are the "improvements" of

the "conventional" arms with which World War II was fought, as shown, for instance, in the Israeli attack on Lebanon/Beirut in 1982. Like all offensive arms they are provocative, lead to arms races, and in all probability to wars—although not necessarily in Europe.

2c. *Transarmament to defensive, nonprovocative arms, and a new military doctrine.* This doctrine would have as its assumption first of all a no-first-use pledge also from the West, then its translation into military posture through withdrawal of (at least) all nuclear arms not belonging to the country itself (Brezhnev proposal, Egon Bahr proposal). Coordination of East and West through talks/negotiations would be needed. But the West would have to take some first steps because of nuclear superiority, and because it is in general more likely that the East will imitate the West than vice versa, for historical reasons. Some conventional, highly defensive armament (meaning with short-range weapons systems that are very precise, with PGM—precision-guided munition), would be needed, carried by small, highly mobile, locally based, autonomous units well dispersed on their own territory so as to make the country as indigestible as possible. Para-military defense would also belong here, and so would nonmilitary/social defense.

2d. *Disarmament down to nonmilitary/social defense.* This defense would be based on a strategy of nonuse of violence against persons, but possibly include use of self-inflicted violence against objects that may be of use to an invader (sabotage). Noncooperation would be used to make the social structure useless. Civil disobedience would be added as acts of utter defiance. But at the same time efforts to build personal and positive relations to the invader/occupant as individuals would be made (fraternization). The problem with this position is that it may work better in some cultures/structures than others (thus, are Germans sufficiently talented in disobedience to do this?). It is also very much a minority position in the countries concerned. But that may change.

Let us now try to combine these two efforts to outline major positions in the current struggle for a New European Peace Order. In principle there are 16 combinations. But four combinations seem right now to cover the discussion space relatively well:

1a + 2a: The conservative ("Blue") option. Conservatives do what conservatives are supposed to do: they stick to the *status quo*. No amount of superpower cruelty, interventionism, invasions, war-mongering, threats and

provocations, and quantitative and qualitative arms race impresses them neg-
atively. Nor do *glasnost'/perestroika* and an INF agreement impress them
positively. Their support of the past is unfailing. And they may not discover
how alone they are before it is too late,[3] and the option is "brown" only.

1b + 2b: The neo-conservative ("Light-Blue") option. This is the combination for the intelligent conservatives who understand that something has
to be done. They hope that less reliance on nuclear and more on highly
offensive conventional strategies/doctrines ("to increase the nuclear thresh-
old") and a militarily strong and more independent Europe-NATO or European Defense Community will take the wind out of the sails of the peace
movement. They are reflecting the debate within the self-appointed military-
bureaucratic-corporate-intelligentsia-political elite that is ruling our countries
in these matters, the *classe politique* as the French say. They are not reflecting the debate in the population. But they are good at marketing their
option as an alternative, riding on—among other factors—the lack of debate
about French foreign policy, and about the crucial distinction (always problematic because of the gray zones) between offensive and defensive arms.[4]

*1c + 2c: The social democratic/liberal ("Light Red/Light Green") op-
tion.* This is probably the position toward which the social democrats are
steering. But it is a long process since many still stick to the first option
and are tempted by the second. I think liberal groupings will tend in this
direction, also with hesitation. Well prepared and better presented than the
SPD and the Labour Party did in 1987, there is probably a population majority for this option in many probably most (with the clear exception of
France) European countries. The defense strategy would have to be a MIX.[5]
This is what the Europe red/green coalition governments could bring about
in the 1990s, stopping the trend toward a "European Defense Pillar" and a
(Western) European Union Army.

1d + 2d: The pacifist ("Green") option. This is the long-term goal, should
always be present in the debate, and stated as clearly as possible. However,
the road to *dissolution* of the alliances is probably through their *transformation* (1c), and the road to *disarmament* is probably through *transarmament* (2c). An immediate move toward dissolution of alliances and total
military disarmament is not in the cards.[6]

Let us now try to spell out a process for transformation of the blocs. For
Europe the position taken above would imply the following:

—A general move toward defensive, nonprovocative weapons, away from
   offensive arms.
—More nationally independent forms of defense.

—Transformation of alliances from military to political alliances used as negotiation partners in transarmament processes.
—Withdrawal of U.S. and Soviet troops in Europe, starting with offensive weapons systems as a continuation of the INF agreement, which should be expanded to include all nuclear weapons on foreign soil.[7]

However, no such changes in the relation between blocs and countries are really meaningful unless there are also changes inside the alliances, and inside the countries; removing sources of conflict, building peace:
For the countries in Eastern Europe:

1. Armed neutrality, commitment to resist attacks on themselves and on neighbors (including the Soviet Union) through their territory (Finnish model—"Finlandization" of Eastern Europe) through/over their territory. Dissolution of the Warsaw Treaty Organization.
2. Trade and cooperation in all directions, on symbiotic and equitable terms, avoiding debt burdens and dependencies (Bulgarian model).
3. Production for social and human growth rather than state/military and capital growth (definition of socialism).
4. Continued experimentation with mixed economic systems, combining market and plan.
5. Democracy in the sense of having elections with real choices, if not multiparty, then multicandidate (Hungarian model, now practiced in several contexts in the Soviet Union).
6. Continued fight against stalinism with all its implications in terms of gross infractions of human rights, including the right to leave the country and return (Polish model, Hungarian model, Soviet model).

For the countries in Western Europe:

1. Armed neutrality, commitment to resist attacks on themselves and on neighbors (including the superpowers) through/over their territory (Swedish model, Austrian, Swiss, Yugoslav model—"Swedification" of Western Europe. Dissolution of NATO.
2. Trade and cooperation in all directions, on symbiotic and equitable terms, avoiding debt burdens and dependencies (Austrian model).
3. Production for social and human growth rather than state/military and capital growth (compatible with social democracy).
4. Continued experimentation with mixed economic systems, combining market and plan.

5. Democracy developed further to include more than parliamentarism and parliamentary rule; more referenda, decentralization, federalization (Swiss model).

6. Fight against unemployment and the dangers immanent in a capitalism in crisis, more particularly fight against gross infractions of human rights outside Western countries, in the Third World—through IMF policies, support to authoritarian dictatorships (as long as they serve Western interests), etc.

For all European countries:

1. Strengthen the UN *Economic Commission for Europe*.
2. Make a UN *Security Commission for Europe*.
3. Expand Council of Europe to include all European countries (with the Soviet Union) as they become democratic for political and cultural cooperation.
4. Keep the CSCE as long as it is useful.

And all of this in solidarity with the emancipation movements in the world— with hunger killing among children 1–5 years old alone being the equivalent of 235 Hiroshima bombs annually.[8] There is no law saying Europeans have to continue forever being bossed and tossed around by superpowers intervening and invading, and being ruled by an invisible, technocratic, military group with militarized civilians on their side, meeting among themselves and usually not even being accountable in public debate, pushing (often manipulated) parliamentarians in front of them. *It is time for a people's Europe.*

And that leaves us with one problem, but a major one, right there in the middle of Europe. Billions of words must have been spent on that issue. Let me try to express a view summarized in some very simple principles:[9]

1. That the two German states are not united is an inalienable right of the European peoples.
2. Unification of the German nation in the sense of free flow of goods and services, persons, capital and ideas is an inalienable right of the Germans.
3. West Germany has neither the right, nor the duty, to claim special status as successor state, *Nachfolgerstaat* (to, among others, the nazi regime) for all Germans.
4. East Germany has no right to keep its citizens locked up behind a

wall and a fence even if conditions have improved and leave of absence is more easily obtained.

5. From basic assumption (1) it follows that (3), the claim as successor
   state, should be given up since the logical consequence is unification
   as one state.
6. From basic assumption (2) it follows that (4), the wall and the fence,
   should be given up since the logical consequence is to make unification as a nation impossible.
7. Giving up (3) in exchange for (4), and *vice versa,* would make it
   possible to satisfy the rights of Germans and other Europeans.
8. A historical decision of that type can be taken only by the two German peoples, not by other countries.
9. Unification of Berlin and special status for all Berlin is an option, as
   host to all-German and all-European institutions.
10. The two Germanys should, like other civilized countries, impose re-
    straints on their own armed forces so as to possess only defensive,
    nonprovocative defense they should not have foreign offensive weap-
    ons stationed on their territories, and not being members of military
    alliances capable of fighting wars of aggression. The idea that the
    two Germanys have to be "controlled" is given up altogether with
    NATO and WTO.

Conclusion: peace in Europe. And an end to World War II. Two goals
very much worth struggling for.

And that concludes our journey through the supercomplex political landscape of Europe, in search of a New European Peace Order. I have tried to
avoid some pitfalls:

—assuming that the Soviet Union is a part of our Common European
  house or home; they have their own project (which may not succeed),
—assuming that the U.S. is a part of Europe; they have their own project
  (which may not succeed),
—assuming that the superpowers could and should be kept completely
  out; they also belong, at least in the CSCE context,
—assuming that European civilization is only good or only bad; it is both,
  and at a high level,
—assuming that the European Community is only about economics and
  1992; it is a part of a coming European superpower,
—assuming that the EC transformation is something new; it is the old

story of nation-building at a higher level, according to a code which itself is badly in need of transformation,

—assuming that "nuclear deterrence has preserved peace in Europe for 40 years"; it was in spite of, not because of,

—assuming that the INF agreement was due to Western strength; it was due to an internal Soviet transformation and such opposition movements as Solidarność, Charta 77, the peace movement, and the Green movement,

—assuming that present military doctrines can be kept but at a lower level of armament; a change of doctrine toward defensive defense is indispensable,

—assuming that the present trade doctrine of comparative advantages is peace-building; a change of doctrine toward equitable trade is indispensable,

—assuming that a peace structure is neat, orderly, contradiction-free; a structure of that kind may easily become a war structure,

—assuming that international architecture is sufficient for peace; some internal changes are indispensable, in both camps.

So, let many Europes, not only one, grow and blossom, in active, peaceful co-existence. Let no one dominate. And we shall have a New European Peace Order.

Notes

Introduction: The Five Europes

1. In discussing incompatibility as the root of conflict, Y. Harkabi makes a useful distinction between "grand design" and "policy" to catch the difference between objectives/goals that are "dreams or abstract aspirations" and those that are "concrete ways of dealing with the political domain." He goes on to say that "the Soviet *grand design* toward the West is to bring about its ruin; but this is not the Soviet policy, which is much less ambitious. I also believe that the U.S. grand design toward the Soviet Union is to bring about the collapse of the Soviet system; whereas the U.S. policy is much more modest, and even acknowledges that the Soviet domination of Eastern Europe will persist" (from "The Fateful Choices Before Israel," The International Center for Peace in the Middle East, *Discussion Paper No. 8,* p. 1). He could have added that the grand design of the two superpowers also included the idea of paving the way for themselves after the collapse of the competitor.

2. The U.S.-Canada Free Trade Area would be a beginning of this construction, which may never be realized as a whole. More than Nicaragua stands in the way. Incidentally, the United States has the same habit as the European Community of using the name of the whole continent when referring to itself, "America" and "Europe."—ignoring the protests from the "others."

3. For an exploration of exchange systems between superpowers and clients, see Johan Galtung, "The Cold War as an Exercise in Autism: The US Government, the Governments of Western Europe—and the People," in *Essays in Peace Research,* Vol. VI (Copenhagen: Ejlers, 1988), ch. 5, pp. 81–106; also in *Alternatives* XIV (1989).

4. As pointed out by Neal Ascherson in "How to live with death of missiles," *Observer* (18 September 1988): "—for 40 years most Europeans, East and West, have been able to blame their problems on external things: the nuclear threat, the Soviet threat, American imperialism. Now we have run out of excuses for the squalor around us." And he adds: "For so long all Polish thoughts have had a little Soviet tank clipped to their edge. How does one start having tankless thoughts?"

5. In Italy the Communists represent a reservoir of political energy that has been used, by and large successfully, only at the local level; the historical compromise (of a coalition government) not yet having been realized. In Poland the non-Communists and not only Solidarnosc represent a corresponding reservoir, so long deprived of legitimate ways of voicing their grievances and measuring their strength against the government in multi-party elections. Two systems impoverishing themselves.

6. I have asked that question a number of times at the beginning of lectures about Europe, practically speaking never getting the correct answer or even a method for finding the correct answer (such as adding the number of members of the two alliances and the NN countries).

7. The ratio Europa Minor:Europa Major in number of countries is 12:29, or 41 percent, and in population 321.3 M:539.1 M or 60 percent (figures from *L'Etat du Monde*, Paris, Editions de la Decouverte, 1985).

8. One reason is separateness: Faroe, Aland, and Greenland are islands non-contiguous with their "motherlands"; Gibraltar and (less so) Monaco have a pen-insular quality; Andorra and San Marino are located far above the surrounding moth-erlands; and the Vatican State even farther above, between heaven and earth.

9. The treaty between Finland, Sweden, and Russia signed in Geneva in October 1921 demilitarized Aland (an archipelago between Finland and Sweden), prohibiting fortifications. The League of Nations settled the conflict between Sweden and Fin-land giving the islands to the latter, but the treaty denied Finland the state prerogative of militarization; like Spitsbergen for Norway.

10. If we count the Soviet Union, the total number is well above 800 M (815.6). India, population-wise number two in the world, had 732.2 M, but should rather be compared to Europa Major with India's 22 states and 9 territories, some of them ministates and city-states. It is interesting to reflect on how much better that southern tip of the Eurasian land mass, the subcontinent of India, has been able to contain its divisions and conflicts than the Western tip, Europe. On the other hand, India may now also be on the way to superpower status; associative peace policies within easily leading via integration to hostility without.

11. What Marx and Engels used as opening sentences in the *Communist Mani-festo* was: "A spectre is haunting Europe—the spectre of Communism. All the Pow-ers of old Europe have entered into a holy alliance to exorcise this spectre: Pope and Czar, Metternich and Guizot, French radicals and German police-spies." History has a tendency to repeat itself. German police spies are certainly as active as ever. For "French radicals" read "French Socialists." For "Guizot" read Mitterand, who said that the East has the missiles and the West the pacifists, when he should have pointed out that France has missiles and (almost) no pacifists. For "Metternich" read Waldheim. For the "Czar" read Eastern European general secretaries. For the "Pope" read the Pope. In a sense the reaction is understandable as the growth from none in early 1983 to Green parliamentarians in 11 countries late 1988, and Green parties in 24 countries, makes "the Green Movement the fastest growing political force the world has ever known"; Sara Parkin, *Green Parties: An International Guide* (Lon-don: Heretic Books, 1989).

12. All extranational experience counts here, from tuning in on foreign broadcasts to cross-national marriages and onward to the international nongovernmental orga-nizations. We actually need one map to mirror the quantity and quality of these links, bilateral and multilateral; and another topologically very complex map of val-ues, interests, and functions to locate all of this in nonterritorial space. Here, too, there is contested territory, e.g., among trade unions and professional associations. Is training of nurses medical or educational, both or neither?

13. The Dual Monarchy derives its name from the dual character of this complex

construction with the same monarch ruling Cisleithania meaning (roughly) Austria, Czechoslovakia, Slovenia (the northernmost republic of Yugoslavia today), and parts of Poland as emperor of Austria; and Transleithania meaning (again roughly) Hungary, Transylvania (today in Romania), and Croatia with parts of Dalmatia (today in Yugoslavia) as king of Hungary. Thus the Habsburg project tied together six of the countries on the map of Europe today, meaning more than the Nordic project. But then the five Nordic countries and the three ministates participate fully, they are not divided internally, and that was one of the many problems of the *Doppelmonarchie*.

14. Thus, in the CSCE Madrid conference Spain was still nonaligned and played a major role as a bridge-builder. .

15. EFTA today has two separated parts; four of the Nordic countries (Denmark could not be a member both of the EC and EFTA) that are contiguous with the exception of Iceland, and Switzerland/Austria that also are contiguous with each other. Of the inner six neutral countries, four are in EFTA; Yugoslavia and Albania are not, nor are the outer three. The remaining two EFTA countries, Iceland and Norway, are NATO members. The population is 31.5 M, giving the EC-EFTA joint free trade area in industrial goods (with reciprocal concessions for agricultural products) a total population of 353 M. EC-EFTA are each other's major trade partners (see footnote 27, Chapter 2).

16. Such as the conflict between Hungary and Romania and between Hungarians and Romanians over Transylvania.

17. *Dao Dezhing*, verse 76; translation by Gia-Fu Feng and Jane English (London: Wildwood House, 1973). In my view, a much more realistic view of Europe than Hans Magnos Enzensberger's *Ach Europa!*—he only sees chaos and divisiveness and thinks it will remain that way and Edgar Morin's *Penser l'Europe*—who also sees chaos and divisiveness and pleads for strength and unity as a true ideologue for the European Union.

1. Europe the Contradictory

1. See footnote 3 in the Introduction.

2. To use EC12 as an example: eight are "rich" and four "poor," by and large north-south, but with one from the south among the rich, Italy, and one from the north among the poor, Eire. There are poor pockets in Italy and rich pockets in Eire reminiscent of the yin in the yang in the yin, and the yang in the yin in the yang—. And these are not plays with words; there is politics everywhere in this multitiered contradiction structure.

3. The countries are clustered along the northwest-southeast diagonal, the correlation being $Q = (13 \times 8 - 3 \times 5):(13 \times 8 + 3 \times 5) = .75$. Obviously this reflects the pattern of small countries in the Nordic area/the Low countries and in the Balkans. Fragmentation in the two peripheries, and in mountainous areas? Through the ages there have been some comments on "trouble regions." But the wars in the northwest and the southeast cannot compete with what has been emanating from the center of Europe in destructiveness. Bigger countries, bigger wars.

4. See Introduction, footnote 13 for the relation of Poland and Yugoslavia to the Habsburg construction.

162

5. Stefanie Abt, "Der Traum von Mitteleuropa," *Neue Zürcher Zeitung,* 26 May 1988, sees Central Europe above all as a way in which several parts of Europe can articulate their protests against other projects; particularly true for Eastern European authors (Konrad from Hungary and Kundera from Czechoslovakia) and philosophers/social scientists (Stojanovic from Yugoslavia).

6. This perspective is developed in Chapters 5 and 6, exploring the peace and Green movements as organic parts of the European historical process, not in the sense that their victory is imminent, but in the sense of articulating another Europe.

7. According to *Women in World Affairs* (Vienna: United Nations, 1989) by Karin Lindgren, Department of Peace and Conflict Research, Uppsala University, the proportion of women increased clearly over the period 1966–76–86 in a number of ministries and a number of countries, but not in the sections of ministries of defense and foreign affairs dealing with security matters. Boys' clubs?

8. This is the law of uneven development made famous by Lenin and by Matthew, in the gospel according to Matthew, "to him who has more shall be given, to him who has nothing the little he has shall be taken away." (Matthew 13;12, also in Luke 8;18 and Mark 4;25)

9. S. Radhakrishnan, *Eastern Religions and Western Thought* (Delhi: Oxford University Press, 1974, first published 1939, p. 10: "Their [the Romans] desire for world dominion transformed the simple faith of Jesus into a fiercely proselytizing creed. After the time of Constantine, authorities, clerical and secular, displayed systematic intolerance towards other forms of religious belief—."

10. For an effort to explore this theme, see Johan Galtung, *Methodology and Development* (Copenhagen: Ejlers, 1988), ch. 4.4, "Contradictory reality and mathematics: A contradiction?"

11. For one formulation of this, see J. Galtung, T. Heiestad, and E. Rudeng, "On the Last 2,500 Years in Western History," in Peter Burke (ed.), *The New Modern Cambridge History, Companion Volume* (Cambridge: Cambridge University Press, 1979), ch. 12.

12. Often derided for this from the left, for obvious reasons, but also from the right as not having the courage to cross the divide into the political-military realm. Lord Chalfont expressed it this way: "It has been obvious since the Treaty of Rome was signed that Western Europe will never be more than an expanded customs union until it takes military security more seriously" (*International Herald Tribune,* 23 July 1987).

13. The three power types can be derived from a simple typology based on negative vs. positive sanctions that are social and institutionalized or personal and internalized. Coercive power is negative-institutionalized, remunerative power positive-institutionalized, and then there is "bad and good conscience."

14. The lack of attention to the development of endogenous productive capacity has been the key to *La decadencia española,* in the book of that title by R. Trevor Davies (Barcelona: Editorial Labor, 1972), for instance, on p. 105 where the number of young people seeking grammar and Latin schools, not productive work is mentioned. C. M. Cipolla takes up the same theme in *European Culture and Overseas Expansion* (Middlesex: Pelican, 1970): "It seemed natural to Spain's rulers that if

and when artillery was needed either the orders should be placed to the famous centres of production in Flanders, Italy and Germany; or Flemish, German and Italian founders should be invited to Spain. . . . after the emergency needs were satisfied, the foreign gunners were sent back to their homes for economic reasons and the few Spanish workers were left without jobs or money" (p. 41). This sounds very much like United States today, but not like Germany, and certainly not Japan.

15. All three are, of course, ambiguous. But if the French Revolution set the merchants free to pursue wealth individually regardless of family and religious status, then the Magna Carta of 1215 only limited the power of the king (including the war-making power) relative to clergy and aristocracy, thereby reinforcing feudalism, and the Glorious Revolution essentially did the same, asserting only the power of the parliament.

16. The opposite would have been almost unthinkable, and the location of the center, Paris, has remained uncontested, as in England (with Wales, Scotland, and Ireland conquered from London).

17. See William McNeill, *A World History* (New York: Oxford University Press, 1971), Parts III and IV called "The Dominance of the West" and "Global Cosmopolitanism From 1850" (p. x).

18. A strong identification with the victims of the Roman Empire and Renaissance Italy would be needed as an antidote to those two eras as models for a twentieth-century reincarnation. Mussolini hardly had more identification with them than with the victims of his own operations in Libya, "Abyssinia" (Ethiopia), and Albania.

19. I am indebted to Gunnar Adler-Karlsson in a presentation at a seminar on socialism, Bochum, November 1988, for this image.

20. The four mini-Japans/Chinas practiced the first part of the theory of self-reliance; do not become dependent on others, but not the second part; do not make others dependent on yourself. They moved up the "degree of processing" ladder, but then treated others like they did not want others to treat them, buying raw materials, selling processed goods. Another factor, often overlooked, was hard work. How many developing countries would be able/willing to work that hard? For a theory of self-reliance, see J. Galtung, P. O'Brien, and A. Preiswerk, *Self-Reliance: A Strategy for Development* (London: Bogle-d'Ouverture, 1980).

21. For a theory of nazism, see Chapter 2 in my *Hitlerism, Stalinism, Reaganism: Three Variations on a Theme by Orwell,* in Norwegian (Oslo: Gyldendal, 1984), Spanish (Alicante: Gil Albert, 1985) and German (Wiesbaden: Nomos, 1987) translations.

2. Europe the Contradiction-Free: From Community to Superpower

1. How much of this was intended can, of course, be discussed. The rhetoric of 9 May 1950 mentioned reconciliation between former Axis and former Allies. Was Yaoundé-Lomé already in the cards in 1950? The effort to create a United States of Europe including Eastern Europe? In a sense yes. With Churchill's Zurich speech as early as 19 September 1946 and the Marshall Plan (the European Recovery

Program) proposed in Marshall's Harvard speech 5 June 1947 all-European integrative concepts and projects had certainly been launched. A leading French politician, Edgar Faure saw a Western European Community as a first step (private communication, 1970). The idea "has been in the air." And what happened in the colonies did not escape their attention.

2. The number of countries and the range of agenda items are indispensable analytical tools, but insufficient as the level of transcendence or supernational integration is not reflected. Domain and scope may remain constant, but when an item is decided by majority vote rather than by consensus, the level of integration has certainly changed. A very useful pamphlet from the EC Commission, *A Journey Through the EC* (Luxemburg: EC, 1988) divides its "landmarks" through time (pp. 48ff) into four parallel columns: "development and organization" (scope and names/events), "enlargement" (domain), "integration," and "external relations." Much of the same information is found in *Steps to European Unity, Community Progress to Date: A Chronology*, with successive dates and events, but no built-in theory of the process. My use of both is hereby gratefully acknowledged.

3. See my *The European Community: A Superpower in the Making*, (London: Allen & Unwin, 1973; also Oslo/Copenhagen: Norwegian Universities Press/Ejlers, 1972; Stockholm: Prisma, 1973; Helsinki: Tammi, 1973; Amsterdam: van Gennep, 1973; Buenos Aires, 1978). For the author's effort to assess the book 10 years later, see "The European Community: a Superpower in the Making?" Chapter 11 in Johan Galtung, *Essays in Peace Research*, Vol. VI (Copenhagen: Ejlers, 1988), pp. 183–194.

4. For a description of images of Self and images of Other built into nazism as an ideology, see the work referred to in Chapter 1, footnote 21. One basic source of steep Self-Other gradients would be a transcendental God and chosenness, based on a god living above, outside our earth, capable of general surveillance of our moral situation.

5. For a theory of associative peace-building, see Johan Galtung, *The True Worlds* (New York: Macmillan, 1980), chapter 3.4, pp. 100–103 or *Essays in Peace Research*, Vol. II (Copenhagen: Ejlers, 1976), "Peacebuilding," Ch. 11, pp. 297ff.

6. This, of course, was also a follow-up to his offer in the darkest hour, spring 1940, to France of a union of the two countries. The concept must have been deep in him. But that union was also proposed by Henri St. Simon in 1814.

7. Very important in this connection are the statements issued in connection with the EC summit meetings such as The Hague Summit of 1969, the Paris Conferences of the Heads of State and Governments of the Member States of the European Community of 1972 and 1974; the declarations issued after the European Council meetings of 1983 and 1984; all leading up to the draft treaty. In short, the integrative process towards union is consistent and has gone on all the time.

8. See Michel de Perrot, "Commercial Fast Breeders: Towards an Integrated European Nuclear Force?" (Geneva, May 1984), abbreviated version published in the *Journal of World Trade Law*, 18, no. 3 (London, May/June 1984) for many details.

9. My own perspective on how the types of power are ordered would see political, decision-making power as "événementielle," economic and military power

as "conjoncturelle," and cultural power as "longue durée," to use terms associated with the *Annales* school in general and Fernand Braudel in particular. In no way ruling out causal links in all directions, the general thrust, in my view, is from the cultural base of deep assumptions (the cosmologies) via the construction of the machineries for the exercise of remunerative and coercive power, in other words, economic and military power to the exercise of political power, seen as the more epiphenomenal of the four. What comes first, economic or military, depends on circumstances; either one is easily converted into the other by well-known mechanisms. But the cultural base casts its shadows into everything that happens in the other domains. Jean Monnet, the other EC father, born 100 years ago, is reputed to have said that if he could have done it all over he would have started with culture. I am not so sure. Deep culture should be assumed, not recited; much of it does not stand the light of day anyhow. Knowingly or not, he started with culture.

10. Michel de Perrot (note 8 above) sees the linkage the following way: "Step by step, the technocratic integration of Europe by means of plutonium opens up possibilities for a new military strategy on the part of the European democracies" (p. 50).

11. The customs union, eliminating tariffs between member states and establishing a common tariff for trade with nonmembers, was achieved 1 July 1968, 18 months ahead of what was envisaged in the EEC Treaty. And from 1970 the customs duties on imports from nonmembers together with 1 percent of the value-added tax levied uniformly within the member states were used to secure an independent financial basis for the European Community as such. An interesting question would be whether this created at the top a disincentive for EC self-reliance. In a budget crisis, given a choice between a self-reliant and a trading option with duties coming to the center, would the center not react like any state?

12. The participation rates probably reflect some disenchantment in Denmark and the UK, which may be related to the circumstance that these are also the two countries with the lowest proportion of their trade inside the EC (46.8 percent and 47.9 percent, respectively, *Eurostat*, 1986). The overall turnout was very much above the close to 50 percent turnout registered in the last three U.S. presidential elections, not to mention the 38.5 percent turnout in the congressional election in November 1986. The June 1989 turnout reflected changes in the level of integration of citizens of the member states, not only the governments of the member states.

13. As 1993 and the single market approaches, German skepticism may increase. Thus the percentage in the German Federal Republic favoring "joining the West European nation together to form a United Europe" was 33 percent in March 1983, 40 percent summer 1985, and only 25 percent October 1988. In January 1988, 51 percent felt the development toward a United Europe should proceed faster; in September 1988 this had dropped to 34 percent. "Germans Less Hopeful About EC, Poll Finds," *International Herald Tribune,* 14 December 1988. Possibly the "inner market" will be more advantageous to smaller companies and smaller countries; the big ones are there already.

14. The list of negative and positive aspects of the European patrimony is not random, but derived from a peculiarity of the hard version of the religion common to the Europeans (with minor exceptions), Christianity. God is above, He is tran-

scendental, and has *homo sapiens* as a chosen species, man as a chosen gender, whites as a chosen race, some nations as more chosen than others, clergy/aristocracy/merchants as chosen classes, and the true believers as chosen persons. The nonchosen may be seen as chosen by anti-God, Satan, anti-Christ. The efforts to correct for these biases and cruelties come from the softer version of Christianity, e.g., the Christianity of St. Francesco, and from the humanist tradition.

15. The picture is not yet clear. "Bolkestein/the Dutch Minister of Defense from fall 1988/oppert vorming brigade met Bondsrepubliek" say Dutch papers December 1988. "The Dutch Defense Ministry said Thursday that the Netherlands would contribute troops to a combined West European unit if Bonn's plan for a French-West German joint military brigade succeeded—as a step toward a united European fighting force. . . . Chancellor Helmut Kohl of West Germany suggested France and West Germany set up the unit to strengthen the European pillar of the North Atlantic Treaty Alliance. . . . France has promoted the use of the West European Union— as a European rallying point within NATO" (from "Dutch back European Brigade Plan," *International Herald Tribune,* 3 July 1987). On 27 October 1987 the Western European Union had a meeting in The Hague where a document on the shared security interests of the members was adopted. The independent nuclear forces of France and Britain were seen as making a contribution to global deterrence and the determination of Paris and London to safeguard the credibility of these forces, meaning to modernize them, was endorsed (*The Guardian Weekly,* November 8, 1987). After that meeting there was a French-German summit in Karlsruhe, confirming the "plans to create a security and defense council in Paris to coordinate military cooperation, including the establishment of a 4,000-man integrated army brigade that will be based near Stuttgart" (*International Herald Tribune,* 14–15 November 1987). When finally that "united European fighting force" is a fact, nobody should be surprised. One of the very few attempts at critical analysis of this development is found in *Militärgrossmacht Westeuropa?* (Bonn: Die Grünen, no date), and *Militärzwillinge Bundesrepublik/Frankreich* (Bonn: Die Grünen, 1988).

16. See the analysis by Bill McSweeney, "Dilemmas of Irish Neutrality," *ADIU Report,* 6, no. 5 (September-October 1984). His basic point is that neutrality will be given up in favor of NATO membership or defense alliance with Britain, in return for "peace in Northern Ireland," as a result of "Civil Service and, predominantly, the Department of Foreign Affairs" pressures.

17. The European Community is the world's leading trader, accounting (1985) for 19.8 percent of world exports and 20.2 percent of imports (deficit 0.4 percent). Number two was the United States with 14.6 percent of the exports and 22.5 percent of the imports (deficit 7.9 percent). Number three was Japan with 12.2 percent of world exports and 8.5 percent of world imports (surplus 3.7 percent). Clearly, at least after 1992 the EC will be the world's largest economy. It is well balanced (but the deficit relative to Japan is 18 billion ecu), whereas the value of U.S. exports was 54 percent above imports, meaning increasing indebtedness. And EC official development aid per capita is twice that of the United States ($.47 against $.24; Japan being in-between at $.35). EC12 has a better spread on the primary, secondary, and tertiary sector than the United States, very similar to Japan, including low productivity in the primary sector. On the other hand, EC12 imports 70 percent of its raw materials from the Third World; oil, gold, diamonds, tin, lead, mercury,

bauxite, cotton, cocoa, vegetable oils, rubber, etc. (from ACP practically speaking customs free). And 31.5 percent of the value of EC exports is to the Third World.

18. Robert Schuman said it already in *La declaration du 9 mai 1950*: "La mise en commun des productions de charbon et d'acier/est la/première étape de la Fédération européenne-." In 1988 the French president, François Mitterand, made the European Union a central point in his campaign for the presidency, telling the French voters that the EC ". . . could, if she wanted, become the first scientific and technical power, the first agricultural power and compete with Japan and the United States for the title of first industrial power . . ." (*Le Monde*, 8 April 1988). The information pamphlet *About Europe* (meaning "About the European Community") is very clear: ". . . the Community has decided—to proceed resolutely towards true European union" (p. 3) and sees the process initiated in 1950 as possibly leading to "the formation of a United States of Europe" (p. 6). But then there is the position of Margaret Thatcher, not only important politically but also very valid, as when she told a European gathering in Bruges, Belgium (where the Europe College is located), that she had "not successfully rolled back the frontiers of the state in Britain only to see them reimposed at a European level, with a European superstate exercising a new dominance from Brussels." This contrasts with the European Commission president, Jacques Delors, who suggested to the European Parliament that the EC was looking forward to an "embryo European government" that would take over 80 percent of economic and social decision making from European capitals within 10 years. Both French Prime Minister Michel Rocard and German Prime Minister Helmut Kohl are in favor of a central bank and a common currency (*The Guardian Weekly*, November 6, 1988).

19. The list is not random but corresponds to six dimensions of cosmology analysis: how a civilization views space, time, knowledge, nature, society, and the transpersonal. That the EC shares the author's perspective is clear: "Europe's cultural dimension is there in the collective consciousness of the people" (*European File: The European Community and Culture*, Luxemburg: EC, 1988, p. 3). The difference comes with the propagandistic bias of the rest of the sentence "characterized by a pluralist humanism based on democracy, justice and liberty."

20. This theme, Europe as the contradiction of "Oriental Despotism," is explored brilliantly in *Europas Opdagelse* (Copenhagen: Ejlers, 1988), Ch. 1 by Mogens Trolle Larsen.

21. The first plan often mentioned in EC pamphlets was by Pierre du Bois, 1306, *De recuperatione terrae sanctae*, with general peace in Christianity to reconquer the Holy Land, in other words anti-Islam. In general these plans, and there are many of them, divide into two groups: a European ingroup against an outgroup (where Russia and Turkey played important roles as foci for negative identification), and the more universal plans of, for instance, Dante, Erasmus, Grotius, Penn, Bentham, and Kant with that ingroup in a key role. The Concert of Europe and the European Community belong to the first category; League of Nations and the United Nations to the second.

22. Language is important. An article in the European monthly magazine *EMOIS* introduces a big section on the rebirth of the Swiss watch industry with the "Swatch" with the title "L'Europe écrase le Japon." And the Japanese watches, the Seiko and

the Citizen, are described as "grenades" (p. 56) endangering the safety of Swiss workers.

23. The failure of the Bush administration to take any step at all may be the result of inability to decide what is worse, return to the days of clarity before *glasnost',/ perestroika,* or reformation of the Soviet Union, possibly making the country attractive again to the billions in the Third World.

24. When asked in 1982 whether Britain should get rid of all nuclear weapons in Britain even if other countries keep theirs, 23 percent said "should" and 72 percent "should not," meaning that 3/4 are opposed to unilateralism. But when asked whether Britain should have its own nuclear deterrent independent of America, 59 percent said "should" and 34 percent said "should not." Only 36 percent wanted to allow American cruise missiles to be stationed in Britain. In short, part of the resistance against these missiles was antinuclear, part was anti-American/pro-British. See T. R. Rochon, *Mobilizing for Peace* (Princeton: Princeton University Press, 1988), p. 40.

25. Two major industrial leaders, Pehr Gyllenhammar from Sweden (Volvo) and Kari Kairamo from Finland (Nokia), published an article (*Aftenposten,* Oslo, 22 oktober 1988) arguing strongly for a Nordic alternative to EC. The structure of the argument is Nordic strength (economically almost as strong as Britain); that EFTA is not an adequate negotiation partner because the secretariat is weak and because the non-Nordic members Austria and Sweden have special interests and also a special negotiation card, transit traffic; that special Nordic qualities can be promoted only in a Nordic context and that Nordic integration has stopped in the last 15 years and should be resumed. They then essentially use EC as a model for further Nordic integration (the Nordic countries were actually ahead of the EC in terms of integration in the 1950s and 1960s). It remains to be seen whether neutral Sweden and Finland can persuade the two NATO countries, Norway and Iceland, to give up entry into the obvious successor to a U.S.-dominated NATO. The Finnish foreign minister Kalevi Sorsa argued the same line in Copenhagen, 13 December 1988, with a Nordic Commission modeled after the EC Commission. In Norway the debate has not started because of Norwegian Labour party refusal to come out openly.

26. Also, on top of the Eastern European agenda is not economics but politics; both the internal pattern of governance and the political relationship to the Soviet Union.

27. This is already the model for EFTA and could be for CMEA, to the benefit of both. And for a possible Nordic alternative. Relations with the EC would then be handled by international negotiations and treaties rather than as members in EC organs. It is not obvious that this would give outside countries less power. EFTA countries have from 40 percent to 64 percent of their trade with the EC without being members, and EFTA is the biggest trade partner of the EC (31.5 percent in 1986, above the United States). On the other hand, the inner market may also be accompanied by higher external tariffs, as pointed out by the vice president of the European Commission, Manuel Marin Gonzalez: "Protectionisme is niet noodzakelijkerwijs een slechte zaak. De zwakken beschermen is niet slecht" (*Nieuwe Rotterdansche Courant,* 14 November 1988).

28. In my 1972 book, *The European Community,* Africa was seen as a major integrative factor; today I would put more emphasis on military integration growing out of arms and nuclear cooperation. The dispatch of 2,700 Belgian and French soldiers, May 1978, to Kinshasa and Kolwezi to save 2,500 Americans and Europeans in the Shaba province of Zaire was the type of action expected—and still expected. As pointed out in an editorial in *Frankfurter Rundschau,* 20 May 1978, "Panthersprung nach Schaba," this must have been discussed in the framework of the European Political Cooperation, and yet does not fit the official style of the EC-ACP relation.

29. The possibility that a vote in many former colonies might be in favor of *de facto* recolonization should not be ruled out.

30. And Europe has many of these minorities, including inside the EC member states: Basques and Corsicans, Alsatians and Bretons, Welsh and Scots, that bleeding ulcer in Ulster, Bavarians and Tirolians that make even EC12 considerably less contradiction-free than it may look at the surface.

3. U.S. and Soviet World Myths

1. This dichotomy between the chosen and the unchosen should not be seen as a characteristic of religion in general, but particularly of transcendental religions with God-above-us. It is not the message of the immanent religions, with God-in-us (such as Buddhism).

2. Johan Galtung, *US Foreign Policy As Manifest Theology* (San Diego: University of California, Institute for Global Conflict and Cooperation, 1987).

3. The point is trivial: our images are governed by simple assumptions of which we are mainly unaware. Even Stephen W. Hawking, in his *A Brief History of Time: From the Big Bang to Black Holes* (New York: Bantam, 1988), seems to be locked into the assumption that there has to be only one Big Bang, and only one universe. Of Black Holes there can be several, however, improving on mono-satanistic theology.

4. And "they" were the wilderness-beasts-savages triad in which the Puritans were inserted, covenanted with God. As John Winthrop, "the beginning of/US/ consciousness," expresses it in his famous sermon, on board the ship bringing them to the New World: "Wee shall finde that the God of Israell is among us, when tenn of us shall be able to resist a thousand of our enemies, when hee shall make us a prayse and glory, that men shall say of succeeding plantacions: the lord make it like that of New England: for wee must consider that wee shall be as a Citty upon a Hill; the eies of all people are uppon us" (quoted from Robert N. Bellah, *The Broken Covenant,* New York: The Seabury Press, 1971).

5. But the Americans did something more. They, meaning John Winthrop, God's New Cana'an and God's New Israel, also stole their myth, seeing Israel as a position vacated by the Jews, to be filled by a new select people instead. Highly anti-Semitic?

6. However, 1988 witnessed a consistent Jewish countertrend to reopen and reconquer positions on the left, the progressive end of the spectrum, with the magazine

Tikkun, and a number of public conferences; no doubt related to the *intifadah* and the rapidly decreasing legitimacy of the present Israeli regime and, by implication, its U.S. supporters.

7. The obvious and highly pessimistic prediction would be a strong wave of anti-Semitism in the United States based on the synergy between economic frustrations in the relation to East Asia and political frustrations in the Middle East having had the U.S. dog wagged by the Israeli/AIPAC tail with its very simplistic and self-serving logic for a very long time. All of this will strengthen an EC12 stance more in favor of the Arab/Palestinian side, and even more so as there are very few Jews left in Europe.

8. One of the reasons why the United States was so late in ratifying the genocide treaty, 40 years after the treaty was first proposed by President Truman and after 97 countries had done so: "Some conservatives in Congress had opposed the treaty on the grounds that its definition of genocide might encourage American Indians to sue the United States Government for their suffering earlier in the nation's history and also that it might result in unsubstantiated charges being brought against the United States by present day adversaries" (*New York Times*, 15 October 1988).

9. For one discussion of this distinction in Marx and particularly Engels, see Miklos Mólnar, *Marx, Engels et la politique internationale* (Paris: Gallimard, 1975), e.g., II, 3, "Les peuples non-historiques," p. 82, where one criterion for being historical is a complete articulation of the feudal formation whereas nonhistorical societies are essentially peasant, with no urban middle class and without a landed aristocracy.

10. On the other hand, it may also be difficult to draw the line. Lenin must have felt that world revolution was around the corner with communist regimes being established not only in Hungary but even in Bavaria (the latter would make anybody believe that basic world change is around the corner). Events then had a sobering effect, and consolidation in one country became the leading idea. Being an example, the first among Socialist countries, having a midwife function when birth of a socialist society is imminent, are not the same as a world empire. But attitudes and behavior are so similar to what would be expected from a country wanting world dominion that many should be forgiven for confusing them.

11. One hunch might be that this is a spillover from the Christian idea of irreversibility of conversion (more Protestant) and baptism (more Catholic). Once accepted into the *corpus mysticum* there is no legitimate way out; once socialist you cannot revert. "Cannot" then becomes "may not" and "should not."

12. There are six steps, not only four: primitive communism-slavery-feudalism-capitalism-socialism-communism, with the "Asiatic mode of production" sometimes being at the bottom, sometimes on the outside. (Marx also had to have something corresponding to Hegel's Orientalism, however much, or precisely because, he "stood Hegel on his head".)

13. Consequently, the Jews fought with Czech aircraft in 1948, and Israel had a progressive, socialist image. All that changed, making it easier for many Europeans to identify with Israel than with many Islamic/Arab countries experimenting with revolution and socialism. And Israel is the only democracy in the region.

14. As shown by the diversity of development styles among the Islamic countries.

15. Two basic documents in this connection are, of course, *Moscow Embassy Telegram # 511: "The Long Telegram,"* of February 22 1946, and "The Sources of Soviet Conduct," *Foreign Affairs,* July 1947, both by George F. Kennan, as U.S. ambassador to the Soviet Union and as "X" respectively; feeding into NSC 68.

4. The Structure of a Myth

1. Here is one statement of the American reaction: "the Russians—would—advance their aims through internal subversion. . . . their agents would be proxies. Indochina and Greece, where indigenous forces were trying to overthrow governments, Bullitt saw only 'active tools of worldwide Communism.' By neglecting the complex jumble of historic, economic, racial, social, and other factors that led to the conflicts and by ignoring the fact that Stalin was giving no active support to the Greek rebels, Chinese Communists, or Viet Minh in Vietnam, Bullitt and the many others in the Administration who thought the way he did oversimplified the problem," from S. E. Ambrose, *Rise to Globalism* (New York: Penguin Books, 1981), p. 123. Of course, if the analysis was that flawed in these three cases, the total analysis of the Cold War might have been equally or more flawed. And might still be, for that matter.

2. The formula can be read many ways. One would be that this is traditional sphere-of-influence politics at its feudal worst, essentially regarding other peoples and their states as property of the greater powers, to be bargained with much like feudal lords with serfs. By 1944–45, at the time of the Moscow and Yalta conferences, the only legitimate value should have been "self-determination." For the Soviet Union's geopolitical concerns, many of them legitimate in the light of history, other ways and means could have been found (nonaggression treaties, collective security), not giving the Soviet Union a free hand in many parts of Eastern Europe and United States/England a free hand in Greece and Italy. For all countries democracy would have been the answer.

3. The conditions making a Soviet intervention likely are explored in more detail in Johan Galtung, *There Are Alternatives,* (Nottingham: Spokesman, 1984), Ch. 2.1, "The global reach: superpower values and interests", pp. 40–48.

4. The dominant interpretation in 1989, however, seems to be that the East German revolt was against their own regime and neither an expression of a desire for reunification with Western Germany, nor of a general desire for more links with the West. But how could the Soviet Union know? They probably overreacted.

5. A more systematic analysis might proceed as follows. The first question is whether there was an intention to attack; the second whether there was a known and credible intention to counterattack whether by the object of the attack or somebody else (extended deterrence); the third whether there was an attack or not. The deterrence hypothesis is that deterrence works: when sufficient deterrence is "on" then and only then will those who intend to attack abstain from doing so. This gives us eight possibilities, but only two cases of "C" for confirm (and "D" for disconfirm):

Attack intended?	Deterrence on?	No attack?	Conclusion:
Yes	Yes	Yes	(1) C
Yes	Yes	No	(2) D
Yes	No	Yes	(3) D
Yes	No	No	(4) C
No	Yes	Yes	(5) 0
No	Yes	No	(6) 0
No	No	Yes	(7) 0
No	No	No	(8) 0

The first four cases are clear as there is something to deter. When deterrence is on and only then should we have no attack, hence C for case 1 and D for case 3. When deterrence is not and only then should we have attack, hence C for case 4 and D for case 2. Military ideology is built around cases 1 and 4 as if these were the only possible. Cases 2 and 3 may then be handled by saying that the attacker, rightly or wrongly, underestimated the deterrence (case 2) or rightly or wrongly overestimated the deterrence (case 3). As he wants to attack, the assumption is that he operates within a deterrence framework even to the point of seeing what is not there and not seeing what is (which may or may not be a correct assumption about his mind-set).

But what if he has no intention of attacking? If there is nothing to deter the hypothesis is neither confirmed nor disconfirmed, indicated by a 0 in all cases. However, the true believer in the deterrence hypothesis may never believe that the other side has no attention of attacking. He will then mentally impute the C-D-D-C sequence also to cases 4–8, and handle the two Ds the way just indicated. With these mental techniques the deterrence hypothesis becomes a tautology.

The view given here is that we are by and large dealing with case 6, meaning that the deterrence hypothesis is neither confirmed nor disconfirmed, meaning that "nuclear deterrence has preserved peace in Europe for 40 years" is a myth. But since case 6 does not directly disconfirm the deterrence hypothesis, it might be said to be "compatible" with that hypothesis—as also with its negation.

For a different road to the same conclusion, see Paul Huth and Bruce Russett, in "What Makes Deterrence Work? Cases from 1900 to 1980," *World Politics* (1984), pp. 496–526: ". . . success was most often associated with close economic and political-military ties between the defender and its protege. . . . Only a marginal contribution was made by the possession of nuclear weapons. . . . A quest for strategic nuclear superiority is unlikely to be the most effective means for providing security to America's friends and allies in a crisis, or to America itself" (pp. 523f).

6. As A. J. P. Taylor expresses it: "In Italy, Togliatti, the Communist leader, returned from Moscow with orders to cooperate with the Allied authorities. And the Italian resistance, composed of 150,000 fighters, surrendered their arms uncomplainingly" ("Daddy, What was Winston Churchill?" in *Essays in English History,* New York: Penguin, 1976, p. 305).

7. In this author's view, fundamentals of a peace structure.

8. A considerable amount of racism and classism would be needed to refer to the nineteenth century with extremes both of slavery, colonialism, and working class

exploitation as "peaceful." Or what in practice is the same: a segmented mind abstracting "the international system" away from the human condition in general.

9. In saying this, I am also saying that even if the data should support the hypothesis that nuclear deterrence had in fact preserved peace in Europe for 40 years, and theory had provided us with an understanding of the mechanisms through which this took place, the "finding" could nevertheless be rejected on value grounds given the cost in terms of psychological terror, the pattern set for the future in terms of preparedness for nuclear exterminism or at least continuation of that terror. For an exploration of this position, see Johan Galtung, "Empiricism, Criticism and Constructivism: Three Aspects of Scientific Activity," *Methodology and Ideology* (Copenhagen: Ejlers, 1977), pp. 41–71. The fact that something is a fact does not make it an acceptable fact. However, the argument is that this special deterrence hypothesis is not factual but fictitious.

5. The Peace Movement

1. The king's last argument, inscribed on a cannon at Wavel castle outside Krakow in Southern Poland.

2. As any exchange-oriented social scientist would take for granted, there will be no human rights, granted by the state (meaning the government) without human duties to the state (also meaning the government); and the supreme duty would be to give up one's own life for the causes defined by the government. See J. E. C. Fuller, *The Conduct of War 1789–1961* (London: Methuen, 1972), Ch. II "The Rebirth of Unlimited War."

3. The Nazis, *Nationalsozialismus*, made this political color combination brilliantly, combining extreme nationalism with welfare state measures—for those considered parts of the nation. And the *Lumpenproletariat* was included, indeed.

4. There is a correspondence here between institutional categories and needs categories, with economic power (potentially) protecting material/somatic well-being, political power freedom, and cultural power identity (with religion, language, etc.).

5. The famous letter by Yuri Zhukov, then president of the Soviet Peace Committee, of 2 December 1982, contains a very bitter critique of the Western peace movement in general and the Bertrand Russell Peace Foundation and the Movement for European Nuclear Disarmament in particular for "efforts to disunite the anti-war movements" with "debates on issues that have nothing to do with this task." These issues include, according to Zhukov, the "German question" and internal problems in the Socialist countries. Underlying the letter is also the concern with the Western peace movement's refusal to hold the West alone responsible for the arms race, thereby concealing and justifying the "aggressive militarist policy of the USA and NATO." As Ken Coates (of the Bertrand Russell Peace Foundation and the END) said in his letter to the editor of *The Guardian* of 23 December 1982: "Mr. Zhukov and the British Government should put their heads together, and they might at least cancel some of each other's misperceptions about the non-aligned peace movement." Events in the Soviet Union, particularly the second Revolution, that of Mikhail Gorbachev, testify to the validity of the approach of the nonaligned peace movement, seeing internal factors in the Socialist countries as major causes of the arms race.

6. In my book *There Are Alternatives!* (Spokesman, Nottingham: 1984), transarmament is seen in terms of a switch from a military doctrine based on offensive arms and retaliatory deterrence to one based on defensive arms and defensive deterrence. But this is seen in a context of a more broadly based alternative security policy with Switzerland as a good, although not unproblematic (for the critical remarks about Switzerland, see pp. 209–211) case. For an early presentation of Swiss foreign policy by an eminent Swiss analyst, Jacques Freymond, see his "Switzerland's Position in the World Peace Structure," *Political Science Quarterly,* Vol. LXVII (December 1952), pp. 521–533. Some examples:

> . . . neutrality was not imposed by an external pressure, but still remained the only way to preserve the existence of the country which, otherwise, would have been divided into two antagonistic camps (p. 527).
> . . . Switzerland at least does not endanger peace and has not been, for a long time, a threat to any of its neighbors. In our era, when not only big states but even small nations have not always refrained from the use of arms for the defense of what they consider as their interests, I think that this readiness for peace and these pacific dispositions are important considerations (p. 521).
> An even more important contribution, however modest, is Swiss self-reliance. This country is not a burden on its neighbors. It is not a satellite of any foreign power. It is not asking help from outside in order to maintain its standard of life, to defend its economic order, to make social experiments, or to build up its military strength (pp. 521f).

Important points, born out of Swiss experience incorporating two articulations of Christianity and three major European nationalities, in a small country that certainly cannot afford to be divided, be dependent on only one of its big neighbors, or aggressive. Other countries can emulate that posture without being conditioned the same way.

7. For a brilliant analysis of the transition from feudalism to the beginnings of the modern state, see Part III, Conclusions in Perry Anderson's monumental *Lineages of the Absolutist State* (London, 1974). The determination to maintain absolute control over military power while at the same time permitting economic decentralization is very clear. The royal princes in Europe are still supposed to become military men, not rejecting military training like the British Prince Edward.

8. For, in my view, the best analysis of the Western European Peace Movement, see Thomas R. Rochon, *Mobilizing for Peace: The Antinuclear Movements in Western Europe* (Princeton: Princeton University Press, 1988). He argues persuasively that the peace movement managed to change the way of thinking about security issues in Western Europe. For another less positive view, see Jeffrey Herf, "War, Peace and the Intellectuals: The West German Peace Movement," *International Security* (1986), pp. 172–200. J. Herf considers peace research and peace movement to be highly political, which is obviously correct: anything dealing directly with politics is highly political. The same applies to his own piece and the type of movement behind the politics of "deterrence" (to use Herf's favorite means of expression, quote-unquote). He also gives much too much credit to peace research, including this author, for inspiring the peace movement.

9. During the cultural revolution in China 1966–76, one impression was that military power was decentralized before at least cultural and political power, into local militia units of the People's Liberation Army. After the cultural revolution, however, central control seems to have been reestablished.

10. For a very strong expression of the view that there has to be basic internal change in the Soviet Union before that country can be counted on for a peace process, see Vladimir Bukovsky, *The Peace Movement and the Soviet Union* (London: The Coalition for Peace Through Security, 1982). For a very sophisticated analysis of this problématique, see Rudolf Bahro, *Über die Logik der Blockkonfrontation; Die Friedensbewegung, die Sowjetunion und die DKP* (Berlin: Olle & Wolter, 1982). For an analysis of the criticism of the European peace movements, see Esko Antola, *Campaigns Against European Peace Movements* (Finland: IPB Peace Union, 1984).

11. See the analysis by Ryuhei Hatsuse, "Indices of Japanese Militarization," International Peace Research Association, 1986. The author sees three stages in post-Tokgawa Japan: 1868–1945: militarization, "strong military, rich country" 1945–50: demilitarization, antinuclearism. 1950–present: remilitarization; self-defense forces from 1954.

12. And why should people in a society where getting rich is a major value not try to do so, emulating the role models available?

13. See "Goals and Processes in Spanish Politics: Western in Corporation or Autonomy?", chapter 12 in my *Essays in Peace Research,* Vol. VI (Copenhagen: Ejlers, 1988) for an effort to explore these processes in the Spanish case.

14. A Catch-22: in a political culture highly skeptical of explicit political ideology the multiple-issue movement will also stand in the way of efficacy.

15. A major point in Manfred Halpern's analysis of politics; reminiscent of the Italian sociologist Alberoni's analysis of love as a revolutionary experience. A reason why revolutionary activity often is carried out by couples in love?

16. Hopefully, the INF agreement December 1987 will lead to more, not less peace movement activity (see chapter 8).

6. The Green Movement

*Originally presented as a lecture at FLACSO, Santiago, Chile, December 1984, and at the Gujarat Vidyapith, Ahmedabad, India, January 1985.

1. The 1985 elections in the Federal Republic of Germany did not work so well for *Die Grünen*; but ups and downs are to be expected as well as internal conflicts over persons and issues. The elections of January 1987 worked very well with the number of mandates in the *Bundestag* increased from 28 to 44.

2. The paradigm underlying this is developed in some detail in the first volume of a forthcoming set of books on development theory and practice—*Development: Goals and Processes; concepts and theories.*

3. The "chemical/circus way of life" is then seen as something accompanying the basic form, the bourgeois way of life, to alleviate some of the loneliness and meaninglessness that may be the way the person experiences BWL.

4. Two basic issues discussed inside any Green movement, viz. "does one start changing the social formation or engaging in alternative ways of life, at the indi-

vidual and micro social levels" or "is a micro level change possible at all without a macro level change" (simply opting out of industrial society as the green fundamentalist Rudolph Bahro would and does advocate). are usually resolved through a "both-and."

5. For a discussion of this, see volume II in the set mentioned in footnote 2 above: *Development and social processes* (forthcoming).

6. There is probably something universal in this. Any social order needing specialists in culture, force (military/police), and economic production/reproduction, although the relative order of those groups in the power structure may vary from one formation to the other and over time, with occasional breakthroughs for the underdog subjects. The Indian philosopher P. R. Sarkar bases reflections of this type on a theory of four types of personality, corresponding to the four classical castes, and develops, like Sorokin, a cyclical theory of history where the groups take power in the order Force-Culture-Economy-People-Force. He forgets, however, and strange for an Indian, that there are two groups of "people": low class and marginalized. The Green Movement mobilizes the latter rather than the former. The marginalized include women, and *die Grünen* are to a large extent a women's party, essentially being founded by one woman (Petra Kelly) and for some period steered by a directorate of three women. For Sarkar's very important theory see R. N. Batra, *The Downfall of Capitalism & Communism, A New Study of History* (London: Macmillan, 1978).

7. In Sarkar's thinking this is the *shudras*, the masses of working people, breaking through the crust provided by the other three. But where are the *pariahs*?

8. All of that is actually happening today around us living in the societies of the Western social formation, all the time. No doubt it will be classified as a revolution in due course of time. But it does not conform to our standard image of revolution, with *one* relatively well defined group exercising tremendous pressure on *one* particular point in the social structure and at *one* short interval of time.

9. The French Revolution must have been equally confusing to the contemporaries; it is only afterward when intellectuals have processed the raw material that the period gains sufficiently in coherence to be upgraded as a revolution, as done in the masterly book by Lefebvre, *The Coming of the French Revolution* (Princeton: Princeton University Press, 1974).

10. Western societies still retain much of the verticality of feudal organization, particularly as related to the great organizations of the classical Western social order, church, land, and military/police and economy, making it natural for these institutions to exhibit conservative political profiles. Voting with their bosses, in other words, rather with that much more abstract entity, the class.

11. At the time being the Liberal party in Great Britain is doing well in its alliance with the social democrats—perhaps exactly for that reason: the element of social democracy.

12. Of course, the dwindling of the secondary sector in postindustrial societies is also a major factor here. The structure keeping workers as an exploited proletariat has to a large extent been demolished by the labor movement, and, whereas retaining gratitude and solidarity of the first generation of workers liberated, their offspring

may use the transition from structure to actor to design highly individual-centered careers and/or to play the market.

13. Of course, new cleavages will appear, new contradictory values and/or interests. Green ideas may also be co-opted by older parties, as to some extent happened in Saar to the social democratic party under the skillful leadership of Oscar Lafontaine, leading to a sweeping victory. The voters liked the new wine, but preferred the old bottles to Green party-style marketing. The basic point, however, is that with the Green Movement the conflict potentials of the traditional Western social formation has been acted out—according to the model presented here.

14. See Galtung, Heiestad, Rudeng, "On the last 2,500 years of Western history, With some remarks on the coming 500," final chapter in the companion volume, *New Cambridge Modern History* (London: Cambridge University Press, 1979), pp. 318–361.

15. See the chapters by the Danish authors in Friberg, Galtung, eds., *Alternativen* (Stockholm: Akademisk förlag, 1986), consistently stressing the theme of closeness as basic to an alternative way of life.

16. And these societies, mainly in the Third World, may be in other phases in their social transformation history. Those most hit by marginalization may not even dream of being actors in any transformation, meaning that the Green parties will tend to cooperate with middle and upper classes in the Third World countries (particularly with the intellectuals), who may have very different interests.

17. The basic point in our ecological predicament is probably very simple: the joint transformation from cyclical to linear ecological processes, and from limited to highly extended economic cycles—due to massive industrialization and world trade—leads to depletion and pollution on the one hand, and lack of direct control on the other. Individuals may engage in some protective measures at the micro level, but they may easily come to naught through the harmful operation of blind macro level processes.

18. In many Third World countries, such as Malaysia, a certain fatigue effect with modern technology is already discernible—simply because the costs seem to outweigh the benefits.

19. For an analysis see Johan Galtung, *There are Alternatives*, (Nottingham: Spokesman, 1984), sections 5.1–2, pp. 162–183.

20. But then a new escalation of the arms race, such as the SDI, may lead to a new explosive burst of peace movement activity.

21. For a good example, see Anne Wilson Schaef, *Women's Reality*, (Minneapolis 1981), particularly chapter 5, "The female system and the white male system: New ways of looking at our culture," pp. 99ff.

22. This brings out the point of not confusing the Green Movement with the Green party. Whether the latter is the most adequate carrier of the basic ideas of the former is an empirical question, not to be decided by semantics alone.

23. This point goes deeper than to political strategy. It is not merely a weak movement advocating change through the synergy of multiple small attacks. This is also the expression of a philosophy/epistemology favoring synchronicity to causality based on a single lever approach to social transformation.

24. If that is the case it should affect the recruitment profile: not many workers but the same (over-)educated, urban middle class that flocked to the socialist parties earlier in this century should join the Green Movement. In fact, what happened to SPD in the March 1983 elections in the Federal Republic of Germany was precisely that they lost (probably three million) workers to the CDU/CSE, and a high number of the country's intelligentsia to *Die Grünen*.

25. It should be pointed out that RAF was also engaged in a large-scale social experiment, testing the hypothesis that their terror would lead to the uprising of the working class with the antiterrorist terror of the state as the intervening factor. The hypothesis was disconfirmed, and the Fascist nature of a group killing others in a social experiment was confirmed in its place. This is one factor underlying the rise of the Green Movement: the fall of the ultrareds.

26. This disinterest should not be confused with loyalty to country/state/government. If that were the dominant underlying sentiment the French would have produced a *levée en masse* against the German invasion in 1940. Rather, it could be seen as profound concern for individual and family welfare over and above the issues affecting society as a whole, except when they touch the private sphere directly, limiting what the French call "liberté." The Greenpeace case, French state terrorism in Auckland harbor against the *Rainbow Warrior,* is an example. There was practically speaking no demonstration against the French government in the streets of Paris.

27. Thus the French Socialist party can be seen as a party of state employees securing their interests.

7. Gorbachev

*The author would like to express gratitude to my many friends in the Soviet Union, so helpful during numerous trips there.

1. According to the Soviet sociologist Igor Bestuzhev-Lada, the Soviet Union has 35 million academics, meaning people with diplomas from tertiary education, including technical colleges and what in the United States is known as community colleges. The 35 million would split, roughly, into 20 million of the latter and 15 million graduates and beyond. These are very high figures, estimated to be 25 percent of the world total of "academics." The total population of the Soviet Union is 285 million, out of whom 60 million are retired and 95 million are children. Of an active population of 130 million 43 million are functionaries (18 million bureaucrats), 6 million are engineers, 3 million teachers, and 1.5 million mechanics.

2. The gap in age between Reagan and Bush is 12 years, and between Brezhnev (not counting his two successors) and Gorbachev 14 years.

3. I am thinking of Amalrik's famous book *Can the Soviet Union Survive Till 1984?* (New York: Harper, 1970).

4. People with one status high and one status low, such as being high on education and low on power, or high on power and low on education. See Johan Galtung, "Rank Disequilibrium Theory," *Essays in Peace Research*, Vol. III (Copenhagen: Ejlers, 1978), chapters 4–6. The high number of academics, presumably high on knowledge, was mentioned in footnote 1 above. According to Bestuzhev-Lada

(in the weekly magazine of *Izvestia, Nedelja*), they had only 5 percent of the quotes in Soviet political documents.

5. Interestingly enough, Gorbachev seems to practice this theory himself; the length of the speeches going down and time allocated to debates with unpredictable outcomes going up.

6. One example possibly being the Soviet tractor *Belorus*. In spring 1988, a Midwest farmer on U.S. TV was asked what it felt like to sit on top of "that pink tractor." His answer: "I do not care what color that tractor has as long as I am not in the red, and this tractor costs one half of the American competitor. True, it doesn't have that many gears forward and backward—."

8. The INF Agreement

1. Highly predictable; what else could they have said after having spent that much money? Never in world history have so few threatened so many with so much destruction, to paraphrase Churchill. Of course, those few and those who believe their story will have to justify what they have done. Moreover, they had to be consistent with the deterrence myth of Chapter 4.

2. ". . . most people believe that it was because of the SS-20 that we modernized. We would have modernized irrespective of the SS-20 because we had this gap in our spectrum of defense developing and we needed to close that gap," according to General Bernhard Rogers in testimony to the Senate Armed Services Committee, March 1983. quoted by T. R. Rochon in his *Mobilizing for Peace* (Princeton: Princeton University Press, 1988), p. 9. The Western argument was usually that Western Europe and more particularly Chancellor Schmid had asked for the INF to be deployed, in response to SS-20. It should be noted that these two motivations do not exclude each other.

3. On the other hand, the Russians left that table first, after the deployment became a fact October 1983—a basic mistake. To show unwillingness to negotiate is also a sign of weakness.

4. Of course, it should never be taken for granted that a party, *in casu* West, NATO, is influenced by moves from the other side at all. The system could be autistic, reacting only to inner stimuli, not reactive to outer stimuli.

5. For details about this see the important book by McGeorge Bundy, *Danger and Survival: Choices About the Bomb in the First Fifty Years* (New York: Random House, 1988).

6. For an interesting analysis along such lines, see Strobe Talbott, "The Road to Zero," *Time*, December 14, 1987, pp. 18–30.

7. The picture drawn in Soviet sources summer 1983, expanding both the number of parties and the range of INF systems, was 938 carriers (missiles and planes) on the Soviet side against 857 for the Western side—a slight superiority for the Soviet Union. In terms of warheads it was 2,155 for the Soviet Union as against 3,056 for the western side, or 1.4 more for the west. If the 108 Pershing II and the 464 Cruise were added, the western side would have had 3,628 warheads; with French and British modernization added (multiple warheads for Trident missiles) their contribution would increase from 290 to 1,326 missiles; meaning 1,036 more. See Johan Galtung, *There Are Alternatives!* (Nottingham: Spokesman, 1984), p. 11.

8. From the fact that demonstrations are small or absent and that demonstrators are arrested even before they demonstrate it does not follow that there is no effective opposition. The leadership may even be deeply influenced by them to the point of wanting to preempt, but horrified by the idea that it might look as if they are yielding to opposition.

9. This may be changing, however. As a matter of fact, Israel could (in early 1989) regain the moral high stand and the influence the country once had (say, before the invasion of Lebanon) by preempting the West and accepting, even welcoming a Palestinian state.

10. For my own views on Star Wars, see the references given in footnote 1 in Chapter 9.

11. This is one of the places where the possibility, remote one would hope, of AIDS as a weapon enters. Even if totally unfounded it is important to note that we live in an era making such speculations far from idle.

12. I am indebted to Stanislav Lem for the observation about the secrecy of secrets.

13. For my own efforts to clarify this type of delayed causation, see *Methodology and Ideology* (Copenhagen: Ejlers, 1977), chapter 4 "Diachronic correlation, process analysis and causal analysis" and Chapter 8 "Positivism and dialectics: A comparison."

14. Norway, Finland, Poland, Czechoslovakia, Hungary, Romania, Turkey, Iran, Afghanistan, China, Mongolia (China again), North Korea. Given recent history one can understand the preference of the Soviet Union for Soviet-Finland relations as the model.

15. The basic mystifying category was the concept of reserves, substitutes if something went wrong (for instance, that the counted missiles were fired?) The 170-page appendix to the INF Treaty mentions 429 deployed U.S. missiles, 80 more than the figures made public at earlier stages. Moreover, 72 Pershing I in Western Germany had been mentioned before, but not the 170 stored in nine states in the United States. And there are similar gaps on the Soviet side. Of course, none of this means that the figures now available necessarily are the true ones; only that so much of the reasoning based on published figures is fictitious.

16. "Making history" was among the favored expressions. History, in the sense of ending the Cold War, was probably made in Helsinki 12 years earlier. What the two summiteers did was to deposit their recording of that fact in the coinage of the nuclear age. Somewhat late, but better late than never.

17. See the excellent series "Weltmacht Droge" in *Der Spiegel,* particularly "Kokain-Republik Kolumbien-das Kartell von Medellin," no. 50, 1988, pp. 120–139 for the self-image of some major drug dealers.

18. To what extent the Brezhnev doctrine, the homologue of the Monroe doctrine, is dead, however, remains to be tested in political practice, and for that experiment not to end badly some more years of *perestroika* might be needed.

19. The INF Treaty was signed Tuesday, 8 December 1987. Friday, 11 December, *The Times* could report that "bombers based in Britain may be armed with cruise missiles as part of the continuing modernization of Nato's nuclear forces, the Prime

Minister said last night." The word "continuing" suggests a high level of autism. On the other hand, if the INF Treaty and the Soviet approach of accepting an asymmetric deal in their disfavor are seen as examples of Charles Osgood's famous GRIT (gradual reduction of international tension), then delayed causation, meaning elapse of time before the other party really responds, would be expected.

20. This, incidentally, is why we need many more peace professionals trained in (fore)seeing such possibilities. The University of Hawaii is planning a two-year Master of Peace Studies program to start Fall 1991 aiming at training people with a high level of concrete knowledge and visioning capacity in the field of peace.

21. The argument in *World Politics of Peace and War* (forthcoming) is that we have had the war between the two superpowers with the Third World as a battlefield and with very many battles. This line of reasoning comes in addition to the line developed in Chapter 4: that nuclear deterrence did not work in Europe essentially because there was nothing to deter. Nuclear deterrence may well have worked between the superpowers, both of them knowing that a nuclear hit on one also spells the end of the other. Consequently the battles were displaced to the Third World where there were real conflicts of interests and values. In some cases (Iran 1946? Korea? China? Vietnam? Cuba?) nuclear deterrence may have worked in the sense of preventing further escalation. But then comes the counterargument: the presence of nuclear weapons may itself have been among the causes leading up to those conflicts.

9. Alternative Security Policies in Europe

*Originally given as a statement before the Political Affairs Committee, Subcommission for Disarmament, European Parliament, Brussels, 25 May 1987; earlier versions at seminars on arms control and disarmament, Princeton University, MIT, and the University of California at Los Angeles and San Diego, Spring 1987. I am grateful to discussants at all places.

1. For the possible offensive uses of SDI (Star Wars) components, see Robert English, "Reagan's 'Peace Shield' Can Attack, Too," *Washington Post* (February 15, 1987); W. J. Broad, "Antimissile Weapon Spurs Debate on Potential for Offensive Strikes," *New York Times,* (February 22, 1987); Johan Galtung, "The Real Star Wars Threat," *The Nation* (February 28, 1987), pp. 248–249; T. B. Taylor, "Third-Generation Nuclear Weapons," *Scientific American,* April 1987, pp. 30–39.

2. However, what is to the right in the figure may be more to the left politically, and *vice versa!*

3. Like many of the categories in the figure, they do not exclude each other: RDF may conceivably be used to get LIC started.

4. For one analysis of the changes in nuclear strategy, see L. Freedman, *The Evolution of Nuclear Strategy* (New York: St. Martin's Press, 1981), p. 246 for MAD (1964), p. 285 for Flexible Response (1967)—McNamara's insistence that all nuclear decisions be made in Washington was unacceptable to de Gaulle—and p. 378 for Schlesinger's Escalation Dominance (in nuclear forces—not included in the figure as it did not "catch on" in the jargon).

5. For the Airland battle, see *Militarpolitik Dokumentation,* Heft 34/35 (prepared by Randolph Nakutta), Frankfurt, Haag/Herchen, 1983; also p. 6 for a brief summary of military doctrines in general.

6. At present both NATO and the Soviet Union can be interpreted as having doctrines of that type, which would designate Eastern Europe as a battlefield based on an underlying consensus—clearly unacceptable to Eastern Europeans.

7. For an elaboration of this, see Johan Galtung, *There Are Alternatives!* (Nottingham: Spokesman, 1984; also in German, Dutch, Norwegian, Swedish, Italian, Spanish, and Japanese editions), chapter 5, particularly 5.1 and 5.2 (the latter also appears as an article in the *Journal of Peace Research,* 1984, pp. 127–139, "Transarmament: from Offensive to Defensive Defense," with references to some of the earlier literature in the field. Most of that literature, however, is marked by a one-sided focus on CMD alone, to the exclusion of PMD and NMD.

8. For an elaboration of the nonmilitary approach in this connection, see Gene Sharp, *Making Europe Unconquerable: The Potential of Civilian-based Deterrence and Defense* (New York: Ballinger, 1985), very positively reviewed by George F. Kennan in *New York Review of Books* (13 February 1986), "A New Philosophy of Defense" (not that new though, even if new to Kennan). Sharp opens for the possibility of mixing nonmilitary and military defense.

9. Who else would be in a position to occupy? There is something feudal in the whole concept: once overlordship has been set up it is not to be contested, except on the terms defined by the lords.

10. Thus the official discourse in the West, dominated by the United States, is still limited to the left hand (but politically right wing) part of the chart of doctrines. But the official discourse has less of a monopolistic position than before. The achievement of the peace movement of the early 1980s was not to bring about any concrete political decision, e.g., about deployment of INF weapons, but to change the thinking and the discourse about security affairs. See T. R. Rochon, *Mobilizing for Peace* (Princeton: Princeton University Press, 1988), chapter 9, "Movements as a Creative Political Force," pp. 203ff.

11. As a very rough rule of thumb, public opinion polls tend to show about 2/3 in favor of NATO, in the five INF stationing countries (which does not mean that as many as 1/3 are against), and about the same fraction skeptical of U.S. nuclear policies, e.g., INF (which does not mean that 1/3 are in favor).

12. Looking at the chart of military doctrines, three political alliance possibilities stand out: pacifist with conventional, defensive military (in Germany roughly the Green "realos" with left to center social democrats); conventional defensive with conventional offensive, against all weapons of mass destruction but less sensitive to the offensive/defensive distinction (in Germany center SPD with FDP?); conventional defense with a clear no first use doctrine for nuclear arms and other arms of mass destruction (in Germany FDP far into CDU?). In other words, the discourse on doctrines may have considerable impact on military politics by filling conceptual gaps. A discontinuous discourse makes for isolation of the "extremists." And for social democrats, traditionally thriving in the middle ("die Vernuft ist in der Mitte") this is a much better point of departure for concrete politics.

13. A particularly acute problem in Switzerland with the harsh treatment of conscientious objectors. A defensive defense system like the Yugoslav system might be better for this particular purpose. There is the "General People's Defense (GPD), instituted in 1957 and 1958, divided into the 260,000 elite forces of the Yugoslavian

People's Army (YPA) and the one million members of the Territorial Defense Forces (TDF)—"ordinary citizens organized at the larger factories, in urban and rural communities, and at the level of the various federal republics." (E. R. Alterman, "Central Europe: Misperceived Threats and Unforeseen Dangers," *World Policy*, 1985, pp. 681–709—the quote is from p. 691). Obviously, TDF could accommodate conscientious objectors.

14. For details, see Johan Galtung, *Environment, Development and Military Activity* (Oslo: Universitetsforlaget, 1982).

15. Defensive defense does not reduce anybody's security since it is incapable of being directed effectively against anybody else's territory. However, defensive defense does provoke anybody whose extraterritorial goals are thwarted. An offensive stance is more conventional in today's world; a defensive stance signals a certain "holier than thou"-ism by saying both "I am not going to attack anybody" and "I am not so sure about others." Unilateral disarmament does not carry the second message.

16. "Strukturelle Nichtangriffsfähigkeit."

17. However, see the remark in footnote 15 above. For an excellent analysis of the origin of the particular military doctrine of Switzerland, see Jacques Freymond, "Switzerland's Position in the World Peace Structure," *Political Science Quarterly*, 1952, pp. 521–533.

18. Of course, a major power like nazi Germany, the Soviet Union, or the United States can invade and overrun the defenses in many other countries. But that is, fortunately, not the whole story. No power, and even less a superpower, wants to be entangled for years, months, perhaps not even for weeks in protracted warfare with no clear victory in sight within an acceptable time horizon. This is not so much because of the human and material losses as because of the loss of prestige. Czechoslovakia 1968 and Grenada 1983 are what superpowers prefer; definitely not Vietnam 1965–75 and Afghanistan 1979–89. Hence deterrence theory has its basis more in the capacity to sustain defense than to stop and evict the invader. The same holds for all the other big-small power relations in this book.

19. There are others, such as the superpower need to be stronger than alliance members as a symbol of political superiority; the need to be strong as the duty of a "chosen people" to project leadership; the economic pressures from inside and outside, not only for corporate profit, for something to reallocate from federal funds and for earnings from arms trade, but also to bolster the national currency by projecting strength in general.

20. A comparison of the military expenditure of neutral and NATO countries in Europe brings out this point to some extent. In 1985 the six neutral countries Austria, Finland, Ireland, Sweden, Switzerland, and Yugoslavia had an average expenditure of $208 per capita whereas NATO Europe had $371 and total NATO had $557 (due to the very high military expenses of the United States). It may be objected that this is because the countries are so small. But their military expenditure per km^2 was 8.9 as against 42.5 for NATO-Europe and 14.7 for total NATO (partly because of the size of Canada). To what extent these countries have a sufficient defensive defense, however, is a matter to be debated. See Vicenc Fisas Armengol, "Los gastos militares en los paises neutrales," *EL PAIS*, 30 August 1986.

21. This point is made very strongly by Freymond, op.cit., p. 527.

22. According to Dietrich Fischer, one method for the Swiss (and also for the Swedes) of not provoking the Germans during World War II was not to have long-range bombers.

23. As Freymond puts it: "Thus, after having seen the dismemberment of the Austrian Empire, after having lived in safety through two world wars in which Germany was destroyed, France and Italy badly damaged, they cannot help feeling that they have succeeded" (op.cit. p. 526).

24. A point that is particularly important in connection with Swedish fighter-bombers, and Austrian missiles—the latter given the location of Austria, bordering on two NATO, two neutral, and two WTO countries.

25. There are many signs that this is now happening. Martin Walker of *The Guardian*, perhaps the best informed of Western journalists in Moscow, reported (*The Guardian*, February 18, 1987) that the discussion between Marshal Ogarkov (victory in a nuclear war remains an "objective possibility") and Marshal Ustinov ("to count on victory in—nuclear war is madness") seems to have ended in favor of Ustinov's position. According to Walker, "a consensus has been achieved within the Soviet government that says not only is nuclear war unthinkable, but that the very idea of war as a continuation of politics by other means must be rethought." Boserup and Neild go one step further (in "The Best Form of Defense is Real Defense," *International Herald Tribune*, July 10 1987): "What is interesting and new is that since Mikhail Gorbachev came to power, the Soviet Union and the Warsaw Pact have taken up these ideas that originated in the West. Mr. Gorbachev has publicly said that the doctrine of the East bloc's nonnuclear forces must be defensive. The Warsaw Pact countries declared that to be their position in June 1986. Then at the end of this May they proposed consultations with NATO at the expert level to compare and analyze military doctrines, and ensure that the doctrines of both blocs "be based on defensive principles." (A personal note: In August 1983 at the Tenth conference of the International Peace Research Association, I was approached by a Soviet researcher very well placed in the Soviet research establishment on these matters. He expressed his frustration at the stalemate with the Reagan administration and asked what I would advise. And my advice was, as it had been for many years: explore transarmament toward defensive defense; call an international conference on military doctrines. He got the message immediately. Many others undoubtedly have given the same advice. But the same points, mentioned in a U.S. setting, tend to draw a blank).

26. For the Bulow-Papier, see *Frankfurter Rundschau*, 13–14 September, 1985. The SPD program from June 1986 states that NATO should be "strikt defensiv" and talks about "Abbau von Drohpotentialen bis hin zur beiderseitigen strukturellen Nichtangriffsfahigkeit."

27. The Labor Party approach is simpler: reliance on nuclear weapons must be brought to an end; NATO's conventional strength must be enhanced.

28. Like SPD, Labor lost elections, possibly partly due to the stance on defense that was new not only to the voters but also to themselves. Thus Kinnock in the United States (Harvard, fall 1986) argued only point one in the preceding footnote, not the more novel point two.

29. This dimension should not be confused with left-right as used in European politics; it is a separate dimension typical of U.S. political discourse.

30. The cost of an antitank, antiaircraft, and antiship missile is very low relative to the target; for antimissile missiles the reverse is the case. However, such comparisons tend to leave out the need for a dense network of defense installations and the logistics to go with it. Thus short takeoff aircraft for intercept, deployed in bunkers all over, using numerous highways as airstrips would cost. So would man-made forests and other barriers, also well dispersed, even randomly. And yet the savings should be considerable, although there are obvious arms manufacturer interests in seeing it otherwise.

31. The general rule is probably that no other country should introduce such measures before the fatherland of socialism does so. Like all rules this one has an exception: Hungary. Why Hungary is the exception is interesting. Neither Slav, nor Orthodox? Hence exceptional anyhow?

32. It should be noted that the Soviet-Finnish treaty has celebrated its fortieth anniversary—a sign that it has stood the test of time given the very high level of support for the treaty in the Finnish public, and for the Soviet Union as a "friend." Alternative security politics is much more than alternative defense. There is also the reduction of the role of the superpowers through processes of decoupling from them; a higher level of economic, political, etc., self-reliance and in general cooperative relations in all directions (in the view of the present author, as spelled out in *There Are Alternatives!*)

10. Active Peaceful Coexistence

1. See, for instance, the German version, "Die künftigen Aufgaben der Allianz" in NATO: *Tatsachen und Dokumente,* Brussels 1971. The declaration hardly mentions weapons in general, and missiles in particular, at all—the content discussed was peace-building. Ten years later the tone of the alliance was totally changed, in the direction of missiles and belligerence, although it was hard to see that there was any objective justification for this basic change.

2. The complete report is published as a book, Johan Galtung and Sverre Lodgaard, *Co-operation in Europe* (Oslo: Universitetsforlaget, 1970). The theory of peace is found on pp. 9–20. A slightly different version is found in Johan Galtung, *The True Worlds* (New York: The Free Press, 1980), p. 101. "Scope" and "domain" have been added as peace factors, and "homology" has been dropped (in addition, "symmetry" is referred to more explicitly as "equity").

3. The key examples in the contemporary world where these conditions by and large can be said to apply would be the Nordic countries and the European Community—in the relation among the members, not in the relation to the rest at the world, which are very far from equitable. The ASEAN countries in Southeast Asia may also be added to this list.

4. The United States was probably against, not so much because it increased Western European dependency on the Soviet Union, as because it decreased the dependence on the Gulf area, and hence the motivation to engage in any "rapidly deployed" action.

5. Thus in both books quoted in footnote 2 above, I argue in favor of a Security Commission for Europe, organized like the Economic Commission for Europe, to carry the "Helsinki process." There is not much of a process at present but should there be any it should be carried by a permanent machinery rather than by a series of frustrating, *ad hoc,* "review conferences." For some further development of the theory of cooperation in Europe by this author, see "Europe, Bipolar, Bicentric or Co-operative?" and "European Security and Cooperation: A Skeptical Contribution," written in 1971 and 1974, respectively, and published as chapters 1 and 2 in Johan Galtung, *Peace Problems: Some Case Studies, Essays in Peace Research,* Vol. V (Copenhagen: Ejlers, 1980).

6. See *Cooperation in Europe,* pp. 9–20.

7. The pipeline itself is a good example: much or most of the technology from the West; the work at laying it and the gas itself from the East. But then U.S. interference forced the Soviet Union to become technologically more self-reliant.

8. This is one of the themes in the article "A Skeptical Contribution" referred to in footnote 5 above, predicting how asymmetrical trade would lead to increased tension. The other article was more normative, more written in the early stage of the process.

9. An exception, besides the giant economy of the Soviet Union, is Bulgaria, with a relatively low debt burden. Bulgaria is worth studying as it seems to have obtained a relatively high living standard without deviating much from a Marxist line.

10. This is explored in more detail in Johan Galtung, *The European Community, A Superpower in the Making* (London: Allen & Unwin, 1973).

11. This policy is then coupled to a theory of the Soviet Union as a giant with clay feet, failing to understand how pressures from the outside can also have an invigorating impact on giants of that type.

12. Thus would a Christian country like Norway accept being a target of programs with a consistently anti-Christian content? Commercial propaganda would be acceptable, perhaps also political propaganda. But anti-Christian? Anti-Royalist?

13. See Johan Galtung, "A Structural Theory of Imperialism," in *Peace and World Structure, Essays in Peace Research,* Vol. IV, chapter 13.

Conclusion

1. Exactly which "allies" are difficult may vary from time to time. Most important in 1989 is probably the entry of the Federal Republic of Germany under the conservative Kohl in this category, related to modernization of the short-range nuclear missiles, and fueled by strong popular reactions against continued NATO air exercises and arms race in general.

2. These two sets of alternatives are not new; they have both been more or less present in the public debate for a long time.

3. For the changes in German public opinion, see, for instance, "Keine Angst mehr vor den Russen," *stern* 1/1989, pp. 10–19.

4. By and large this is the option predicted for the European Community/Western European Union in Chapter 2, at least in the near term.

5. However, in the numerous conferences and research papers in Europe over and around this issue, the approach taken is in terms of short-range conventional options, not including militia and nonmilitary defense. But they may enter the debate later, as argued in my *There Are Alternatives!* Discourses do not change that quickly; the first opening for the defensive/offensive dimension is already a great step forward.

6. But this alternative should always be not only in the air but also on the table, not only as a reminder but to check whether there really still are good arguments against.

7. This would probably have to be done with some denuclearized zones as a first step to get the process started. The arguments from Chapter 5 would point to where those zones should be located: in the European northwest and particularly the Nordic countries because the popular peace movement is strong, and in the European southeast, the Balkans, because the official peace movement is strong.

8. In other words, structural violence is much more important quantitatively than direct violence. Even World War II with an annual casualty rate of 8 million does not come anywhere near the 14 million children dying annually from highly avoidable diseases, linked to malnutrition and unhygienic conditions. I am indebted to George Kent for this observation.

9. The prerogative of the outsider, not thereby saying that the simplicity of the outsider is a necessary or sufficient condition for validity.

About the Author

Johan Galtung, one of the founders of peace research as a discipline, was born in Norway in 1930. After receiving degrees in mathematics and sociology from the University of Oslo, he taught sociology and methodology at Columbia University, founded (1959) the International Peace Research Institute in Oslo (PRIO), the Journal of Peace Research, and was awarded (1969) one of the first chairs in peace studies in the world at the University of Oslo. He has been a consultant to ten UN organizations.

 He has published and edited close to 50 books and more than one thousand articles in the fields of conflict, peace development and future studies, and in theory and methods of social science. Among the books are *Theory and Methods of Social Research, Essays in Peace Research Vols. I–VI,* and *Essays in Methodology Vols. I–III.* He is honorary doctor or professor at six universities and has been a visiting professor at 40 universities around the world. He was given the Right Livelihood Award, also known as the Alternative Nobel Peace Prize, in 1987.

Presently Johan Galtung is Professor of Peace Studies at the University of Hawaii (where his wife, Fumiko Nishimura, is lecturing on Japan–US images) and Professor of Social Sciences at the University of Witten/Herdecke in Germany. In addition to his continuing work on conflict and peace theory, he has for many years been working on civilization theory, exploring the peace and development potential of various civilizations.

Books Published 1953–1989

For a complete bibliography up to 1980, with 676 entries, see Gleditsch et al., *Johan Galtung: A Bibliography of His Scholarly and Popular Writings 1951–1980,* PRIO, Oslo, 1980.

1. *Statistisk Hypoteseproving,* 1953
2. (with Arne Naess): *Gandhis politiske etikk,* 1955

3. *Fengselssamfunnet: Et forsok pa analyse,* 1959
4. *Forsvar uten militarvesen: Et pasifistisk grunnsyn,* 1959
5. (with Arne Naess): *Innforing i logikk og metodelare,* 1960
6. *Fredsforskning,* 1967 (Norwegian, Swedish, German editions)
7. *Theory and Methods of Social Research,* 1967 (English, Spanish)
8. *Members of Two Worlds: A Development Study of Three Villages in Western Sicily,* 1971
9. *The European Community: A Superpower in the Making,* 1973 (Danish, Swedish, Finnish, Dutch, German, Argentinian editions).
10. *A Structural Theory of Revolutions,* 1974
11. *Essays in Peace Research,* Short Edition, 1974, 1975, 1975, 1982, 1986 (Norwegian, Swedish, German, German, Spanish editions).
12. (with Fumiko Nishimura): *Can We Learn From the Chinese?* (Norwegian, Swedish, German editions)
13. *Peace: Research. Education. Action. ESSAYS Vol. I,* 1975
14. *Peace, War and Defense. ESSAYS Vol. II,* 1976.
15. *Hvordan skal det ga med Norge?: Artikler 1953–1977,* 1977
16. *Imperialismo e rivoluzioni: Una teoria strutturale,* 1977
17. *Methodology and Ideology,* 1977
18. *Peace and Social Structure. ESSAYS Vol. III,* 1978
19. *Toward Self-reliance and Global Interdependence: A New International Order and Global Interdependence,* 1978
20. *Papers on Methodology,* 1979
21. *Development, Environment and Technology,* 1979 (English, French, Spanish editions)
22. *Peace and World Structure, ESSAYS Vol. IV,* 1980
23. *Peace Problems: Some Case Studies, ESSAYS Vol. V,* 1980
24. *The True Worlds: A Transnational Perspective,* 1980
25. *Schooling, Education and the Future,* 1982
26. *Self-Reliance. Beitrage zu einer alternativen Entwicklungsstrategie,* 1983
27. *Environment, Development and Military Activity: Towards Alternative Security Doctrines,*
    English edition: Norwegian Universities Press, Oslo, 1982.
    Italian edition: Abele, Torino, 1984
28. *There Are Alternatives: Four Roads to Peace and Security*
    English edition: Spokesman Press, Nottingham, March 1984
    German edition: Westdeutscher Verlag, Wiesbaden, February 1984
    Spanish edition: tecnos, Madrid, April 1984
    Dutch edition: Horstink, Nijmegen, May 1984
    Norwegian edition: PAX/FMK, Oslo, January 1985
    Swedish edition: Gidlund, November 1985
    Italian edition: Abele, Torino, November 1985
    Japanese edition: Shobo-kozo, Tokyo, 1989
29. *Hitlerism, Stalinism, Reaganism: Three Variations on a Theme by Orwell*
    Norwegian edition: Gyldendal, Oslo, 1984
    Spanish edition: Gil Albert, Alicante, April 1985
    German edition: Nomos, Hamburg, May 1987

30. *The Struggle for Peace: The Bajaj Memorial Lectures* Ahmedabad: Navajivan Publishing House, 1984
31. *Gandhi Today*
    Italian edition: Torino, Abele, 1987
    German edition: Wuppertal, Peter Hammer Verlag, 1987
32. *United States Foreign Policy as Manifest Theology,* San Diego: University of California, 1987
33. *Transarmament and the Cold War, ESSAYS, Vol. VI* Copenhagen: Ejlers, 1988
34. *Methodology and Development* Copenhagen: Ejlers, 1988
35. *Buddhism: A Quest for Unity and Peace* Honolulu: Dae Won Sa Buddhist Temple, 1988
36. *Solving Conflicts: A Peace Research Perspective* Honolulu: University of Hawaii Press, 1989
37. *Nonviolence and Israel/Palestine* Honolulu: University of Hawaii Press, 1989
38. *Peace and Development in the Pacific Hemisphere* Honolulu: University of Hawaii Press, 1989

Books Edited
1. (with Aanderaa, Brandrud): *Sovjet-et naboland,* 1954
2. (with Robert Jungk): *Mankind 2000,* 1969
3. (with Sverre Lodgaard): *Co-operation in Europe,* 1970
4. (with Dieter Senghaas): *Kann Europa abrusten? Friedenspolitische Optionen fur die siebziger Jahre,* 1973
5. (with Ornauer, Wiberg, Sicinski): *Images of the World in the Year 2000: A Comparative Ten Nation Study,* 1976
6. (with Eleanora Masini): *Visiones de sociedades deseables,* 1979
7. (with Lederer, Antal): *Human Needs: A Contribution to the Current Debate,* 1980
8. (with Poleszynski, Rudeng): *Norge foran 1980-arene,* 1980
9. (with O'Brien, Preiswerk): *Self-reliance: A Strategy for Development,* 1980
10. (with Wallensteen, Portales): *Global Militarization,* 1985
11. (with Mats Friberg): *Krisen,* 1983
12. (with Mats Friberg): *Rorelserna,* 1984
13. (with Mats Friberg): *Alternativen,* 1986